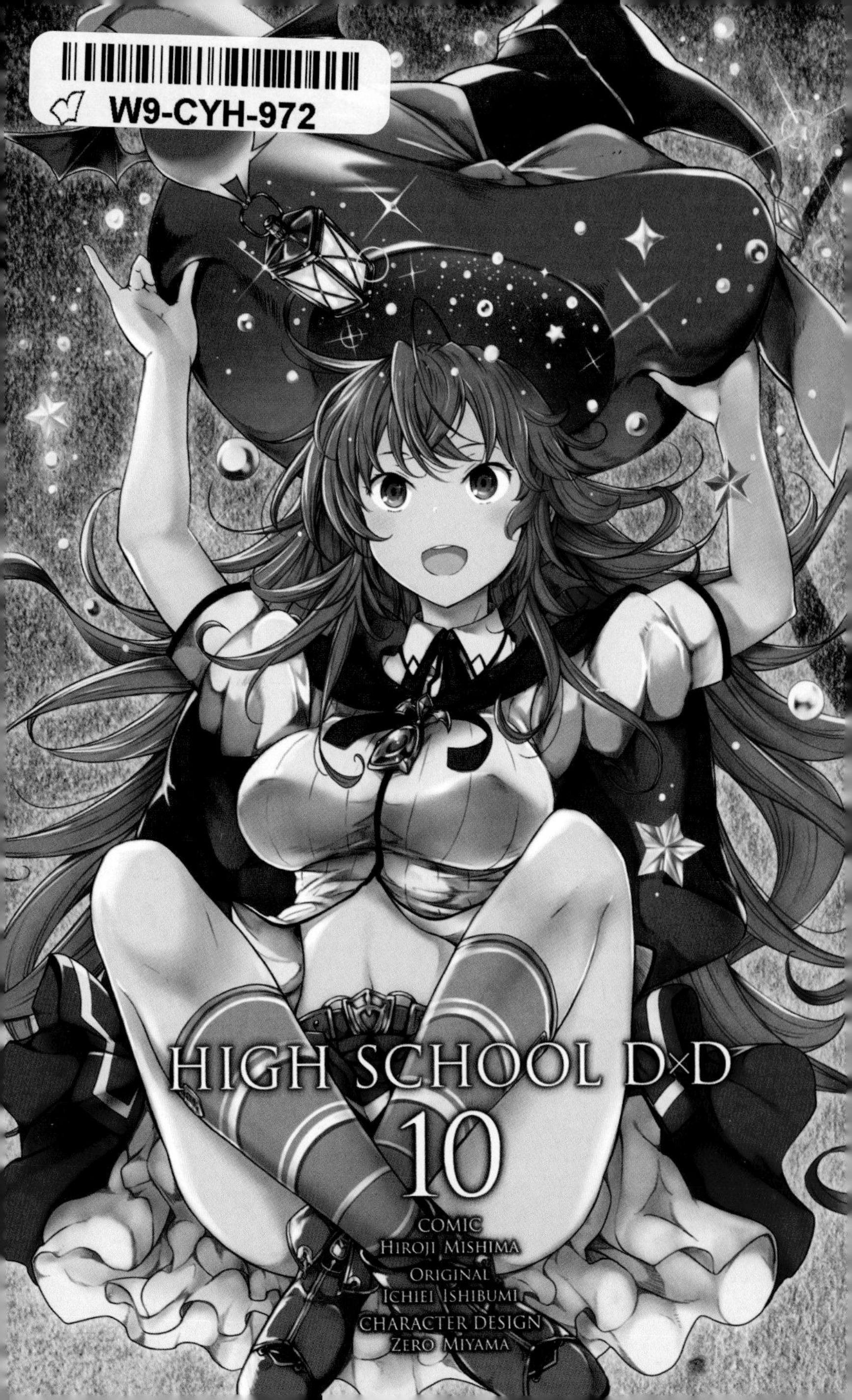
HIGH SCHOOL D×D
10
COMIC
Hiroji Mishima
ORIGINAL
Ichiei Ishibumi
CHARACTER DESIGN
Zero Miyama

10

COMIC
HIROJI MISHIMA
ORIGINAL
ICHIEI ISHIBUMI
CHARACTER DESIGN
ZERO MIYAMA

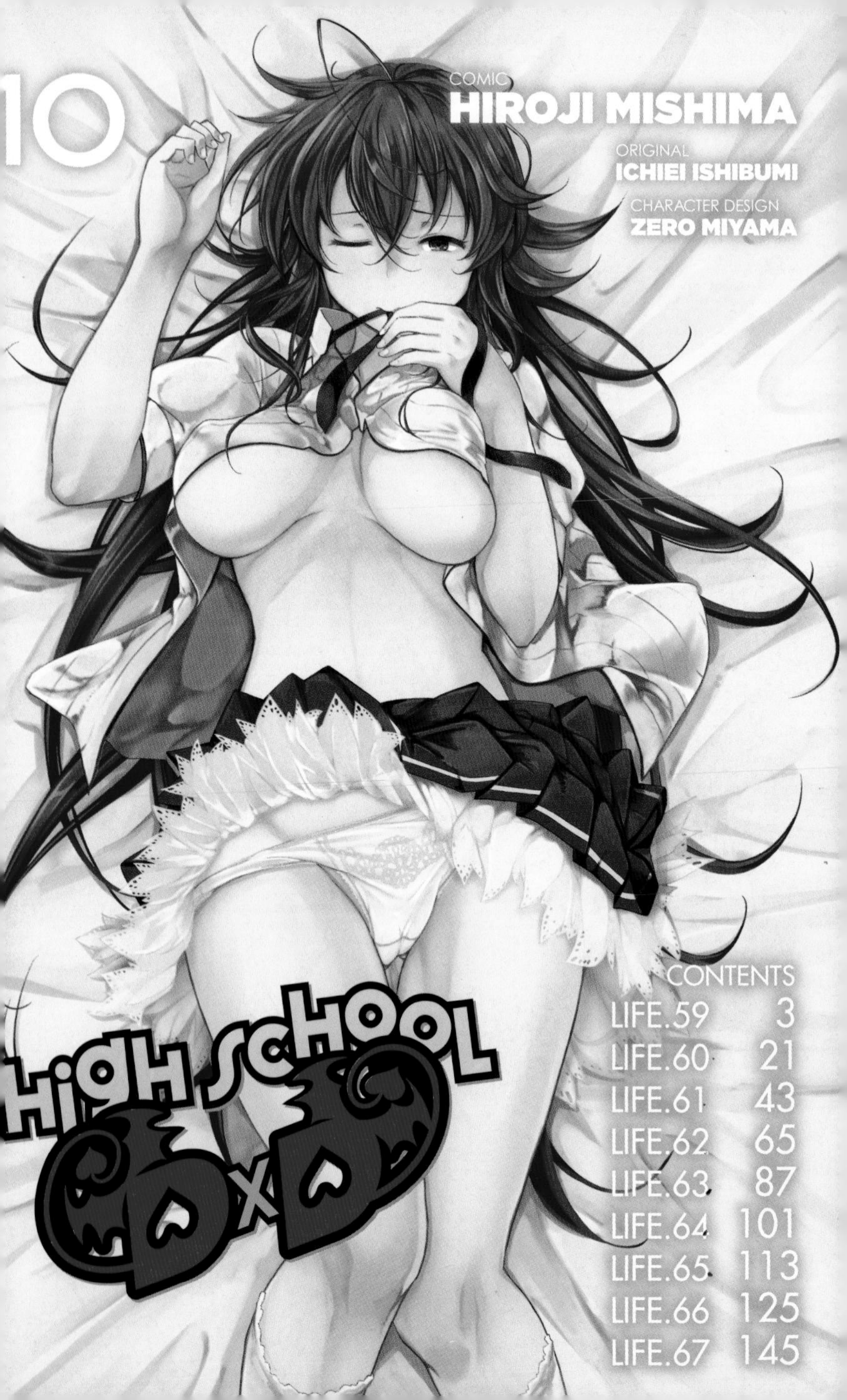

HIGH SCHOOL DxD

CONTENTS

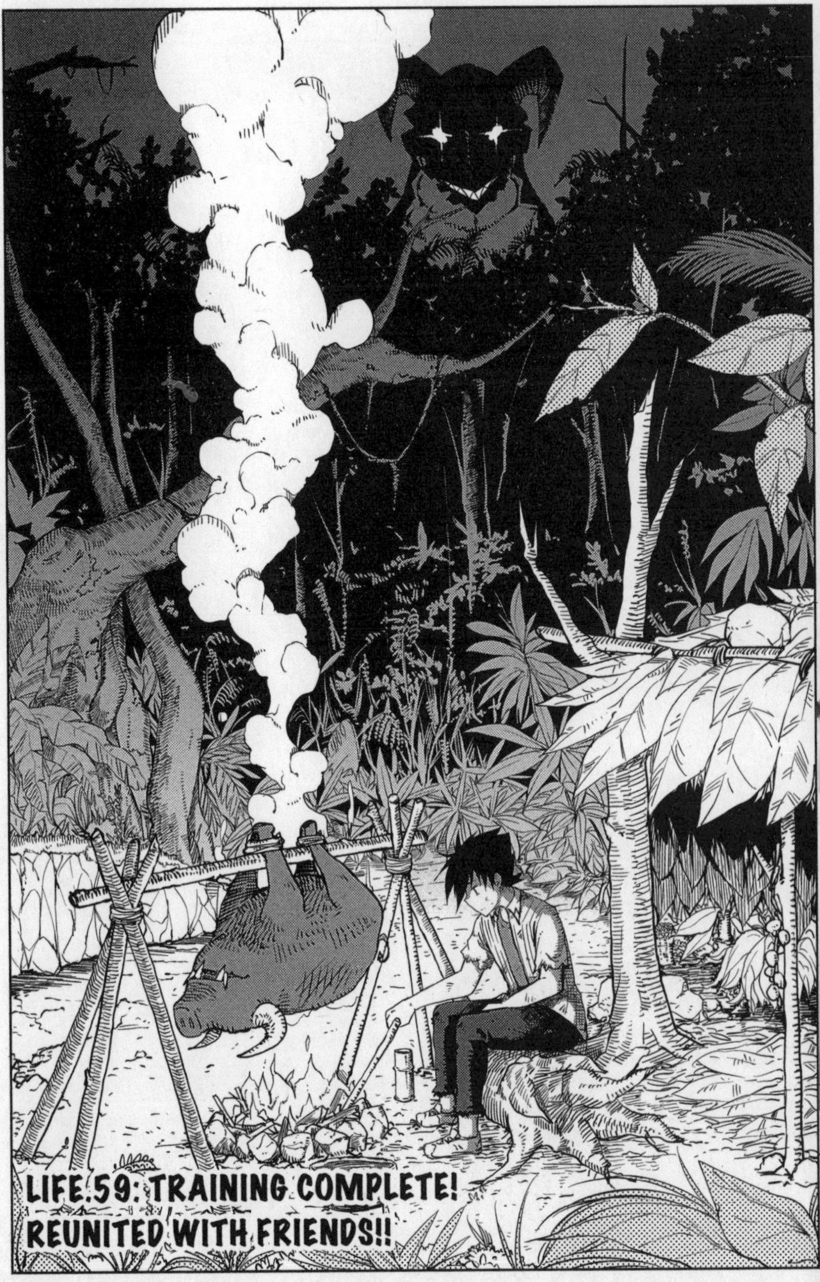
LIFE.59: TRAINING COMPLETE!
REUNITED WITH FRIENDS!!

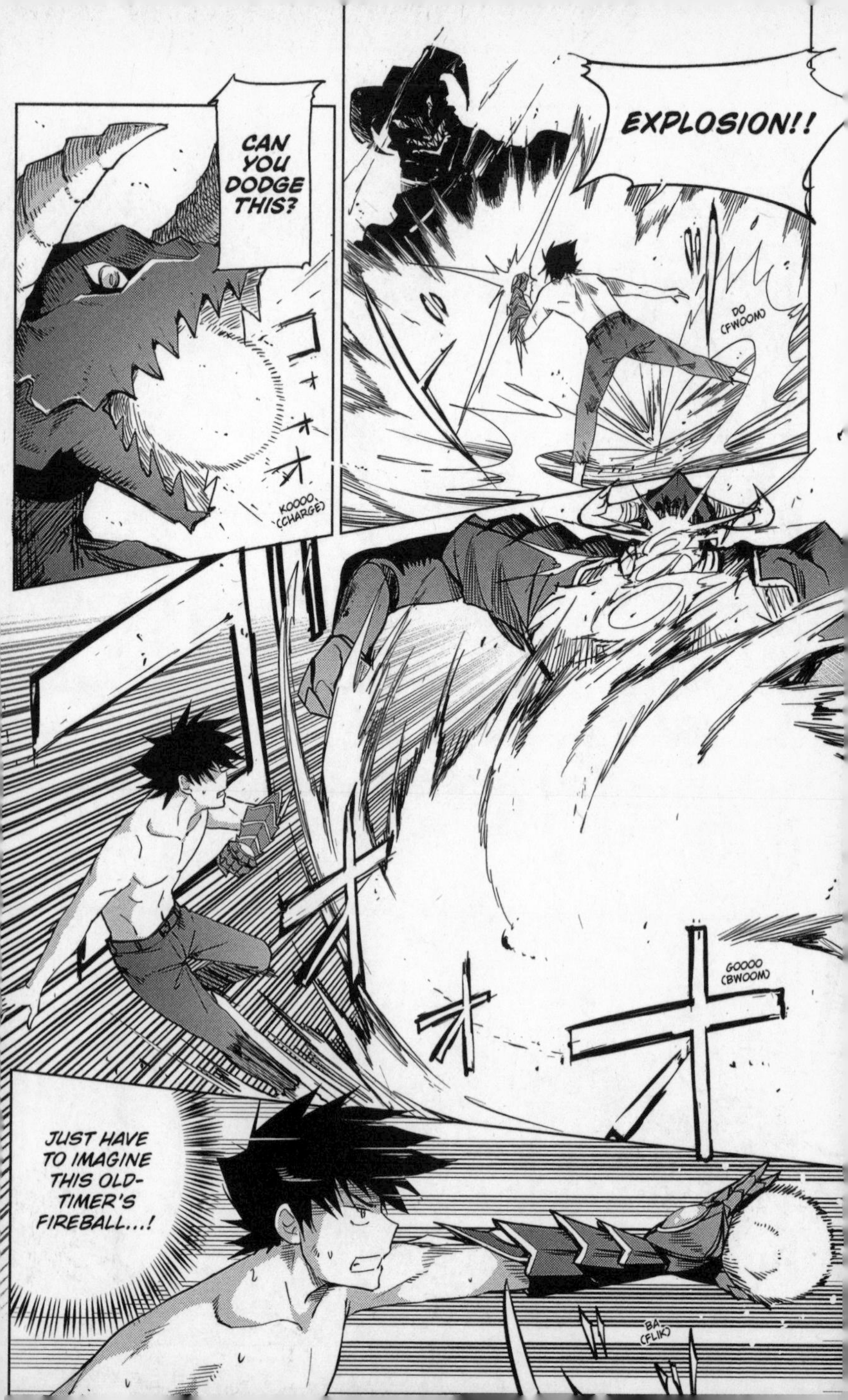
EXPLOSION!!
DO (FWOOM)
CAN YOU DODGE THIS?
KOOOO (CHARGE)
GOOOO (BWOOM)
JUST HAVE TO IMAGINE THIS OLD-TIMER'S FIREBALL...!
BA (FLIK)

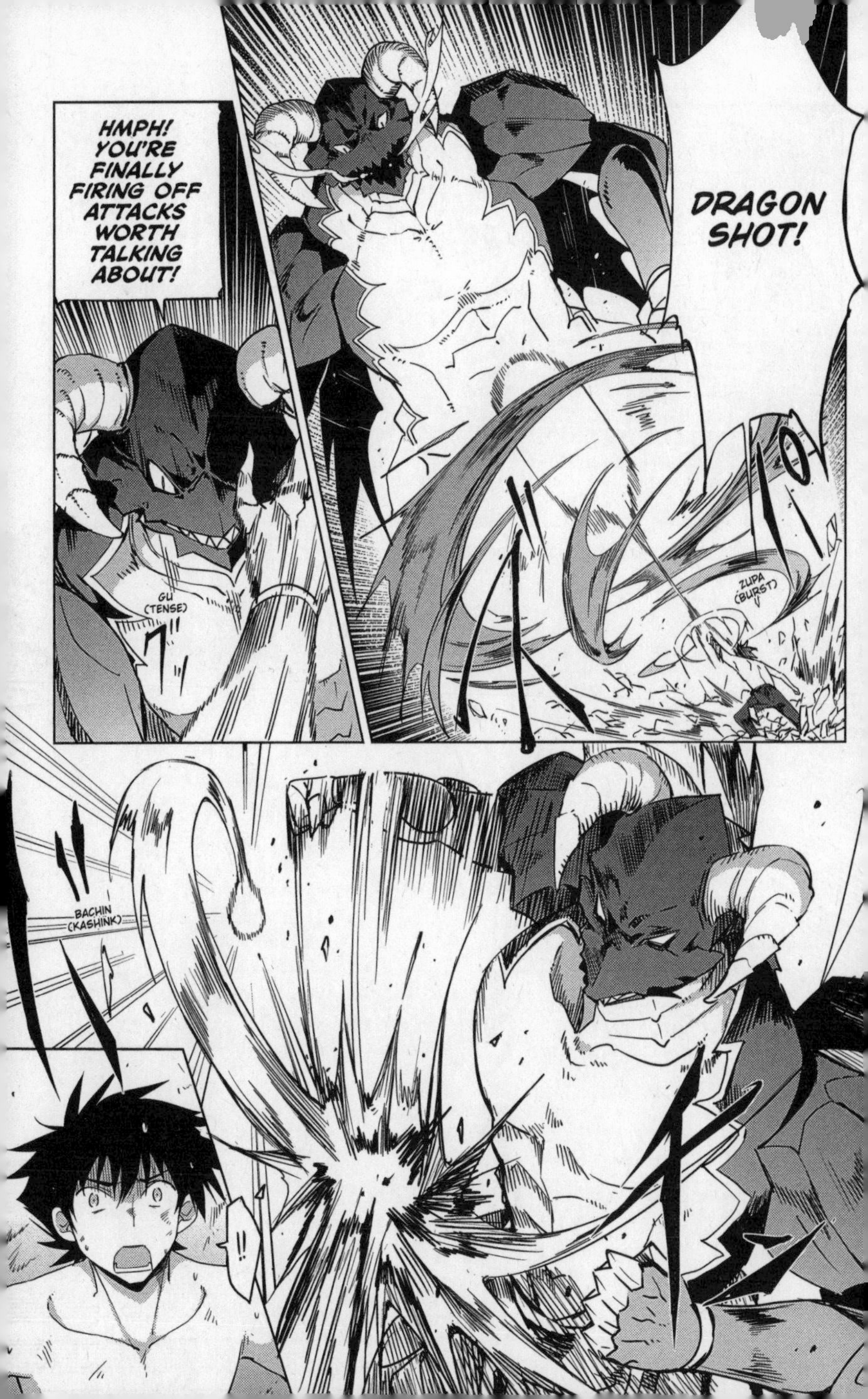
DRAGON SHOT!
ZUPA (BURST)
HMPH! YOU'RE FINALLY FIRING OFF ATTACKS WORTH TALKING ABOUT!
GU (TENSE)
BACHIN (KASHINK)
!!

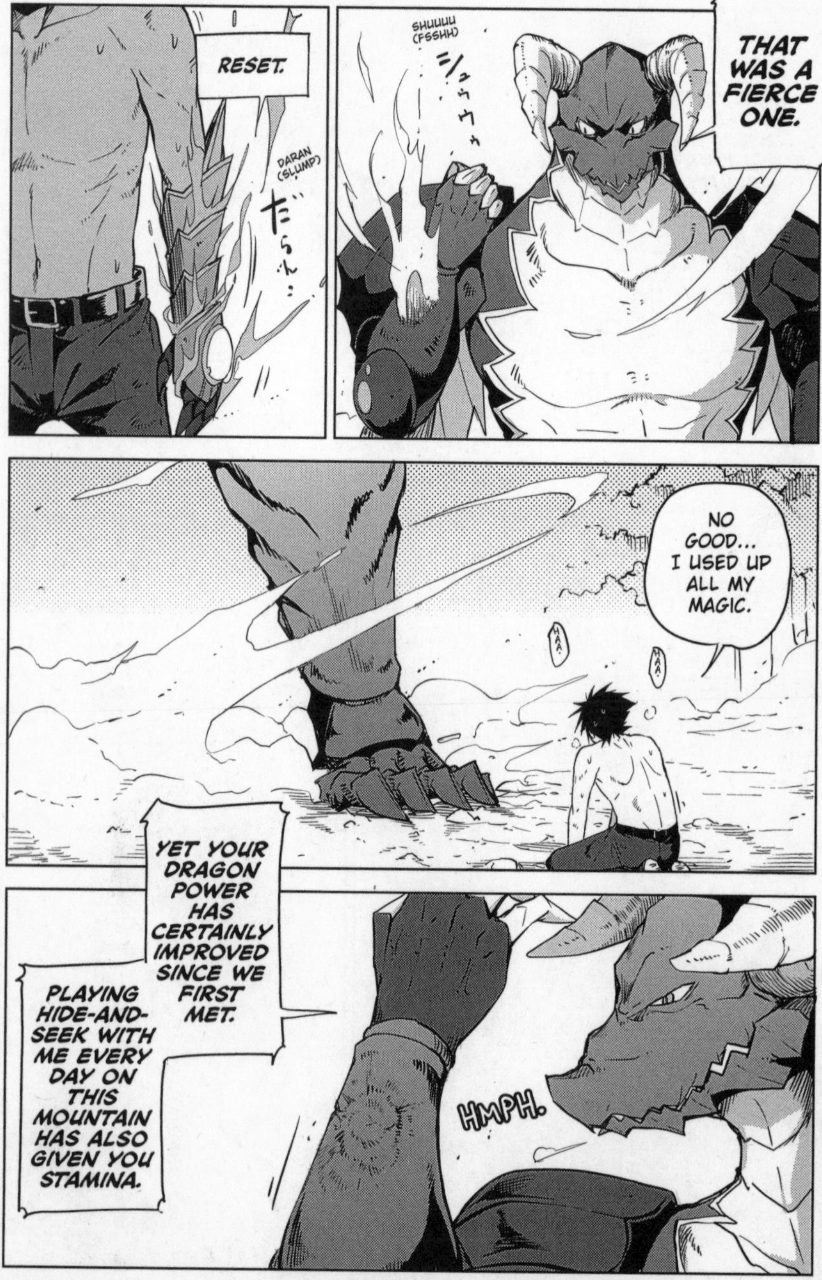

THAT WAS A FIERCE ONE.
SHUUUU (FSSHH)
RESET.
DARAN (SLUMP)
だらん
NO GOOD... I USED UP ALL MY MAGIC.
HAA
HAA
YET YOUR DRAGON POWER HAS CERTAINLY IMPROVED SINCE WE FIRST MET.
PLAYING HIDE-AND-SEEK WITH ME EVERY DAY ON THIS MOUNTAIN HAS ALSO GIVEN YOU STAMINA.
HMPH.

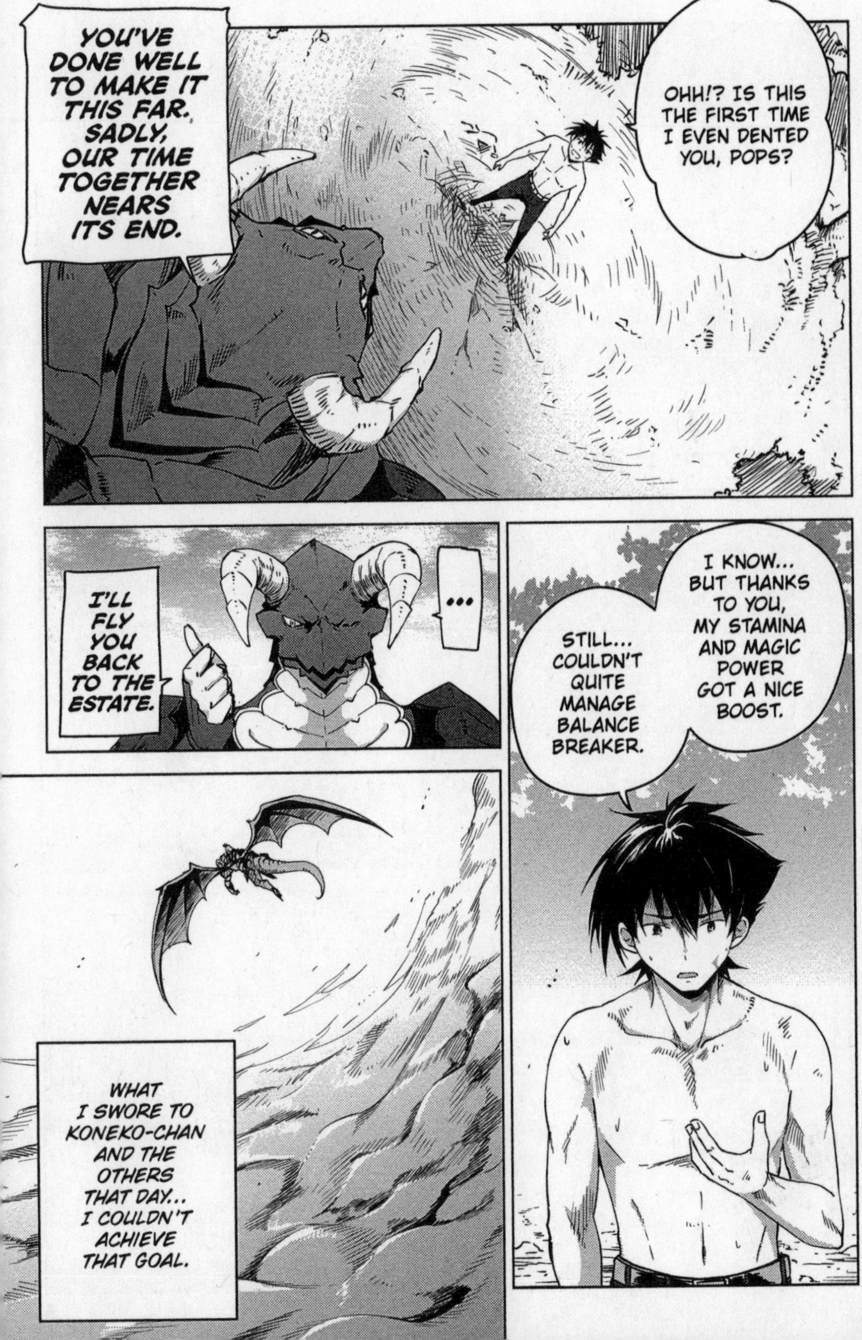
OHH!? IS THIS THE FIRST TIME I EVEN DENTED YOU, POPS?
YOU'VE DONE WELL TO MAKE IT THIS FAR. SADLY, OUR TIME TOGETHER NEARS ITS END.
I KNOW... BUT THANKS TO YOU, MY STAMINA AND MAGIC POWER GOT A NICE BOOST.
STILL... COULDN'T QUITE MANAGE BALANCE BREAKER.
...
I'LL FLY YOU BACK TO THE ESTATE.
WHAT I SWORE TO KONEKO-CHAN AND THE OTHERS THAT DAY... I COULDN'T ACHIEVE THAT GOAL.

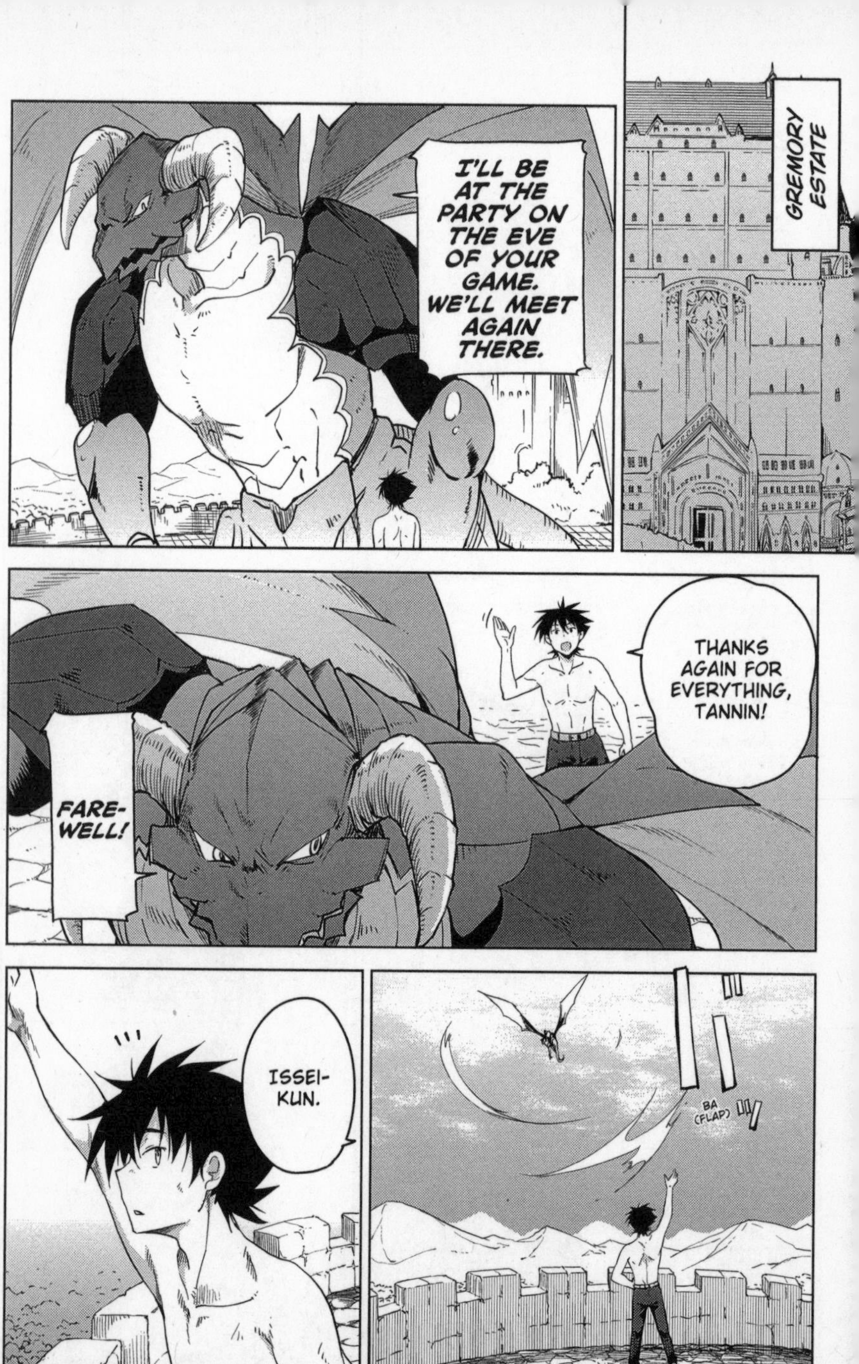
GREMORY ESTATE
I'LL BE AT THE PARTY ON THE EVE OF YOUR GAME. WE'LL MEET AGAIN THERE.
THANKS AGAIN FOR EVERYTHING, TANNIN!
FARE-WELL!
BA (FLAP)
ISSEI-KUN.

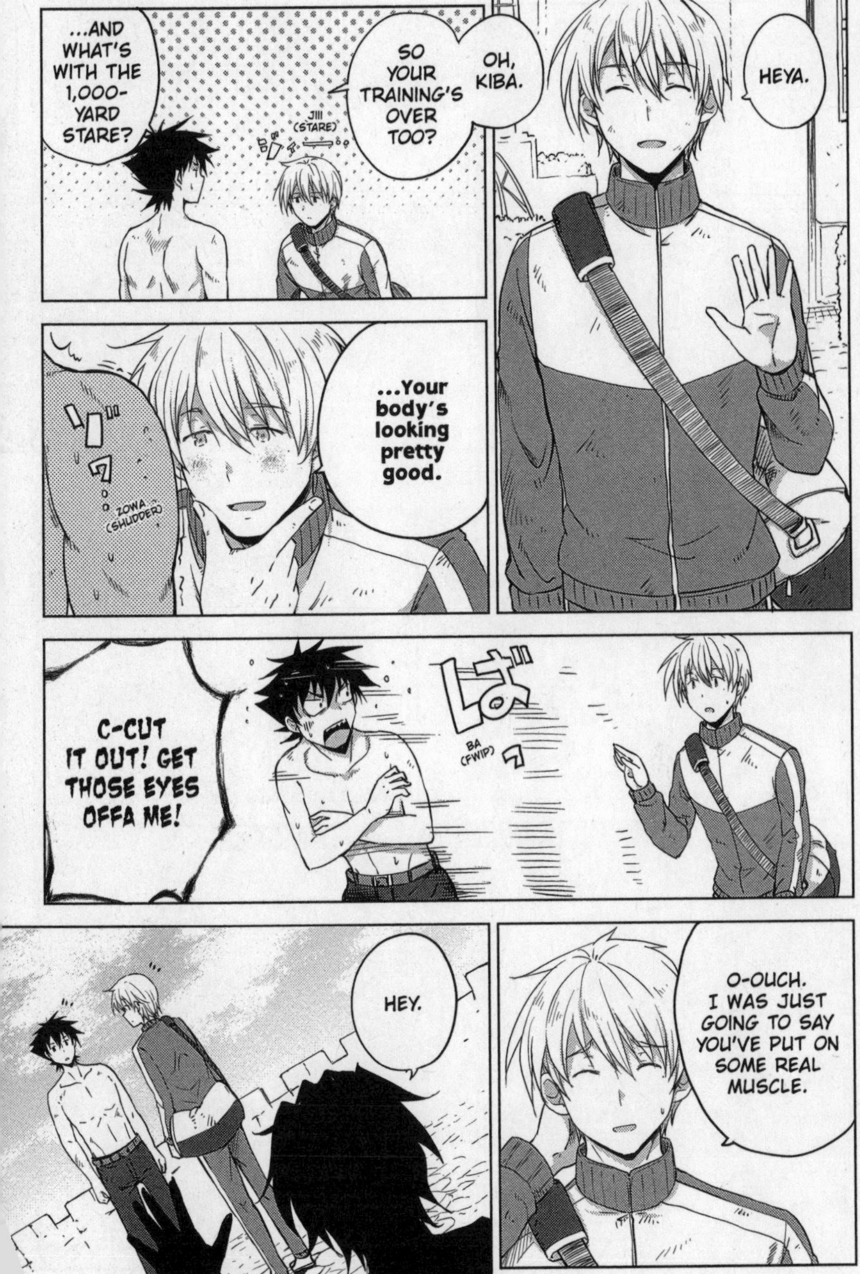
HEYA.
OH, KIBA.
SO YOUR TRAINING'S OVER TOO?
JIII (STARE)
...AND WHAT'S WITH THE 1,000-YARD STARE?
...Your body's looking pretty good.
ZOWA (SHUDDER)
BA (FWIP)
C-CUT IT OUT! GET THOSE EYES OFFA ME!
O-OUCH. I WAS JUST GOING TO SAY YOU'VE PUT ON SOME REAL MUSCLE.
HEY.

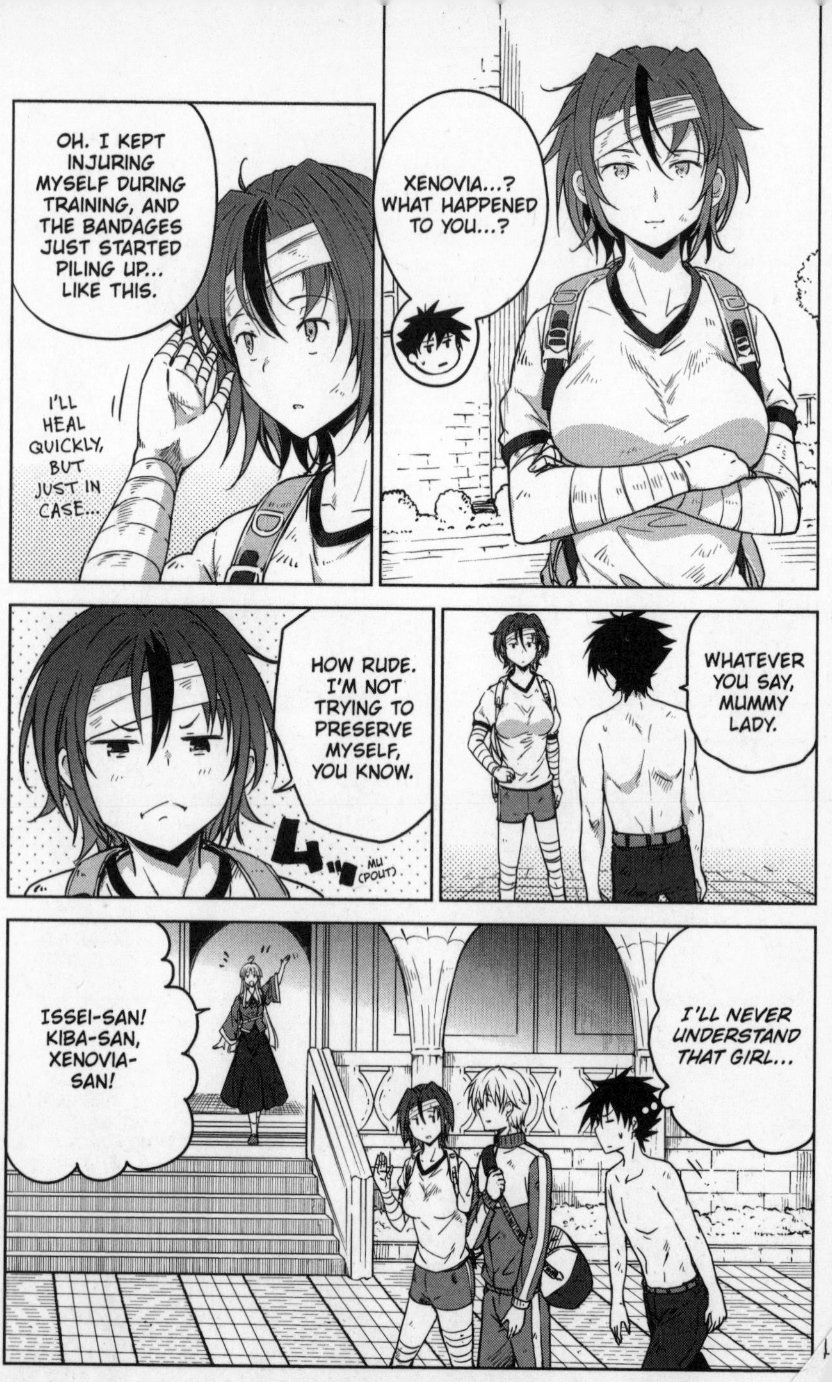
XENOVIA...? WHAT HAPPENED TO YOU...?
OH. I KEPT INJURING MYSELF DURING TRAINING, AND THE BANDAGES JUST STARTED PILING UP... LIKE THIS.
I'LL HEAL QUICKLY, BUT JUST IN CASE...
WHATEVER YOU SAY, MUMMY LADY.
HOW RUDE. I'M NOT TRYING TO PRESERVE MYSELF, YOU KNOW.
MU (POUT)
I'LL NEVER UNDERSTAND THAT GIRL...
ISSEI-SAN! KIBA-SAN, XENOVIA-SAN!

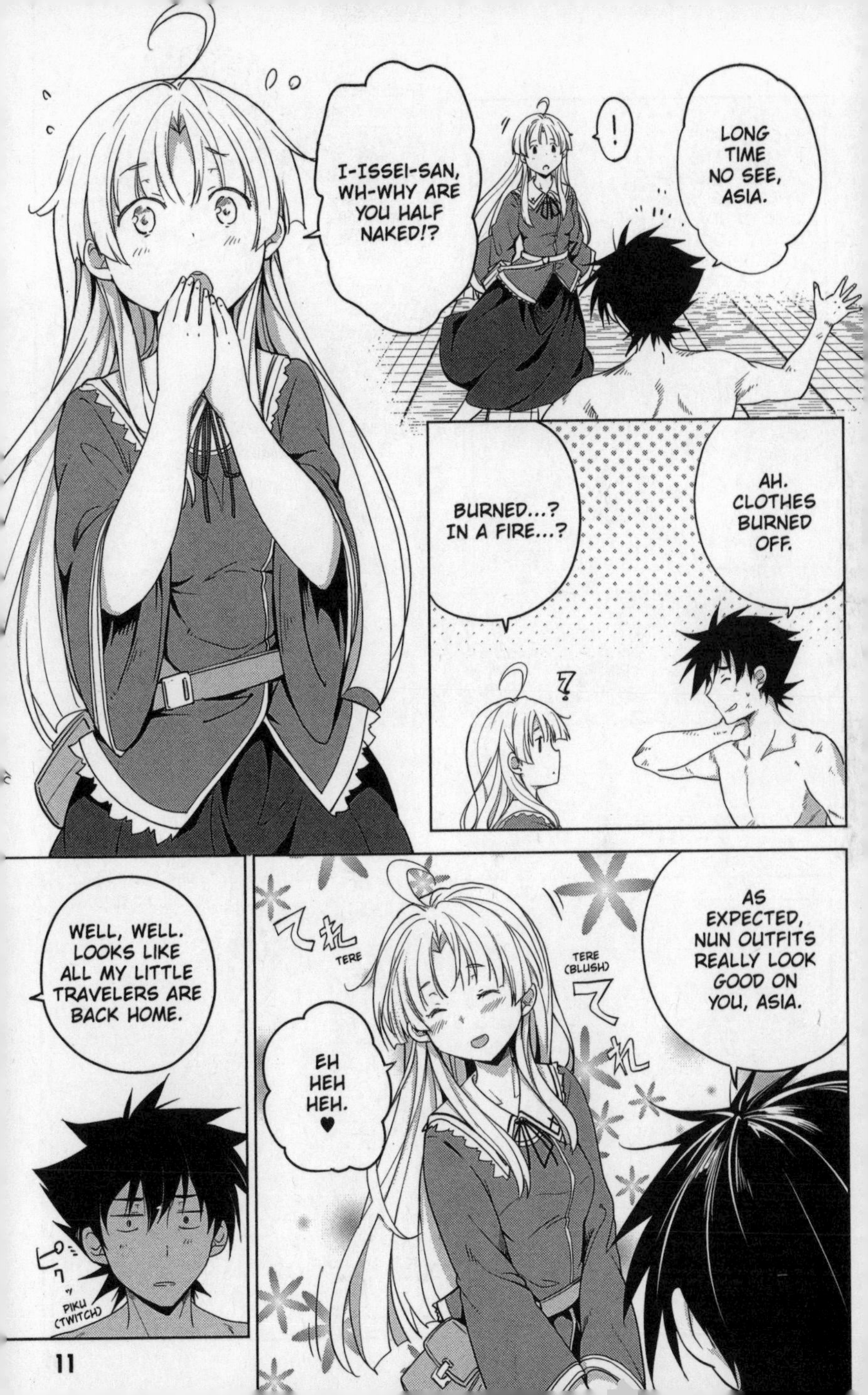
LONG TIME NO SEE, ASIA.
!
I-ISSEI-SAN, WH-WHY ARE YOU HALF NAKED!?
AH. CLOTHES BURNED OFF.
BURNED...? IN A FIRE...?
?
AS EXPECTED, NUN OUTFITS REALLY LOOK GOOD ON YOU, ASIA.
てれ
TERE (BLUSH)
EH HEH HEH. ♥
てれ
TERE
WELL, WELL. LOOKS LIKE ALL MY LITTLE TRAVELERS ARE BACK HOME.
ピクッ
PIKU (TWITCH)

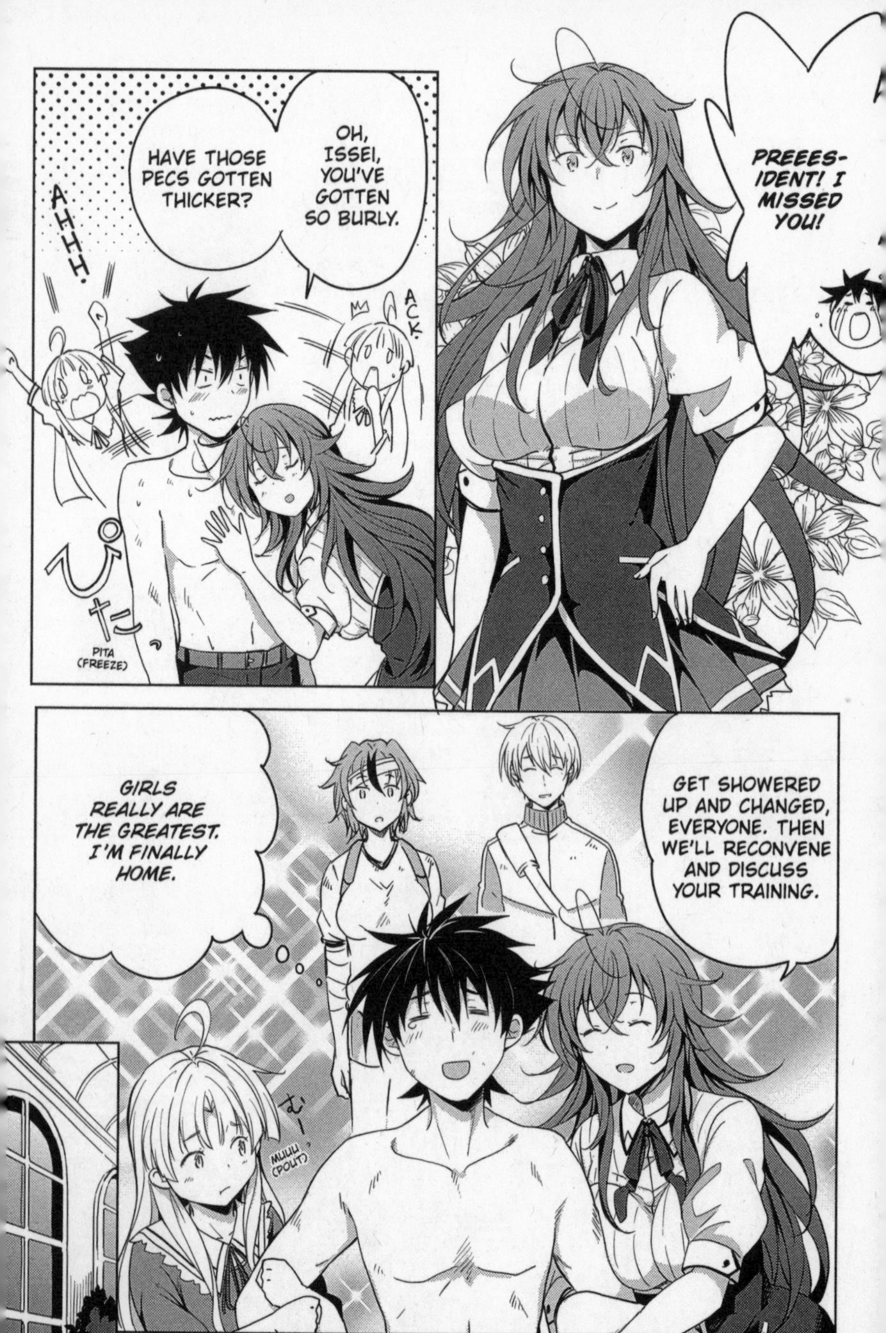
PREEES-IDENT! I MISSED YOU!
OH, ISSEI, YOU'VE GOTTEN SO BURLY.
HAVE THOSE PECS GOTTEN THICKER?
ACK.
AHHH!
PITA (FREEZE)
GET SHOWERED UP AND CHANGED, EVERYONE. THEN WE'LL RECONVENE AND DISCUSS YOUR TRAINING.
GIRLS REALLY ARE THE GREATEST. I'M FINALLY HOME.
MUUU (POUT)

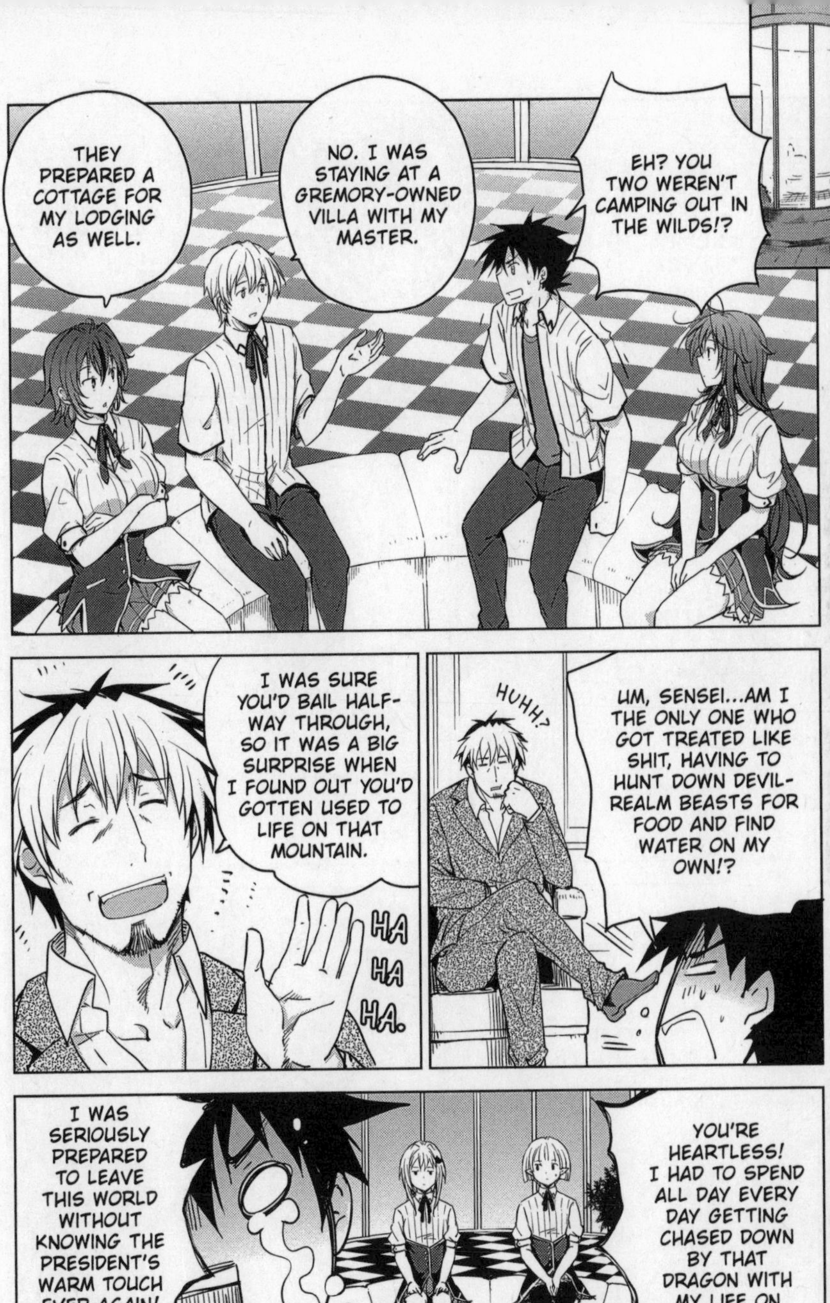
EH? YOU TWO WEREN'T CAMPING OUT IN THE WILDS!?
NO. I WAS STAYING AT A GREMORY-OWNED VILLA WITH MY MASTER.
THEY PREPARED A COTTAGE FOR MY LODGING AS WELL.
UM, SENSEI...AM I THE ONLY ONE WHO GOT TREATED LIKE SHIT, HAVING TO HUNT DOWN DEVIL-REALM BEASTS FOR FOOD AND FIND WATER ON MY OWN!?
HUHH?
I WAS SURE YOU'D BAIL HALF-WAY THROUGH, SO IT WAS A BIG SURPRISE WHEN I FOUND OUT YOU'D GOTTEN USED TO LIFE ON THAT MOUNTAIN.
HA HA HA.
YOU'RE HEARTLESS! I HAD TO SPEND ALL DAY EVERY DAY GETTING CHASED DOWN BY THAT DRAGON WITH MY LIFE ON THE LINE!
I WAS SERIOUSLY PREPARED TO LEAVE THIS WORLD WITHOUT KNOWING THE PRESIDENT'S WARM TOUCH EVER AGAIN! TOO MUCH, MAN!

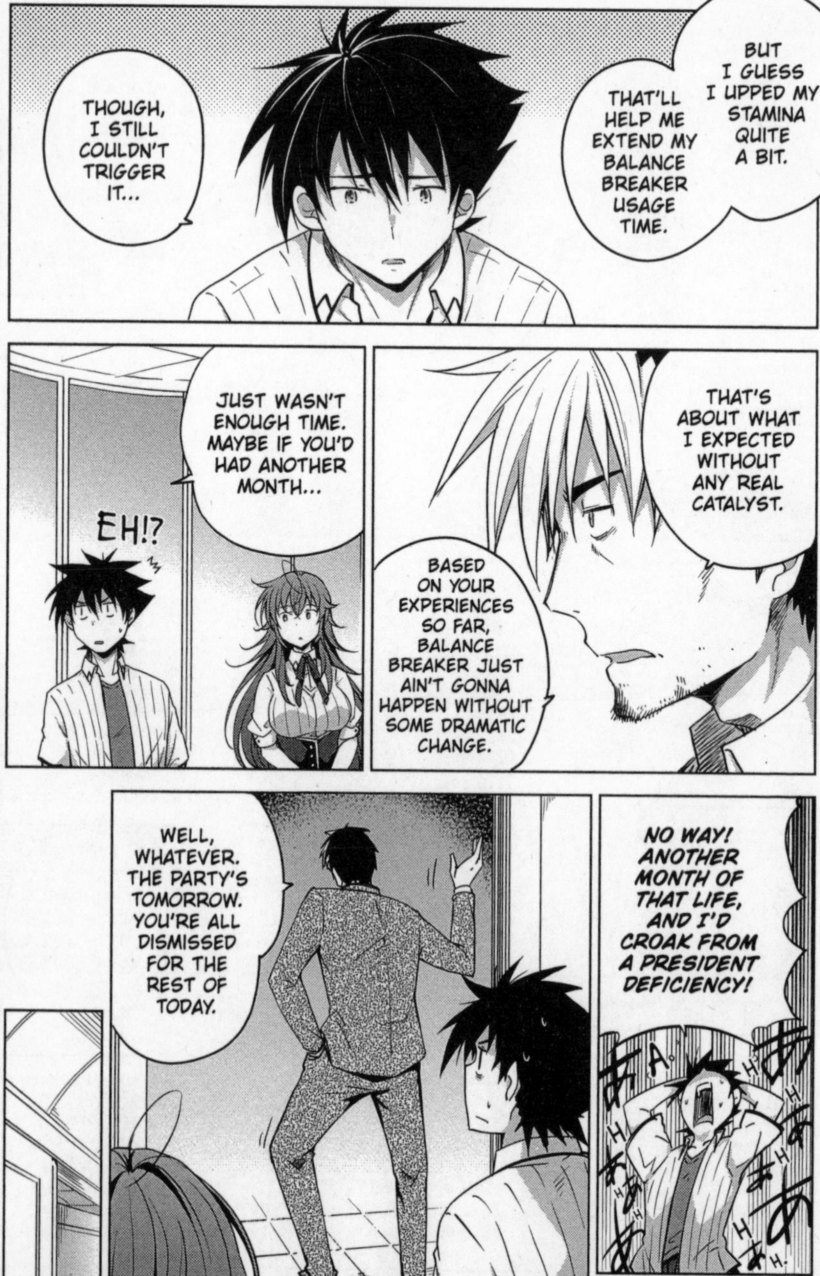
BUT I GUESS I UPPED MY STAMINA QUITE A BIT.
THAT'LL HELP ME EXTEND MY BALANCE BREAKER USAGE TIME.
THOUGH, I STILL COULDN'T TRIGGER IT...
THAT'S ABOUT WHAT I EXPECTED WITHOUT ANY REAL CATALYST.
BASED ON YOUR EXPERIENCES SO FAR, BALANCE BREAKER JUST AIN'T GONNA HAPPEN WITHOUT SOME DRAMATIC CHANGE.
JUST WASN'T ENOUGH TIME. MAYBE IF YOU'D HAD ANOTHER MONTH...
EH!?
NO WAY! ANOTHER MONTH OF THAT LIFE, AND I'D CROAK FROM A PRESIDENT DEFICIENCY!
WELL, WHATEVER. THE PARTY'S TOMORROW. YOU'RE ALL DISMISSED FOR THE REST OF TODAY.

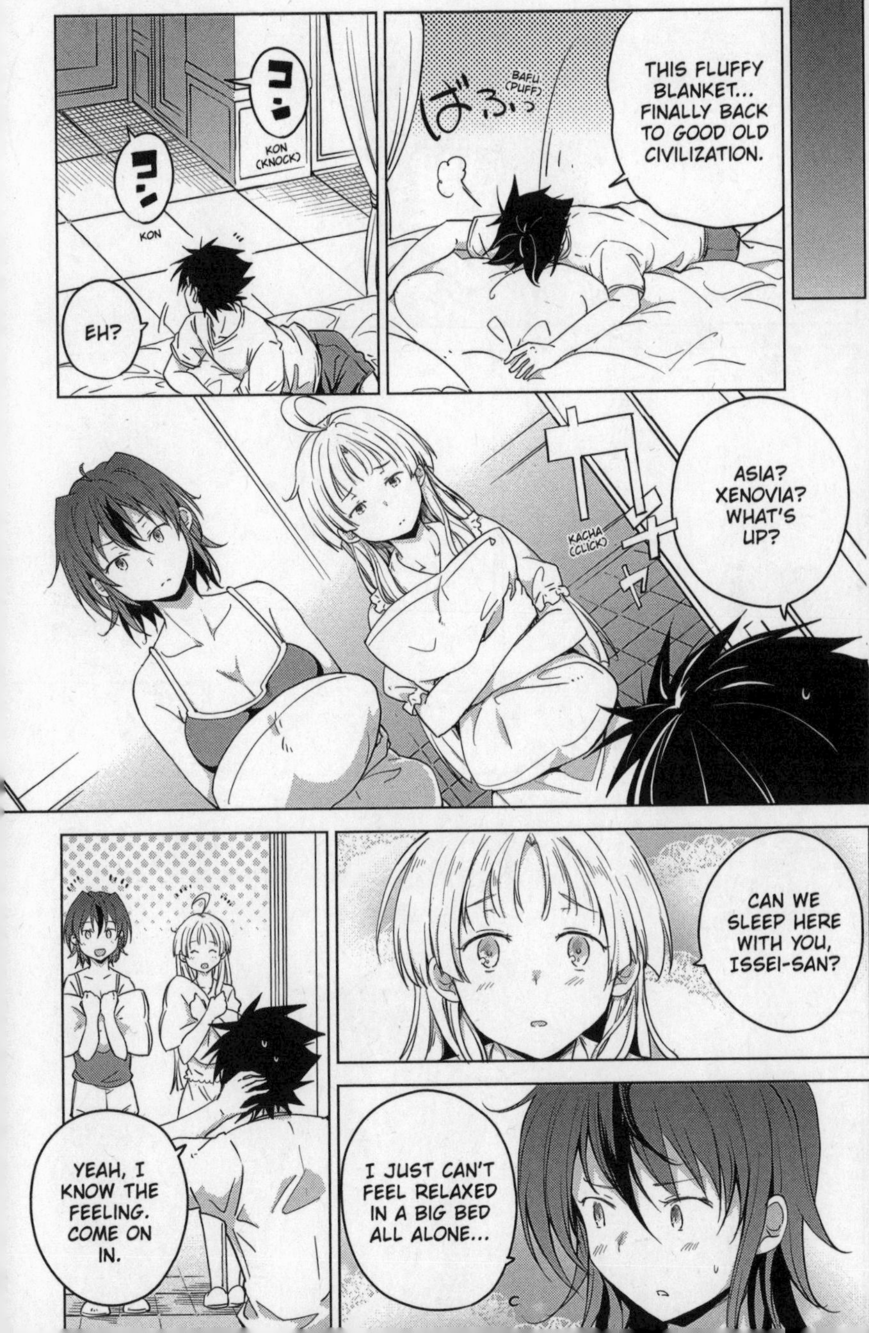

ばふっ
BAFU (PUFF)
THIS FLUFFY BLANKET... FINALLY BACK TO GOOD OLD CIVILIZATION.
コン
KON (KNOCK)
コン
KON
EH?
KACHA (CLICK)
ASIA? XENOVIA? WHAT'S UP?
CAN WE SLEEP HERE WITH YOU, ISSEI-SAN?
I JUST CAN'T FEEL RELAXED IN A BIG BED ALL ALONE...
YEAH, I KNOW THE FEELING. COME ON IN.

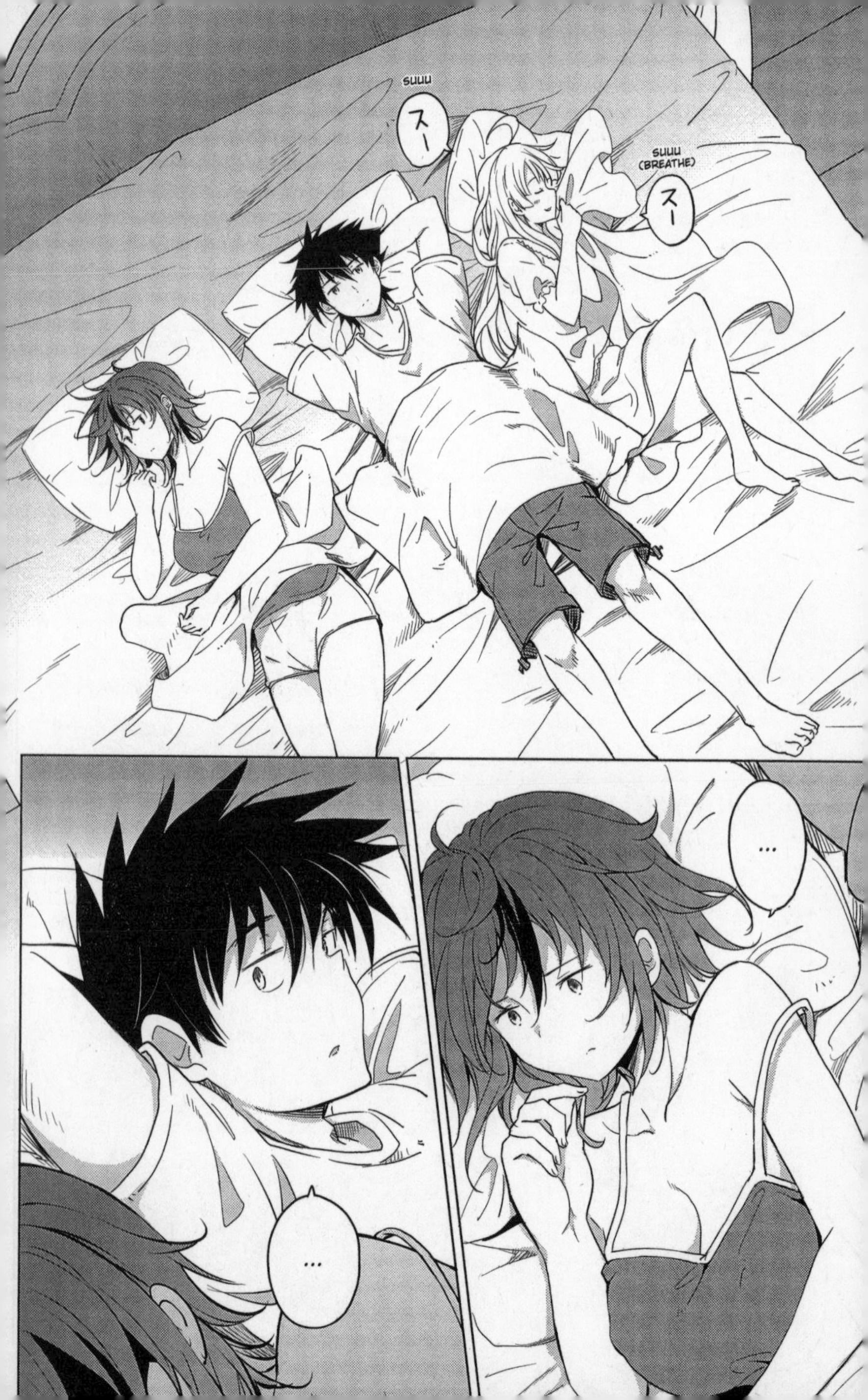
SUUU (BREATHE)
スー
SUUU
スー
...
...

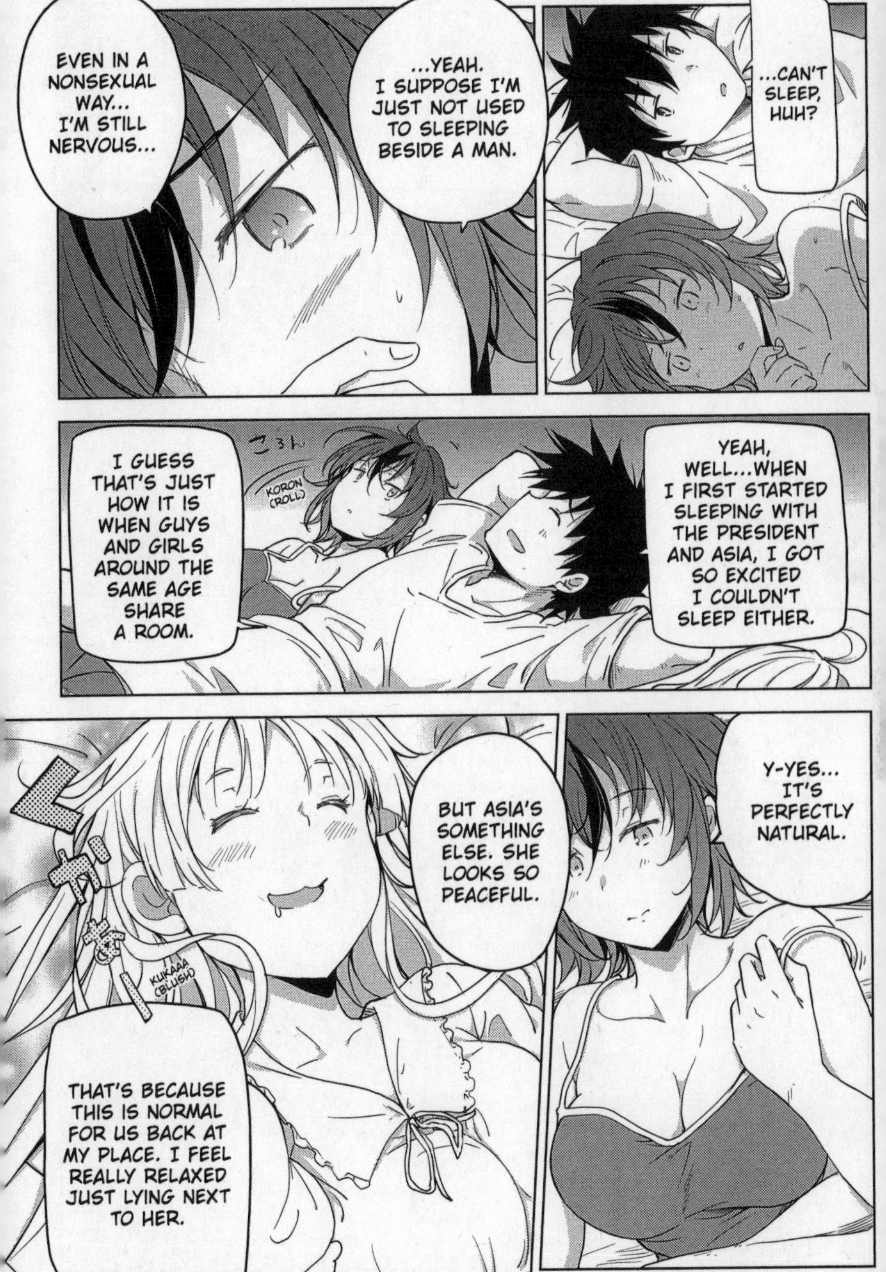
...CAN'T SLEEP, HUH?
...YEAH. I SUPPOSE I'M JUST NOT USED TO SLEEPING BESIDE A MAN.
EVEN IN A NONSEXUAL WAY... I'M STILL NERVOUS...
YEAH, WELL...WHEN I FIRST STARTED SLEEPING WITH THE PRESIDENT AND ASIA, I GOT SO EXCITED I COULDN'T SLEEP EITHER.
ころん
KORON (ROLL)
I GUESS THAT'S JUST HOW IT IS WHEN GUYS AND GIRLS AROUND THE SAME AGE SHARE A ROOM.
Y-YES... IT'S PERFECTLY NATURAL.
BUT ASIA'S SOMETHING ELSE. SHE LOOKS SO PEACEFUL.
KUKAAA (BLUSH)
THAT'S BECAUSE THIS IS NORMAL FOR US BACK AT MY PLACE. I FEEL REALLY RELAXED JUST LYING NEXT TO HER.

GABA
(RISE)

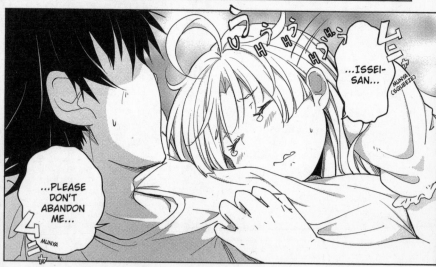

...ISSEI-
SAN...

MUNYA
(SQUEEZE)

...PLEASE
DON'T
ABANDON
ME...

MUNYA

FU-FU-FU.
NOW I SEE WHY
YOU AND THE
PRESIDENT
FAWN OVER
ASIA SO MUCH,
ISSEI.

RIGHT?
ASIA-CHAN'S
JUST THE
CUTEST.

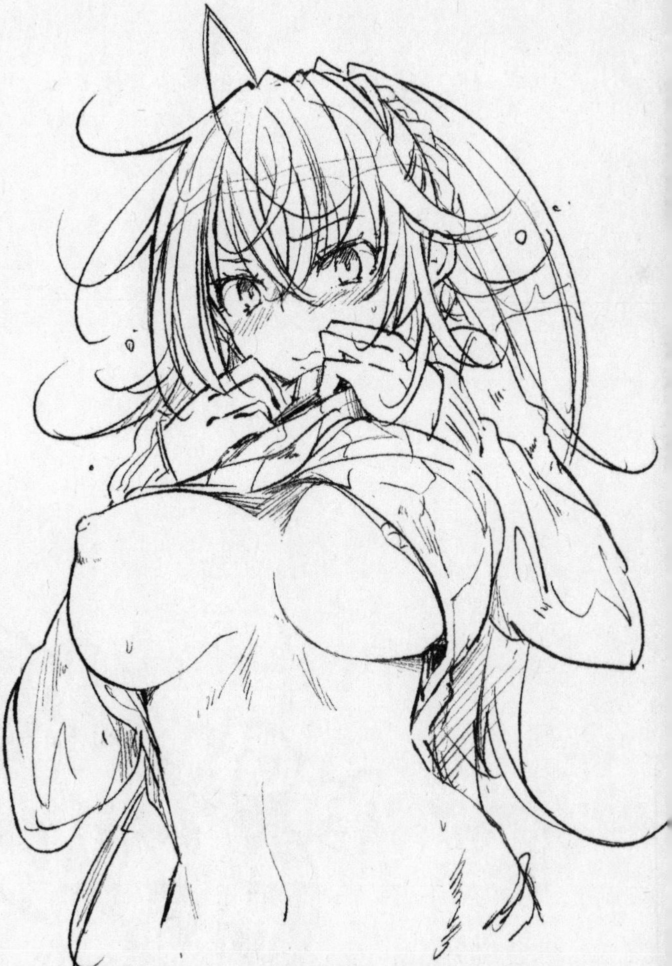

HIGH SCHOOL DxD

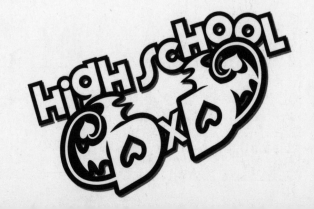

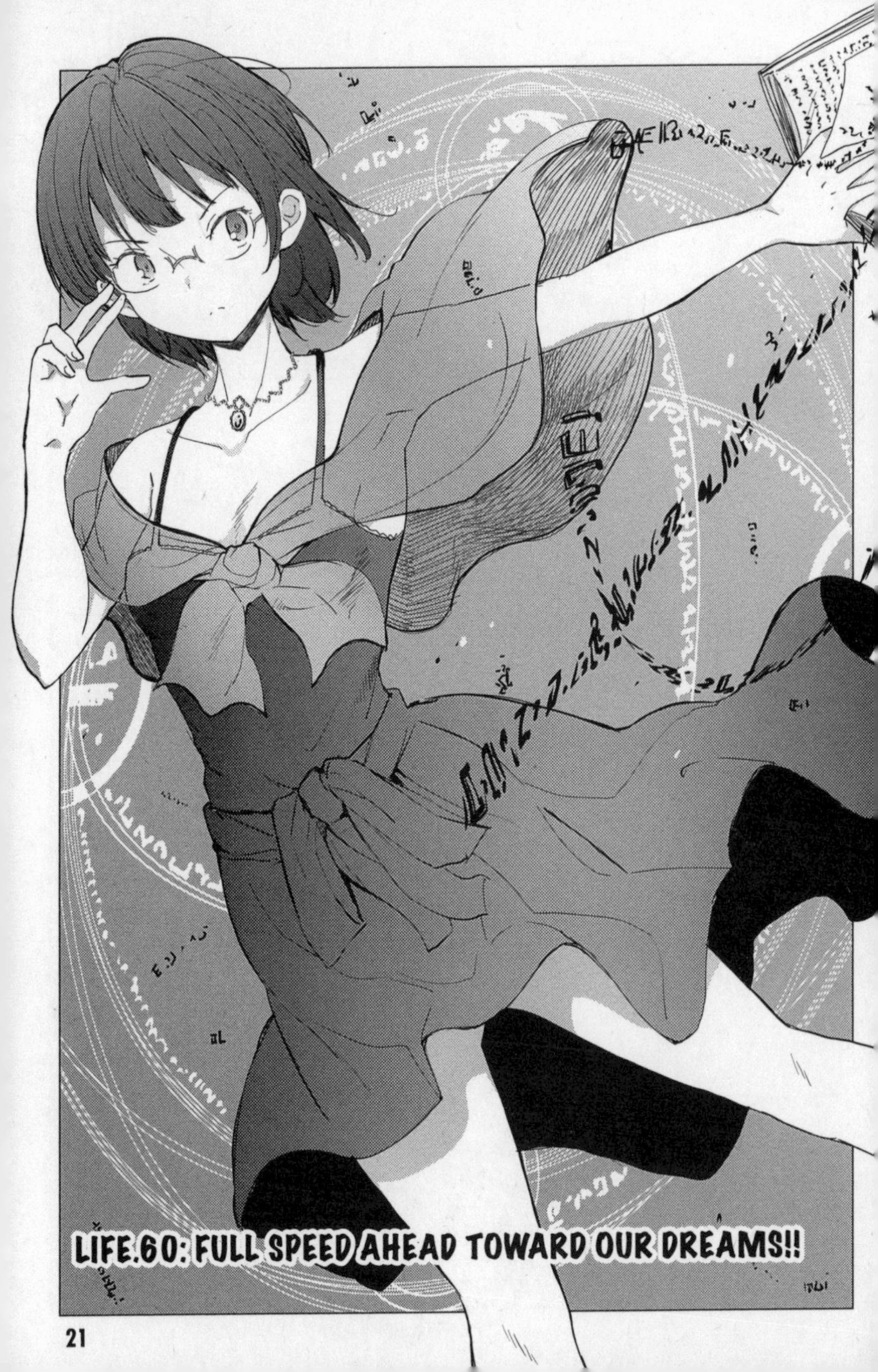
LIFE.60: FULL SPEED AHEAD TOWARD OUR DREAMS!!

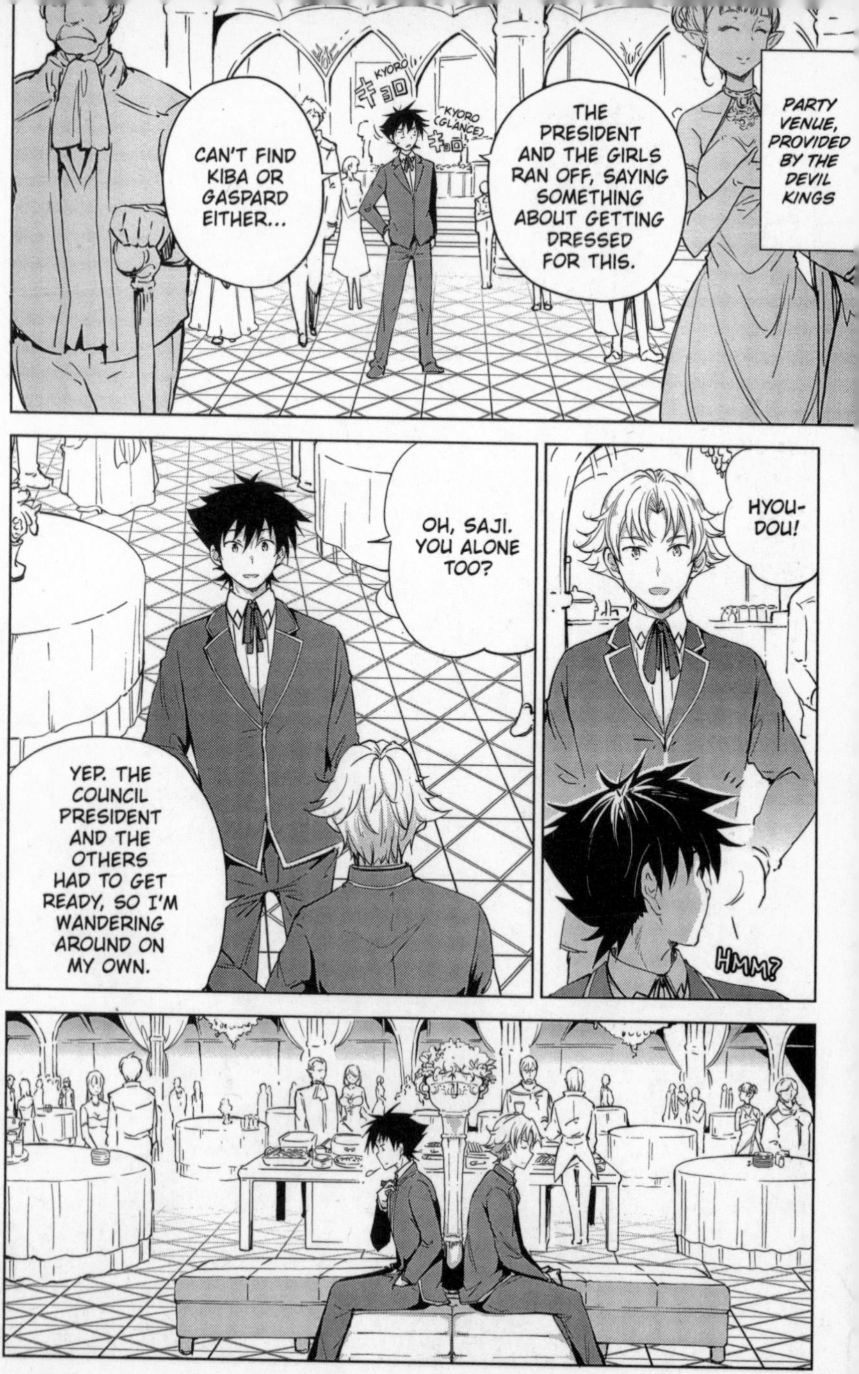
PARTY VENUE, PROVIDED BY THE DEVIL KINGS
THE PRESIDENT AND THE GIRLS RAN OFF, SAYING SOMETHING ABOUT GETTING DRESSED FOR THIS.
KYORO (GLANCE)
KYORO
CAN'T FIND KIBA OR GASPARD EITHER...
HYOU-DOU!
HMM?
OH, SAJI. YOU ALONE TOO?
YEP. THE COUNCIL PRESIDENT AND THE OTHERS HAD TO GET READY, SO I'M WANDERING AROUND ON MY OWN.

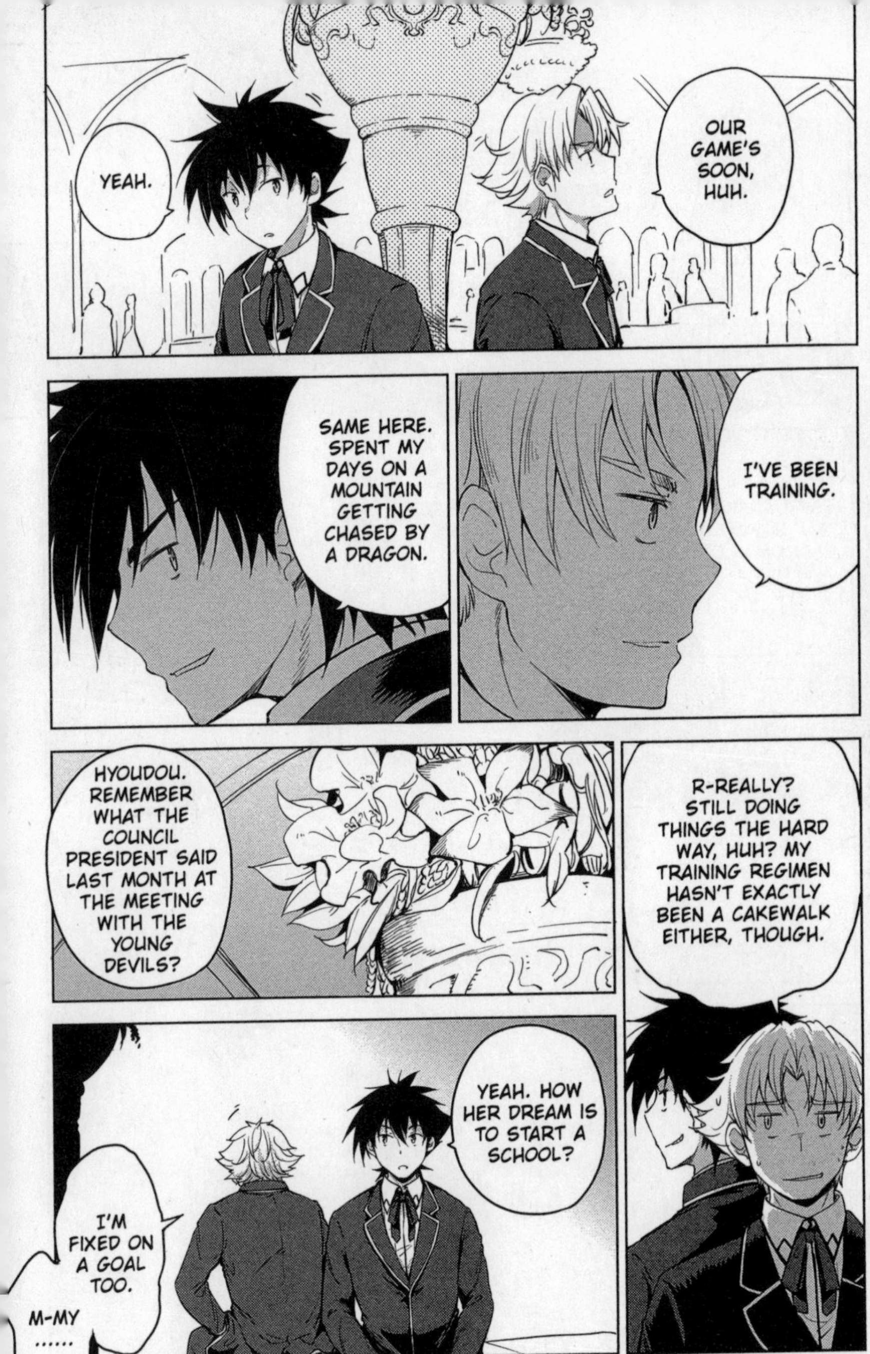
OUR GAME'S SOON, HUH.
YEAH.
I'VE BEEN TRAINING.
SAME HERE. SPENT MY DAYS ON A MOUNTAIN GETTING CHASED BY A DRAGON.
R-REALLY? STILL DOING THINGS THE HARD WAY, HUH? MY TRAINING REGIMEN HASN'T EXACTLY BEEN A CAKEWALK EITHER, THOUGH.
HYOUDOU. REMEMBER WHAT THE COUNCIL PRESIDENT SAID LAST MONTH AT THE MEETING WITH THE YOUNG DEVILS?
YEAH. HOW HER DREAM IS TO START A SCHOOL?
I'M FIXED ON A GOAL TOO.
M-MY ......

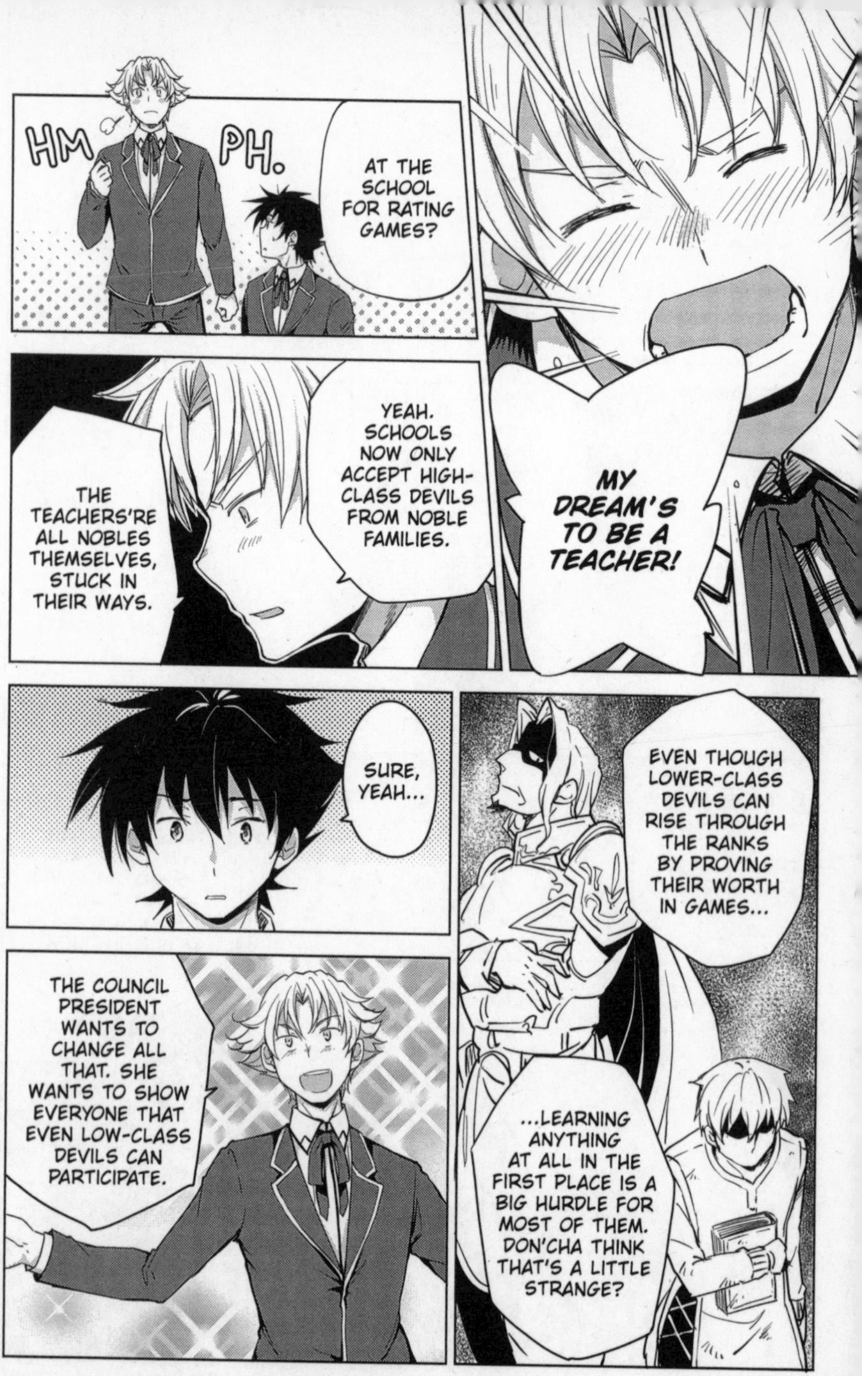
MY DREAM'S TO BE A TEACHER!
AT THE SCHOOL FOR RATING GAMES?
HMPH.
YEAH. SCHOOLS NOW ONLY ACCEPT HIGH-CLASS DEVILS FROM NOBLE FAMILIES.
THE TEACHERS'RE ALL NOBLES THEMSELVES, STUCK IN THEIR WAYS.
EVEN THOUGH LOWER-CLASS DEVILS CAN RISE THROUGH THE RANKS BY PROVING THEIR WORTH IN GAMES...
...LEARNING ANYTHING AT ALL IN THE FIRST PLACE IS A BIG HURDLE FOR MOST OF THEM. DON'CHA THINK THAT'S A LITTLE STRANGE?
SURE, YEAH...
THE COUNCIL PRESIDENT WANTS TO CHANGE ALL THAT. SHE WANTS TO SHOW EVERYONE THAT EVEN LOW-CLASS DEVILS CAN PARTICIPATE.

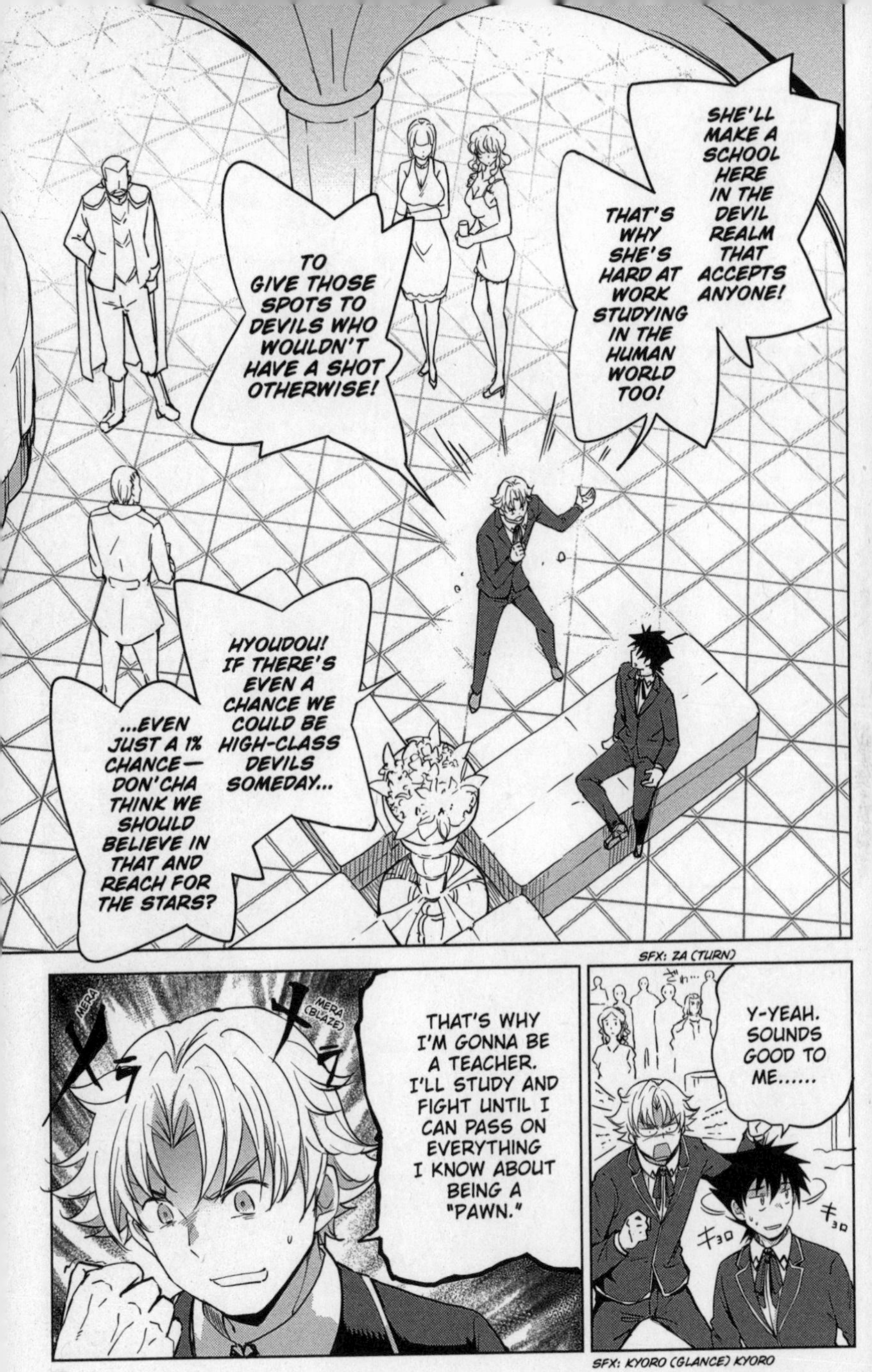
SHE'LL MAKE A SCHOOL HERE IN THE DEVIL REALM THAT ACCEPTS ANYONE!
THAT'S WHY SHE'S HARD AT WORK STUDYING IN THE HUMAN WORLD TOO!
TO GIVE THOSE SPOTS TO DEVILS WHO WOULDN'T HAVE A SHOT OTHERWISE!
HYOUDOU! IF THERE'S EVEN A CHANCE WE COULD BE HIGH-CLASS DEVILS SOMEDAY...
...EVEN JUST A 1% CHANCE—DON'CHA THINK WE SHOULD BELIEVE IN THAT AND REACH FOR THE STARS?
SFX: ZA (TURN)
Y-YEAH. SOUNDS GOOD TO ME......
SFX: KYORO (GLANCE) KYORO
MERA
MERA (BLAZE)
THAT'S WHY I'M GONNA BE A TEACHER. I'LL STUDY AND FIGHT UNTIL I CAN PASS ON EVERYTHING I KNOW ABOUT BEING A "PAWN."

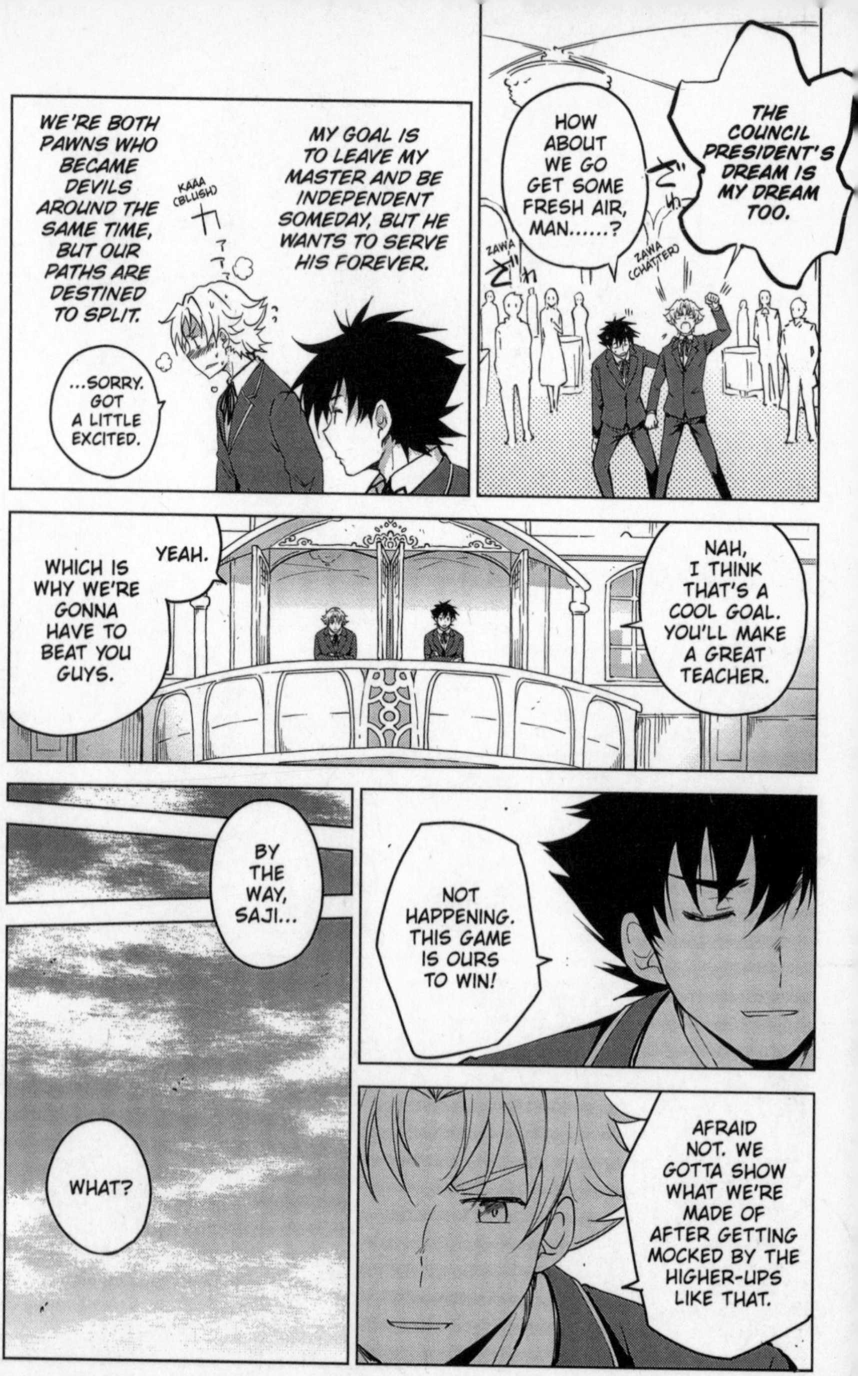
THE COUNCIL PRESIDENT'S DREAM IS MY DREAM TOO.
HOW ABOUT WE GO GET SOME FRESH AIR, MAN......?
ZAWA (CHATTER)
ZAWA
MY GOAL IS TO LEAVE MY MASTER AND BE INDEPENDENT SOMEDAY, BUT HE WANTS TO SERVE HIS FOREVER.
WE'RE BOTH PAWNS WHO BECAME DEVILS AROUND THE SAME TIME, BUT OUR PATHS ARE DESTINED TO SPLIT.
KAAA (BLUSH)
...SORRY. GOT A LITTLE EXCITED.
NAH, I THINK THAT'S A COOL GOAL. YOU'LL MAKE A GREAT TEACHER.
YEAH.
WHICH IS WHY WE'RE GONNA HAVE TO BEAT YOU GUYS.
NOT HAPPENING. THIS GAME IS OURS TO WIN!
AFRAID NOT. WE GOTTA SHOW WHAT WE'RE MADE OF AFTER GETTING MOCKED BY THE HIGHER-UPS LIKE THAT.
BY THE WAY, SAJI...
WHAT?

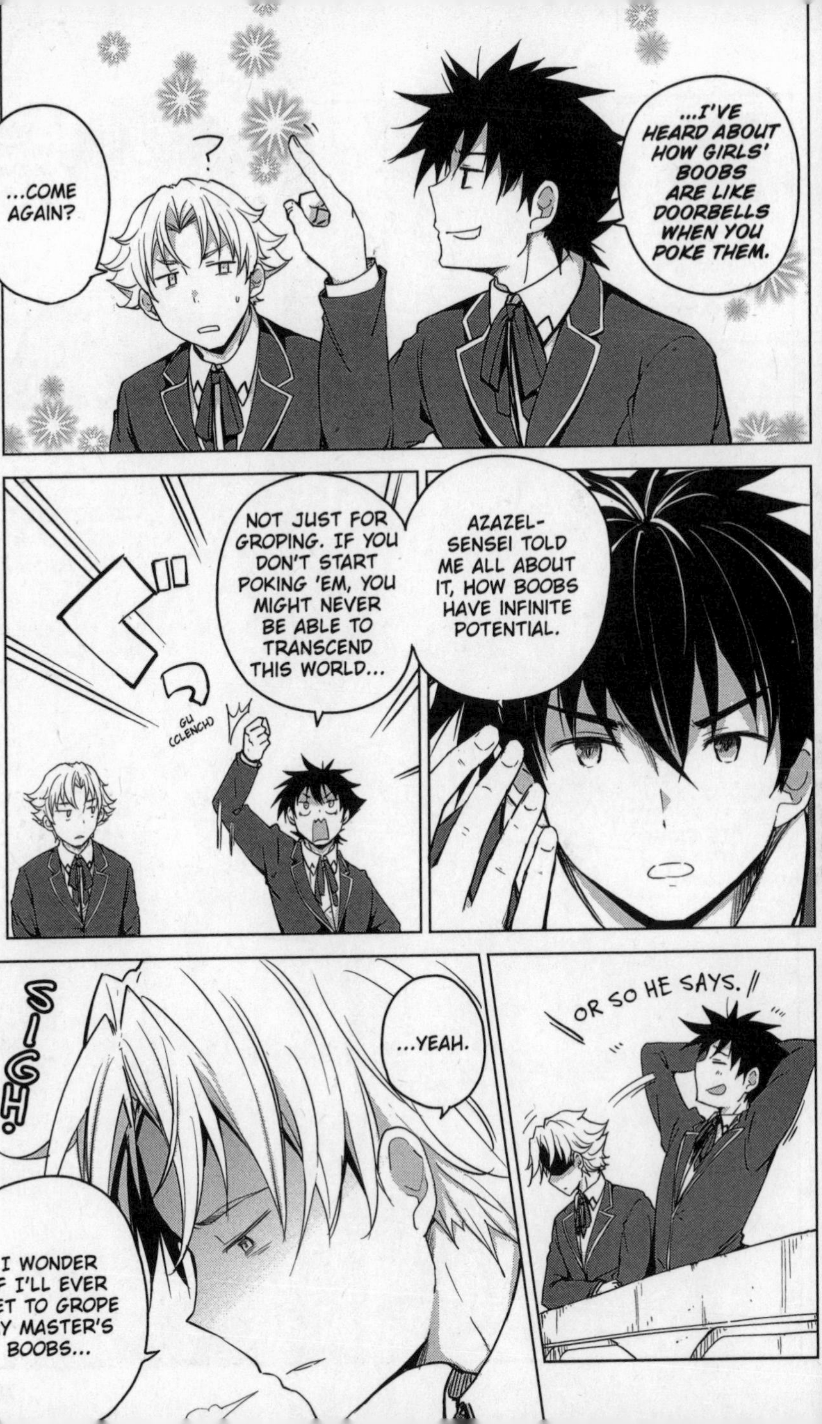

...I'VE HEARD ABOUT HOW GIRLS' BOOBS ARE LIKE DOORBELLS WHEN YOU POKE THEM.
?
...COME AGAIN?
AZAZEL-SENSEI TOLD ME ALL ABOUT IT, HOW BOOBS HAVE INFINITE POTENTIAL.
NOT JUST FOR GROPING. IF YOU DON'T START POKING 'EM, YOU MIGHT NEVER BE ABLE TO TRANSCEND THIS WORLD...
GU (CLENCH)
OR SO HE SAYS.
...YEAH.
SIGH!
I WONDER IF I'LL EVER GET TO GROPE MY MASTER'S BOOBS...

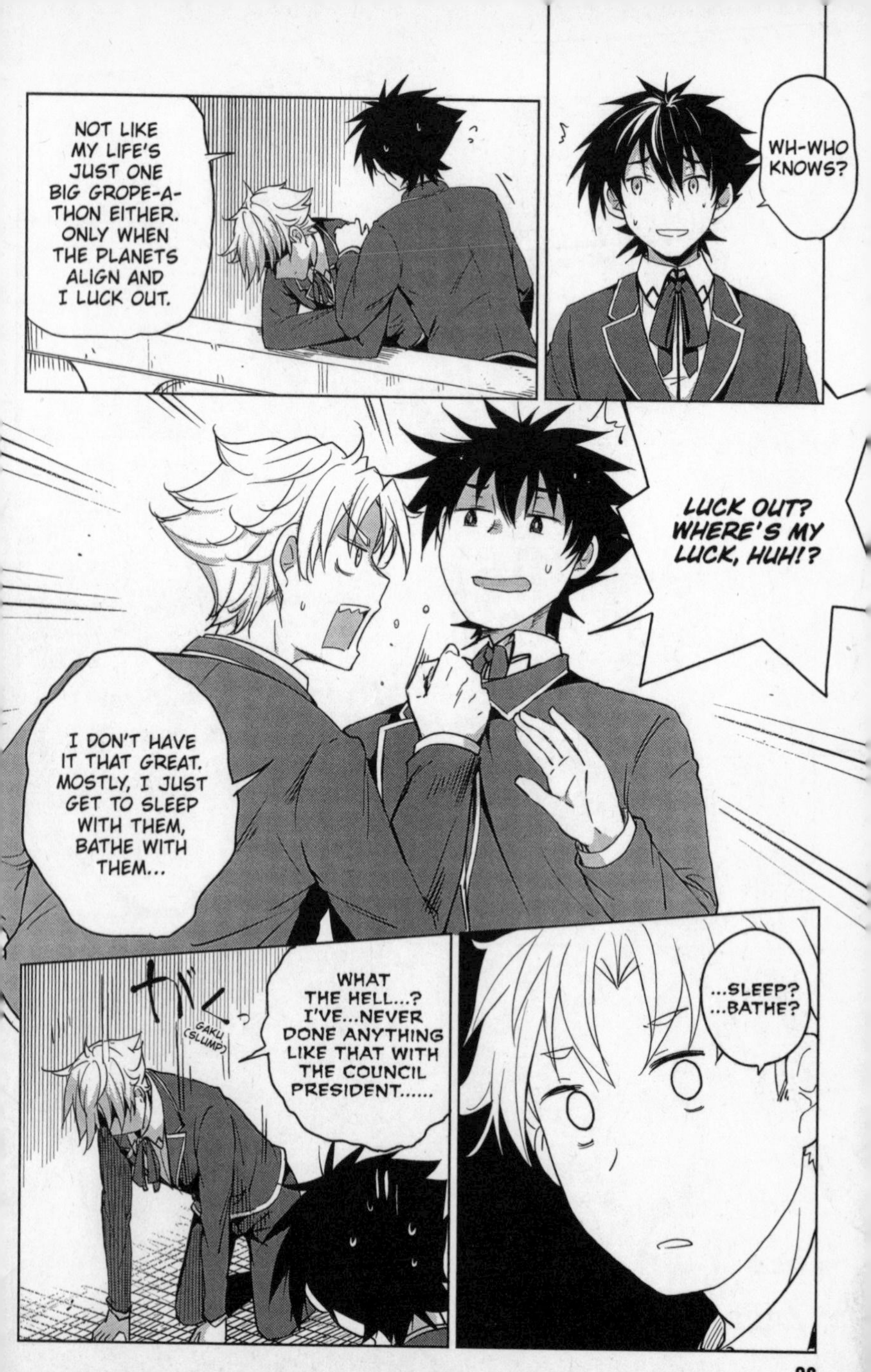
WH-WHO KNOWS?
NOT LIKE MY LIFE'S JUST ONE BIG GROPE-A-THON EITHER. ONLY WHEN THE PLANETS ALIGN AND I LUCK OUT.
LUCK OUT? WHERE'S MY LUCK, HUH!?
I DON'T HAVE IT THAT GREAT. MOSTLY, I JUST GET TO SLEEP WITH THEM, BATHE WITH THEM...
...SLEEP? ...BATHE?
WHAT THE HELL...? I'VE...NEVER DONE ANYTHING LIKE THAT WITH THE COUNCIL PRESIDENT......
GAKU (SLUMP)

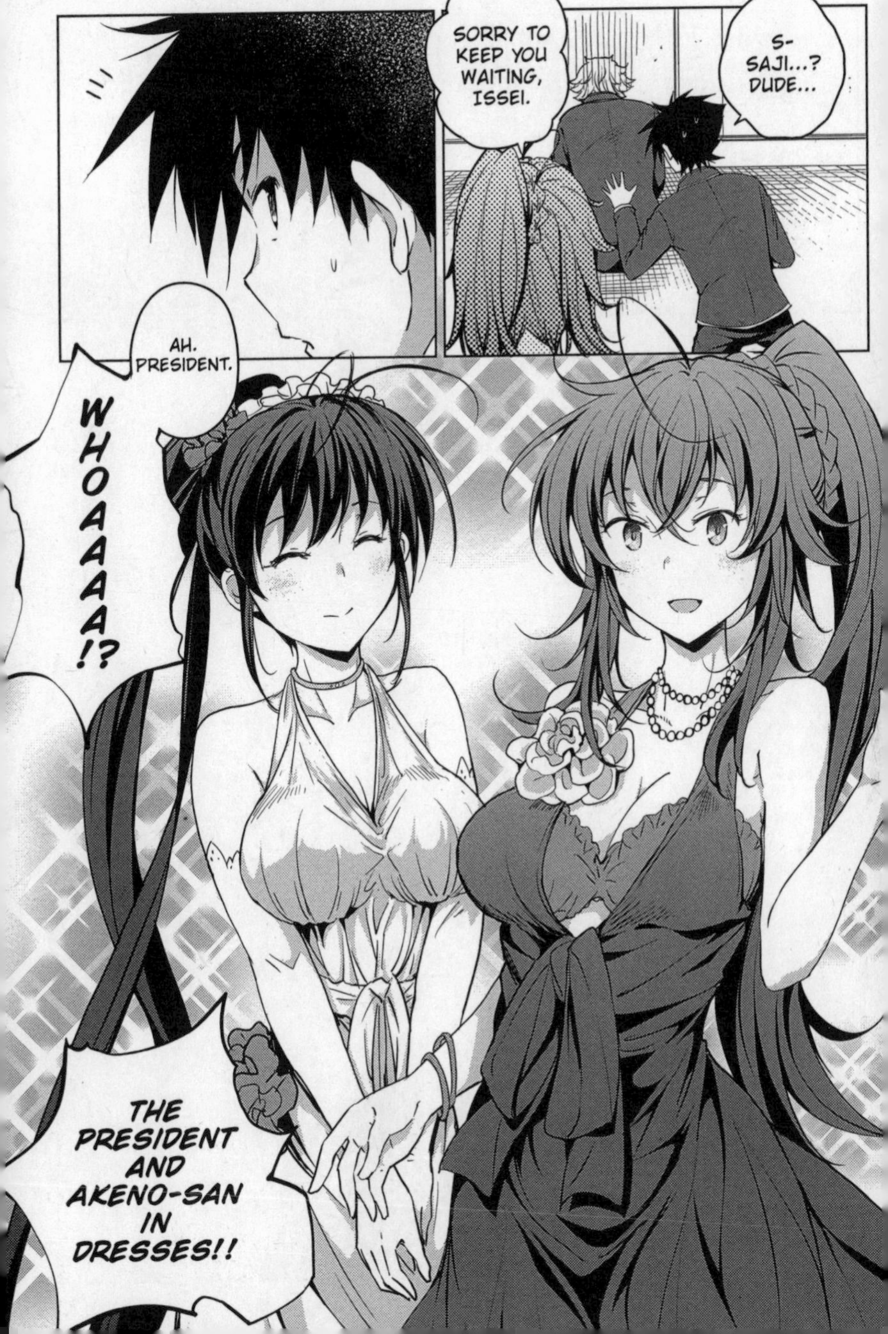
S- SAJI...? DUDE...
SORRY TO KEEP YOU WAITING, ISSEI.
AH. PRESIDENT.
WHOAAAAA!?
THE PRESIDENT AND AKENO-SAN IN DRESSES!!

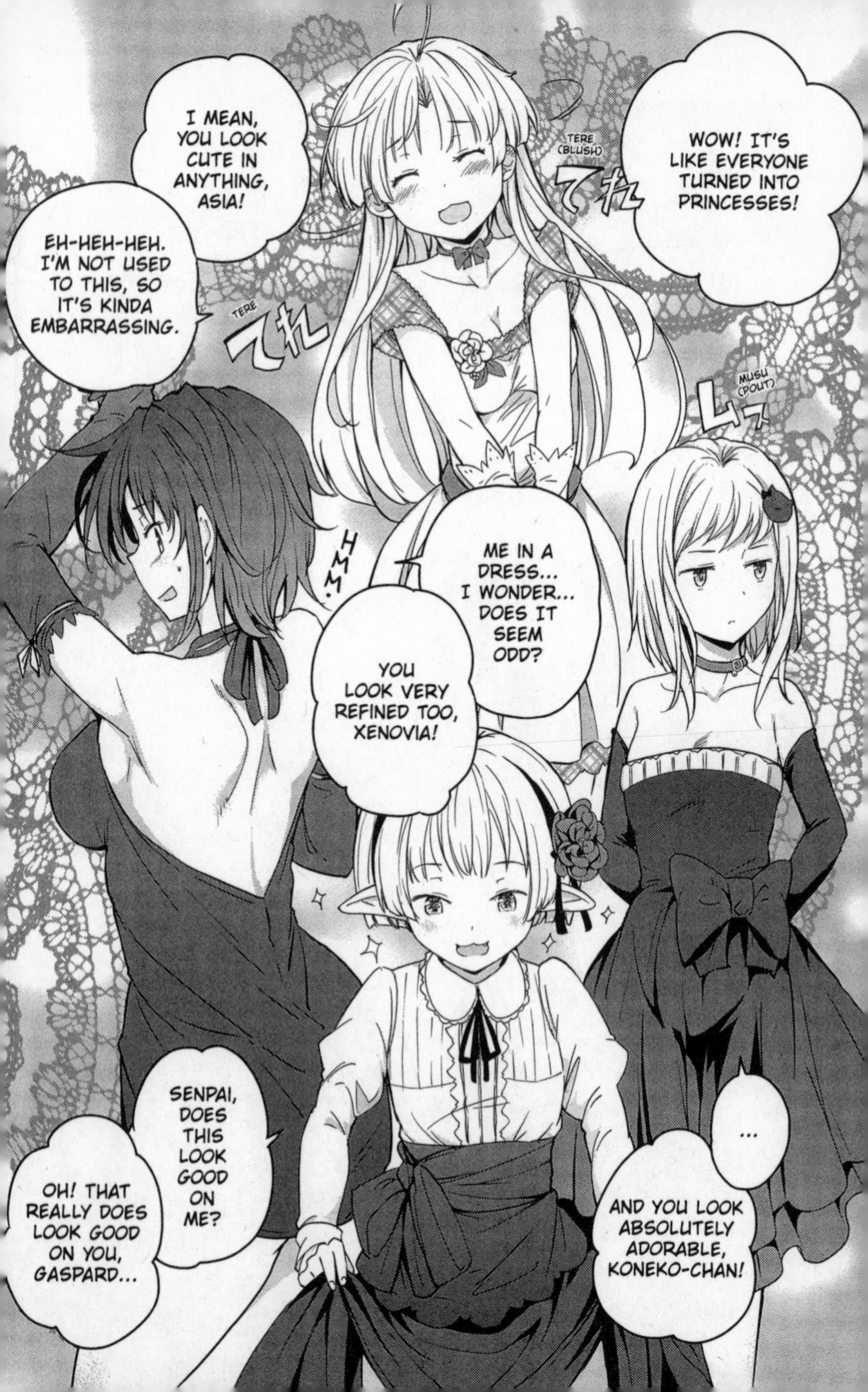
WOW! IT'S LIKE EVERYONE TURNED INTO PRINCESSES!
TERE (BLUSH)
てれ
I MEAN, YOU LOOK CUTE IN ANYTHING, ASIA!
EH-HEH-HEH. I'M NOT USED TO THIS, SO IT'S KINDA EMBARRASSING.
TERE
てれ
MUSU (POUT)
ムッ
ME IN A DRESS... I WONDER... DOES IT SEEM ODD?
HMM...
YOU LOOK VERY REFINED TOO, XENOVIA!
...
AND YOU LOOK ABSOLUTELY ADORABLE, KONEKO-CHAN!
SENPAI, DOES THIS LOOK GOOD ON ME?
OH! THAT REALLY DOES LOOK GOOD ON YOU, GASPARD...

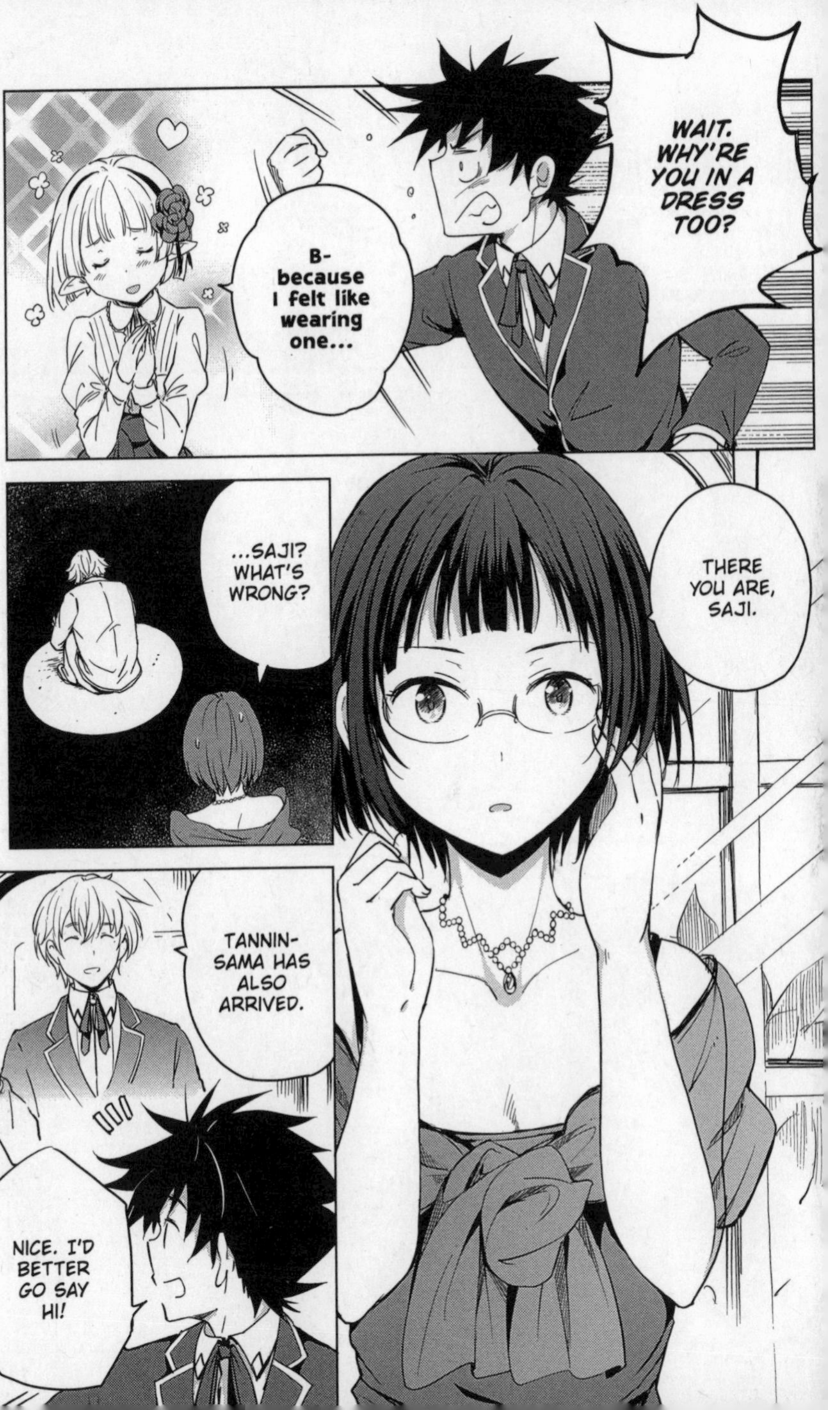
WAIT. WHY'RE YOU IN A DRESS TOO?
B-because I felt like wearing one...
THERE YOU ARE, SAJI.
...SAJI? WHAT'S WRONG?
TANNIN-SAMA HAS ALSO ARRIVED.
NICE. I'D BETTER GO SAY HI!

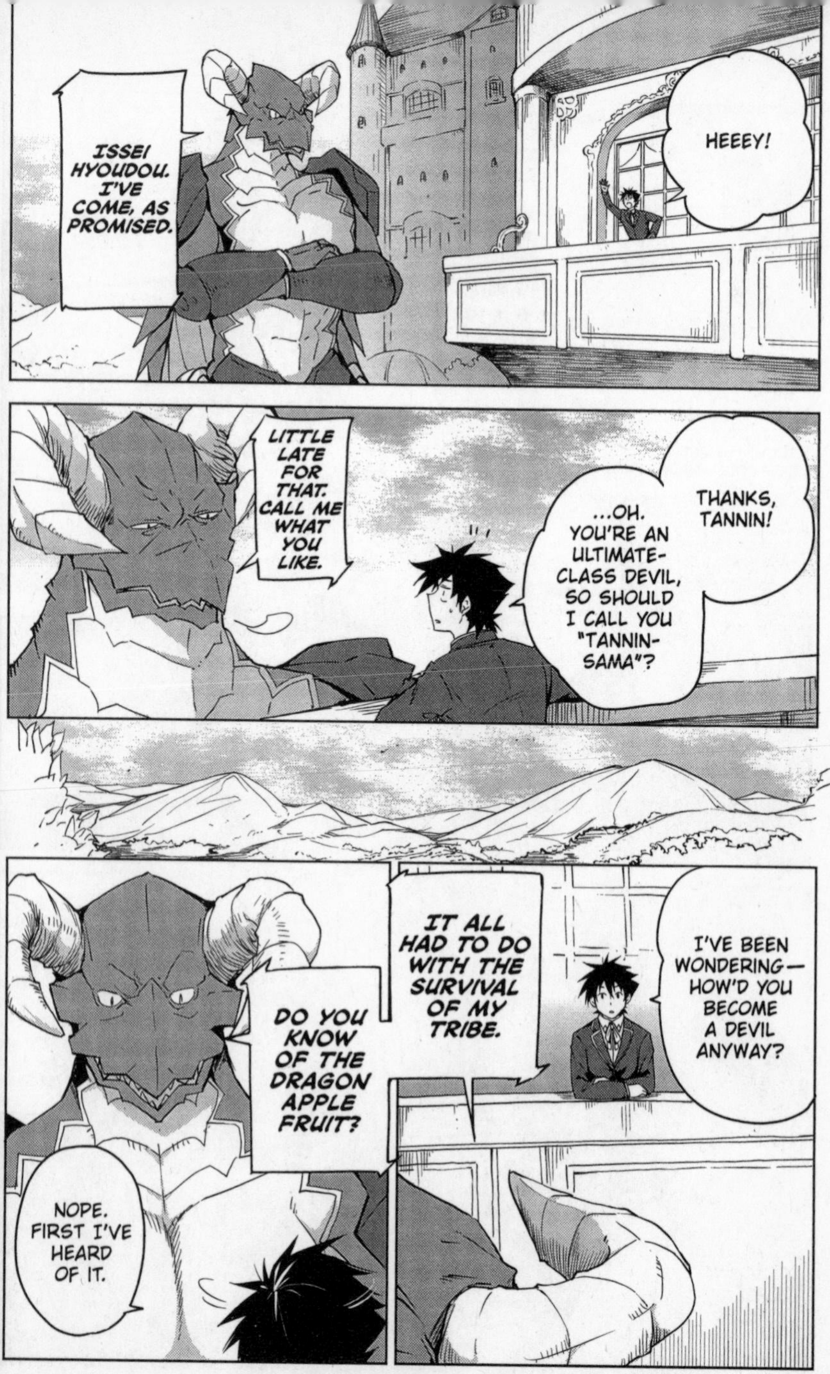
HEEEY!
ISSEI HYOUDOU. I'VE COME, AS PROMISED.
THANKS, TANNIN!
...OH. YOU'RE AN ULTIMATE-CLASS DEVIL, SO SHOULD I CALL YOU "TANNIN-SAMA"?
LITTLE LATE FOR THAT. CALL ME WHAT YOU LIKE.
I'VE BEEN WONDERING—HOW'D YOU BECOME A DEVIL ANYWAY?
IT ALL HAD TO DO WITH THE SURVIVAL OF MY TRIBE.
DO YOU KNOW OF THE DRAGON APPLE FRUIT?
NOPE. FIRST I'VE HEARD OF IT.

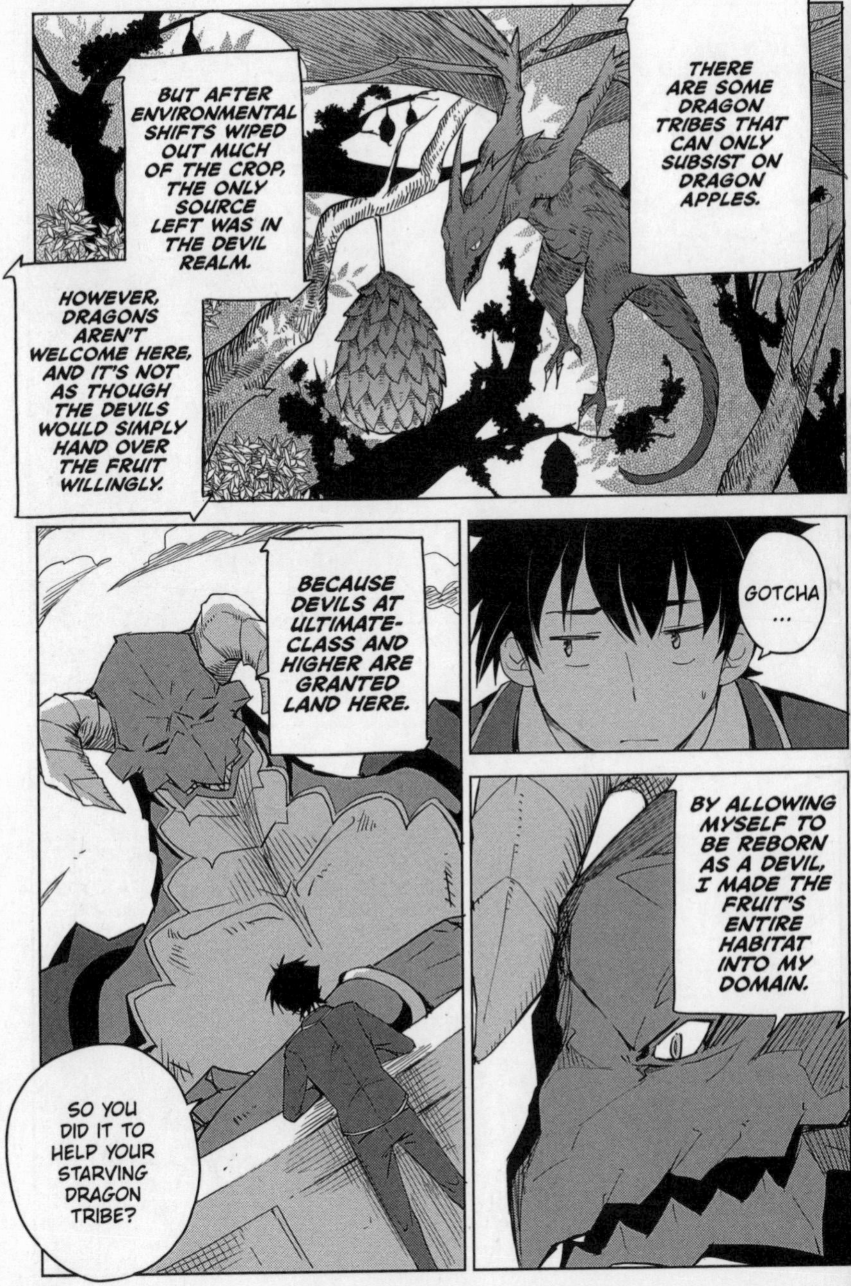
THERE ARE SOME DRAGON TRIBES THAT CAN ONLY SUBSIST ON DRAGON APPLES.
BUT AFTER ENVIRONMENTAL SHIFTS WIPED OUT MUCH OF THE CROP, THE ONLY SOURCE LEFT WAS IN THE DEVIL REALM.
HOWEVER, DRAGONS AREN'T WELCOME HERE, AND IT'S NOT AS THOUGH THE DEVILS WOULD SIMPLY HAND OVER THE FRUIT WILLINGLY.
GOTCHA...
BY ALLOWING MYSELF TO BE REBORN AS A DEVIL, I MADE THE FRUIT'S ENTIRE HABITAT INTO MY DOMAIN.
BECAUSE DEVILS AT ULTIMATE-CLASS AND HIGHER ARE GRANTED LAND HERE.
SO YOU DID IT TO HELP YOUR STARVING DRAGON TRIBE?

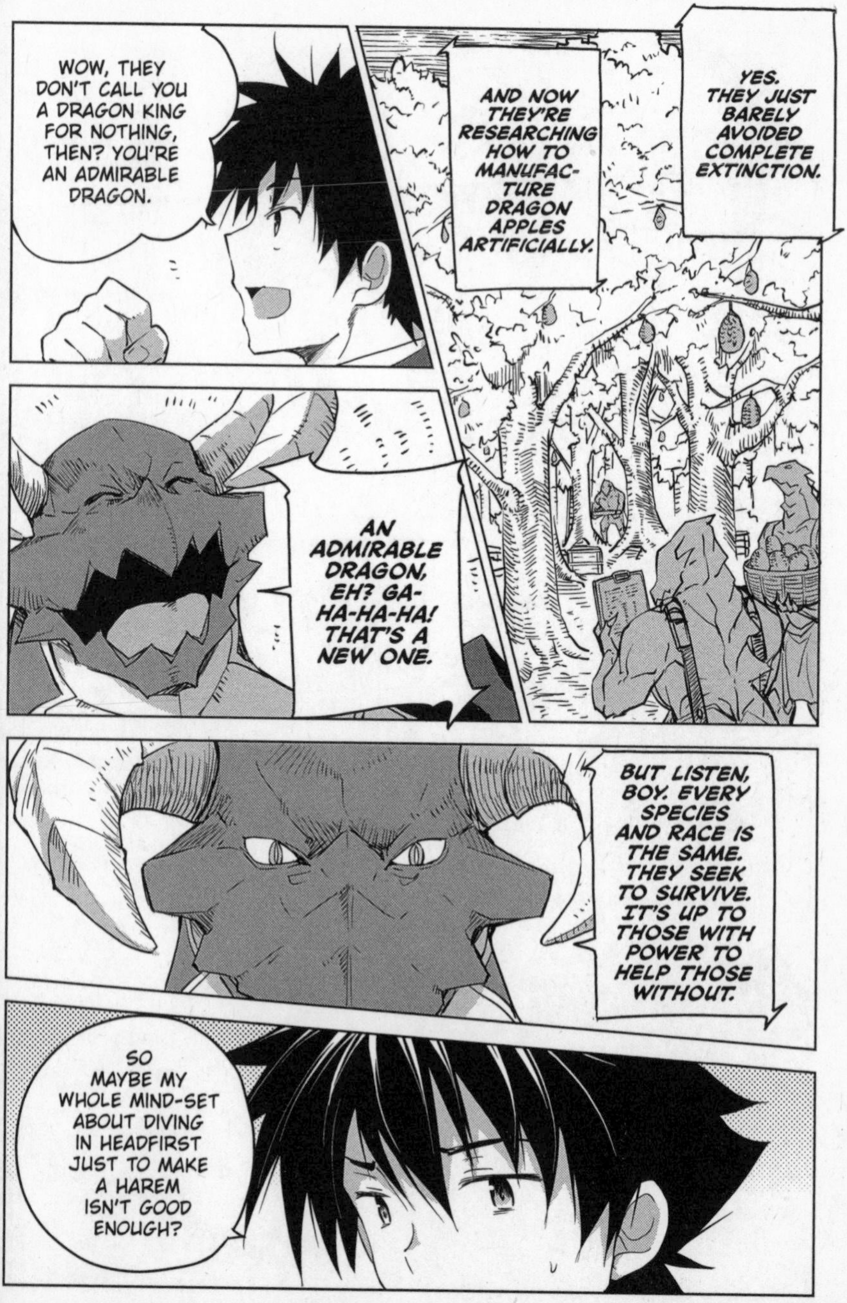
YES. THEY JUST BARELY AVOIDED COMPLETE EXTINCTION.
AND NOW THEY'RE RESEARCHING HOW TO MANUFAC-TURE DRAGON APPLES ARTIFICIALLY.
WOW, THEY DON'T CALL YOU A DRAGON KING FOR NOTHING, THEN? YOU'RE AN ADMIRABLE DRAGON.
AN ADMIRABLE DRAGON, EH? GA-HA-HA-HA! THAT'S A NEW ONE.
BUT LISTEN, BOY. EVERY SPECIES AND RACE IS THE SAME. THEY SEEK TO SURVIVE. IT'S UP TO THOSE WITH POWER TO HELP THOSE WITHOUT.
SO MAYBE MY WHOLE MIND-SET ABOUT DIVING IN HEADFIRST JUST TO MAKE A HAREM ISN'T GOOD ENOUGH?

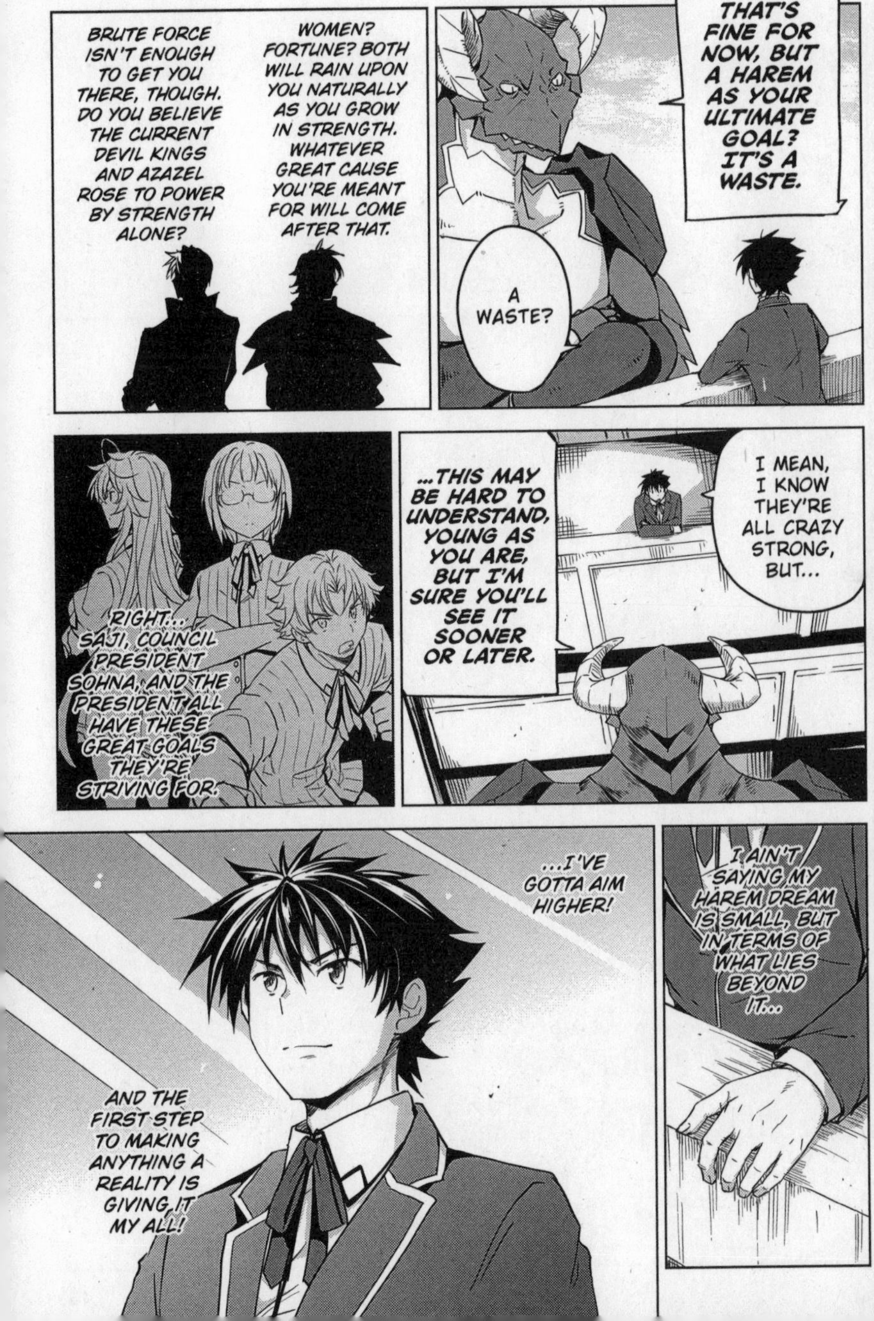
THAT'S FINE FOR NOW, BUT A HAREM AS YOUR ULTIMATE GOAL? IT'S A WASTE.
A WASTE?
WOMEN? FORTUNE? BOTH WILL RAIN UPON YOU NATURALLY AS YOU GROW IN STRENGTH. WHATEVER GREAT CAUSE YOU'RE MEANT FOR WILL COME AFTER THAT.
BRUTE FORCE ISN'T ENOUGH TO GET YOU THERE, THOUGH. DO YOU BELIEVE THE CURRENT DEVIL KINGS AND AZAZEL ROSE TO POWER BY STRENGTH ALONE?
I MEAN, I KNOW THEY'RE ALL CRAZY STRONG, BUT...
...THIS MAY BE HARD TO UNDERSTAND, YOUNG AS YOU ARE, BUT I'M SURE YOU'LL SEE IT SOONER OR LATER.
RIGHT... SAJI, COUNCIL PRESIDENT SOHNA, AND THE PRESIDENT ALL HAVE THESE GREAT GOALS THEY'RE STRIVING FOR.
I AIN'T SAYING MY HAREM DREAM IS SMALL, BUT IN TERMS OF WHAT LIES BEYOND IT...
...I'VE GOTTA AIM HIGHER!
AND THE FIRST STEP TO MAKING ANYTHING A REALITY IS GIVING IT MY ALL!

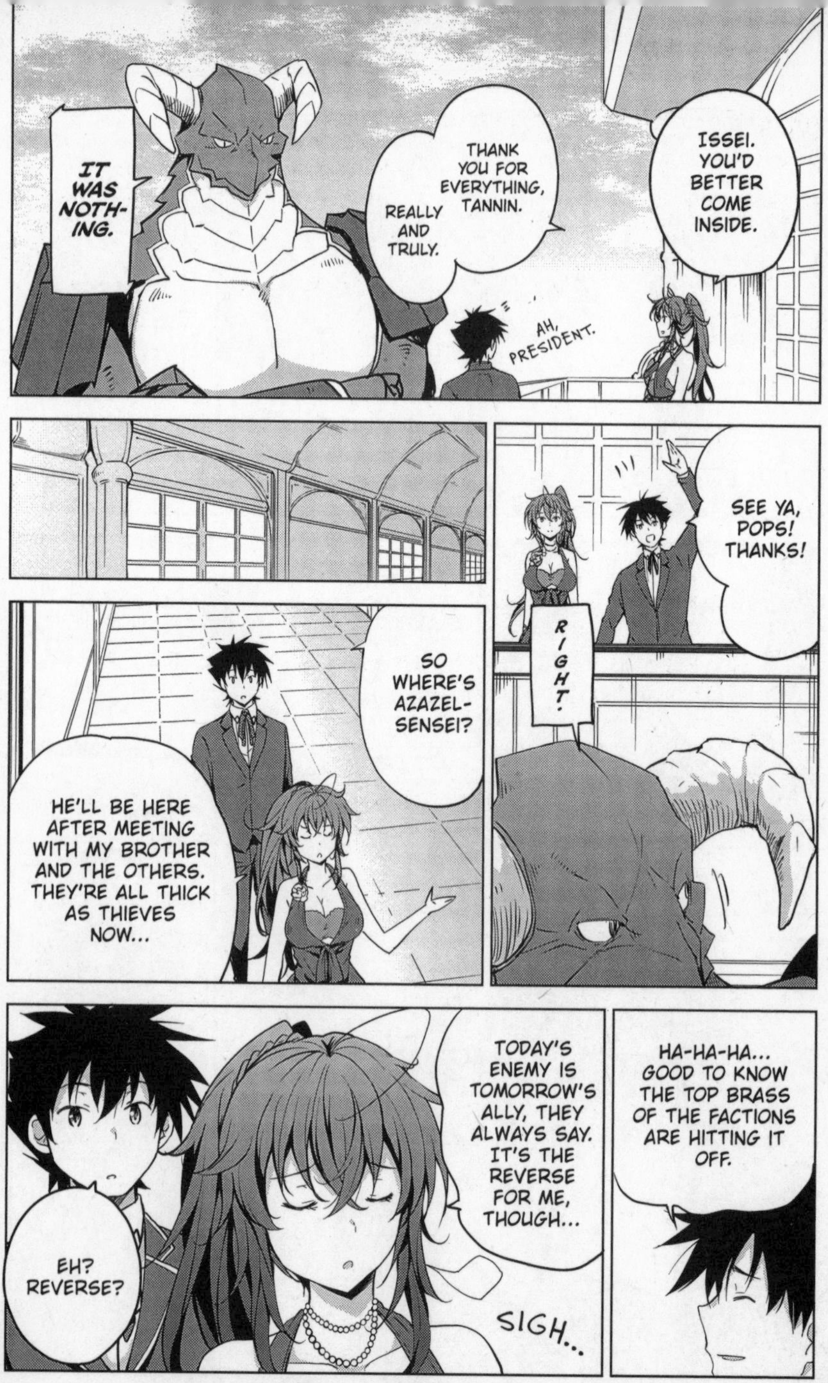
ISSEI. YOU'D BETTER COME INSIDE.
AH, PRESIDENT.
THANK YOU FOR EVERYTHING, TANNIN.
REALLY AND TRULY.
IT WAS NOTHING.
SEE YA, POPS! THANKS!
RIGHT.
SO WHERE'S AZAZEL-SENSEI?
HE'LL BE HERE AFTER MEETING WITH MY BROTHER AND THE OTHERS. THEY'RE ALL THICK AS THIEVES NOW...
HA-HA-HA... GOOD TO KNOW THE TOP BRASS OF THE FACTIONS ARE HITTING IT OFF.
TODAY'S ENEMY IS TOMORROW'S ALLY, THEY ALWAYS SAY. IT'S THE REVERSE FOR ME, THOUGH...
SIGH...
EH? REVERSE?

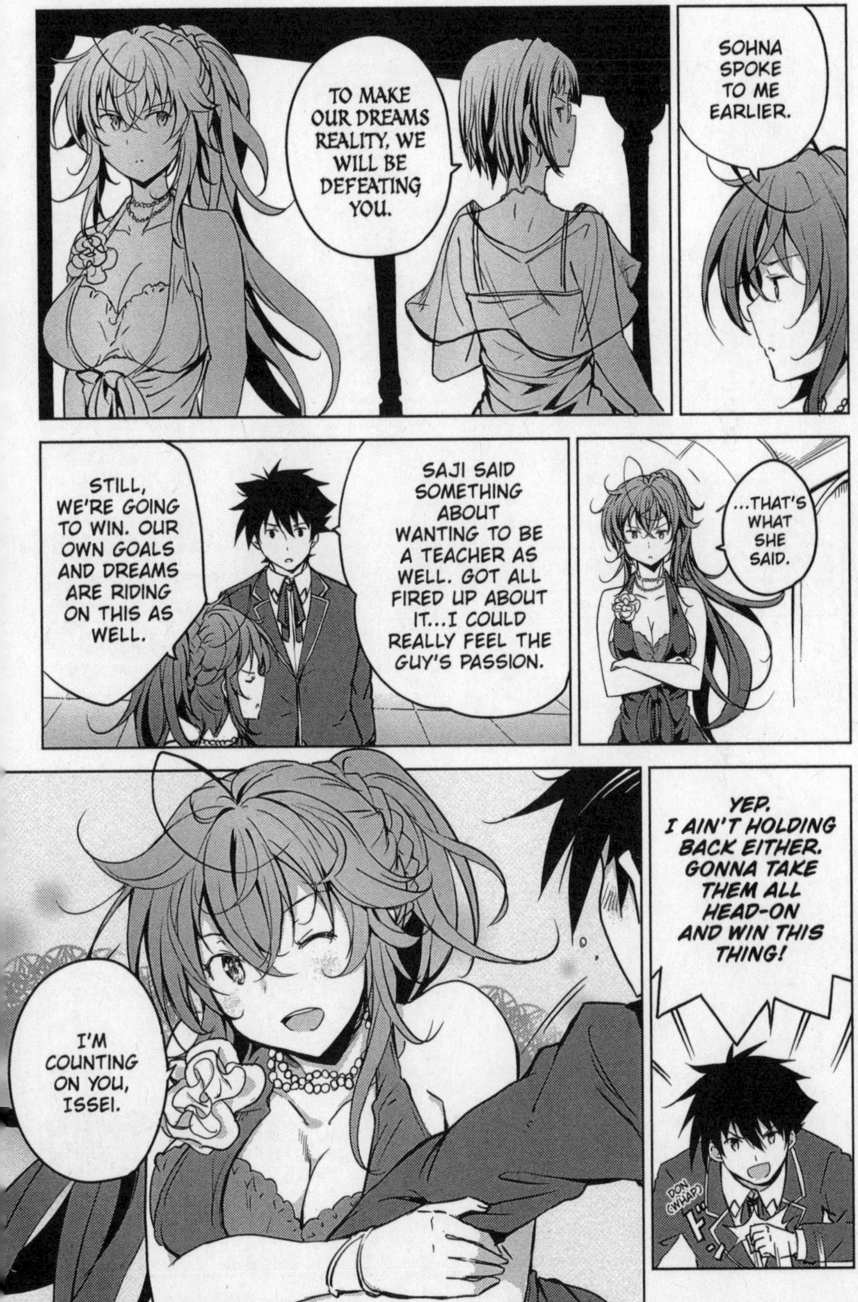
SOHNA SPOKE TO ME EARLIER.
TO MAKE OUR DREAMS REALITY, WE WILL BE DEFEATING YOU.
...THAT'S WHAT SHE SAID.
SAJI SAID SOMETHING ABOUT WANTING TO BE A TEACHER AS WELL. GOT ALL FIRED UP ABOUT IT...I COULD REALLY FEEL THE GUY'S PASSION.
STILL, WE'RE GOING TO WIN. OUR OWN GOALS AND DREAMS ARE RIDING ON THIS AS WELL.
YEP. I AIN'T HOLDING BACK EITHER. GONNA TAKE THEM ALL HEAD-ON AND WIN THIS THING!
DON (WHAP)
I'M COUNTING ON YOU, ISSEI.

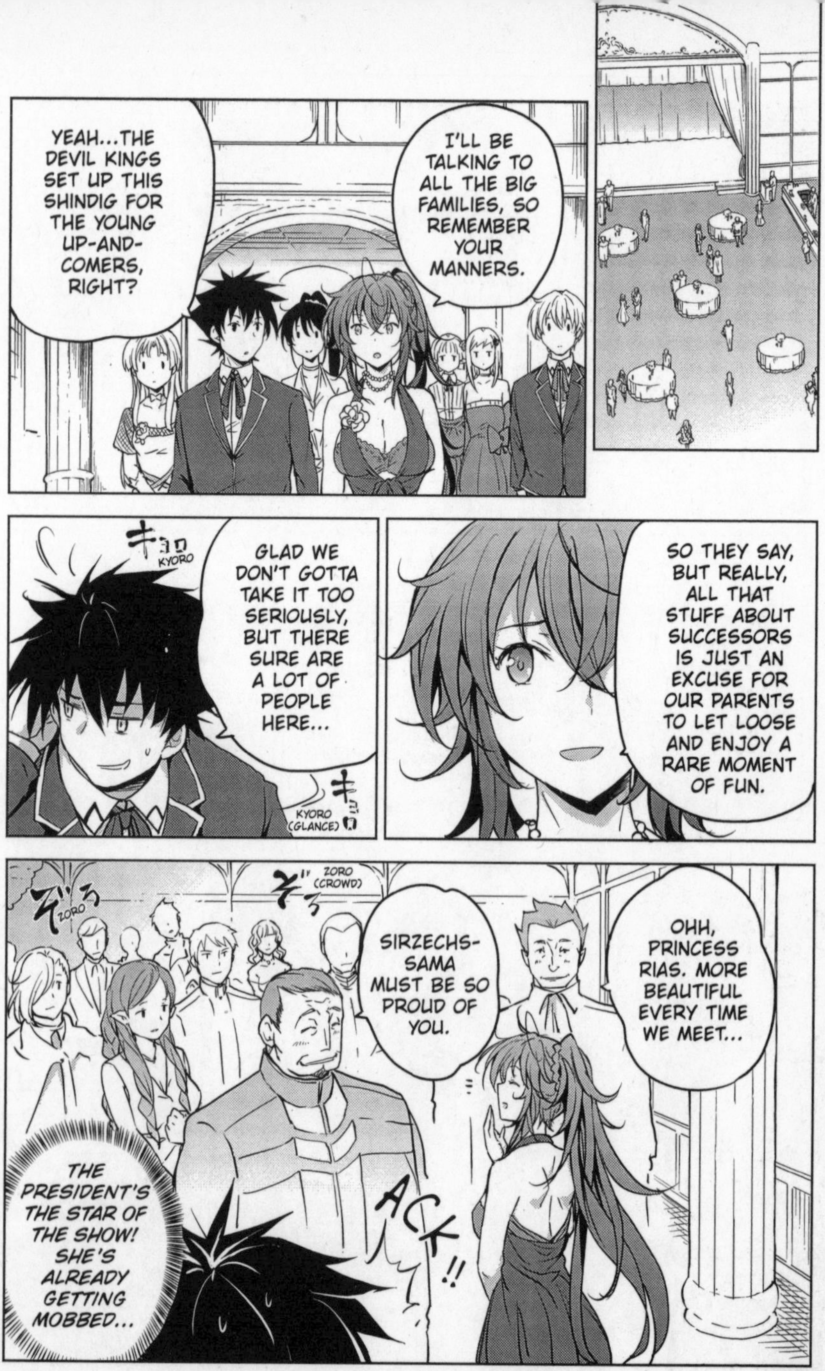
I'LL BE TALKING TO ALL THE BIG FAMILIES, SO REMEMBER YOUR MANNERS.
YEAH...THE DEVIL KINGS SET UP THIS SHINDIG FOR THE YOUNG UP-AND-COMERS, RIGHT?
SO THEY SAY, BUT REALLY, ALL THAT STUFF ABOUT SUCCESSORS IS JUST AN EXCUSE FOR OUR PARENTS TO LET LOOSE AND ENJOY A RARE MOMENT OF FUN.
KYORO
GLAD WE DON'T GOTTA TAKE IT TOO SERIOUSLY, BUT THERE SURE ARE A LOT OF PEOPLE HERE...
KYORO (GLANCE)
OHH, PRINCESS RIAS. MORE BEAUTIFUL EVERY TIME WE MEET...
SIRZECHS-SAMA MUST BE SO PROUD OF YOU.
ZORO (CROWD)
ZORO
THE PRESIDENT'S THE STAR OF THE SHOW! SHE'S ALREADY GETTING MOBBED...
ACK!!

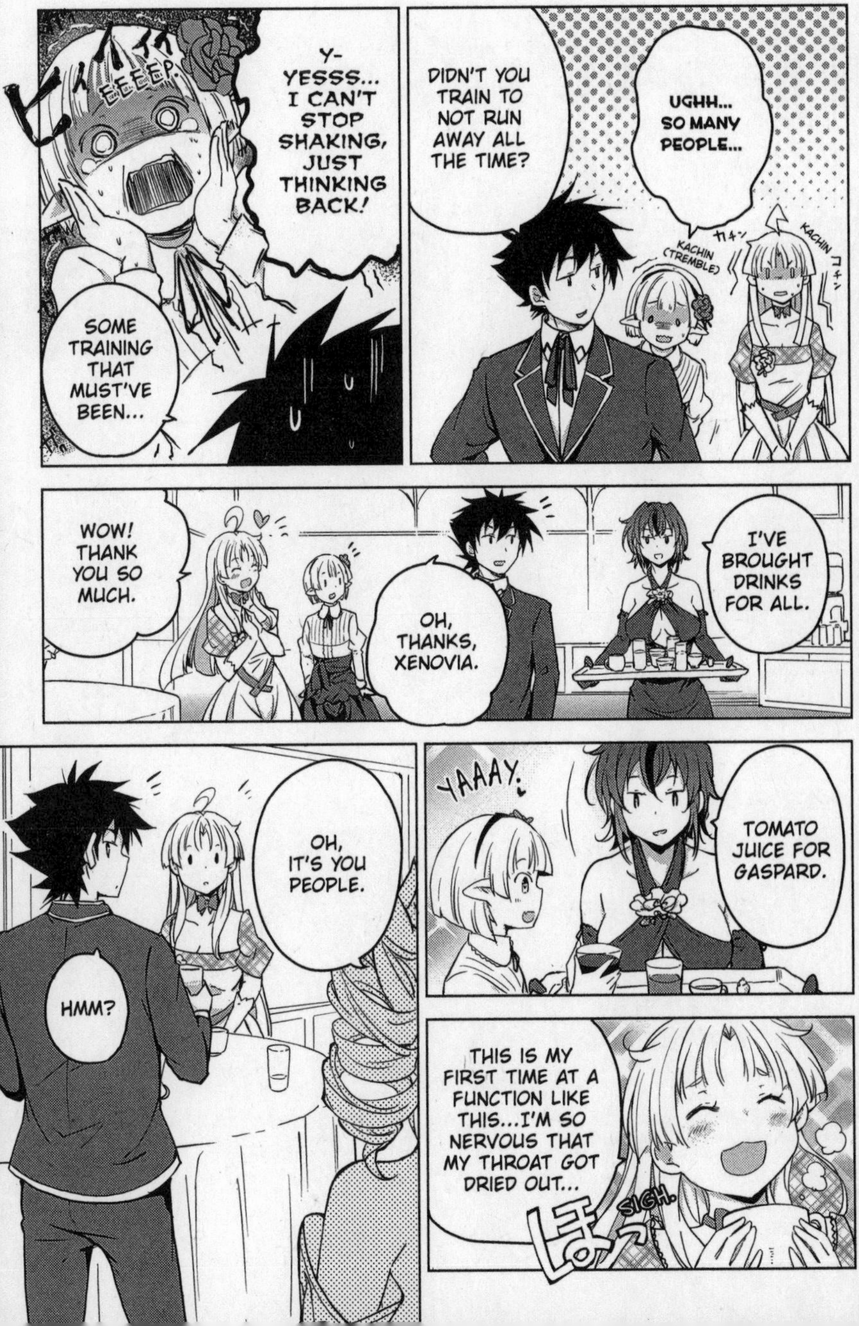
UGHH... SO MANY PEOPLE...
KACHIN
KACHIN (TREMBLE)
DIDN'T YOU TRAIN TO NOT RUN AWAY ALL THE TIME?
EEEEEP.
Y-YESSS... I CAN'T STOP SHAKING, JUST THINKING BACK!
SOME TRAINING THAT MUST'VE BEEN...
I'VE BROUGHT DRINKS FOR ALL.
OH, THANKS, XENOVIA.
WOW! THANK YOU SO MUCH.
TOMATO JUICE FOR GASPARD.
YAAAY.
THIS IS MY FIRST TIME AT A FUNCTION LIKE THIS...I'M SO NERVOUS THAT MY THROAT GOT DRIED OUT...
SIGH.
OH, IT'S YOU PEOPLE.
HMM?

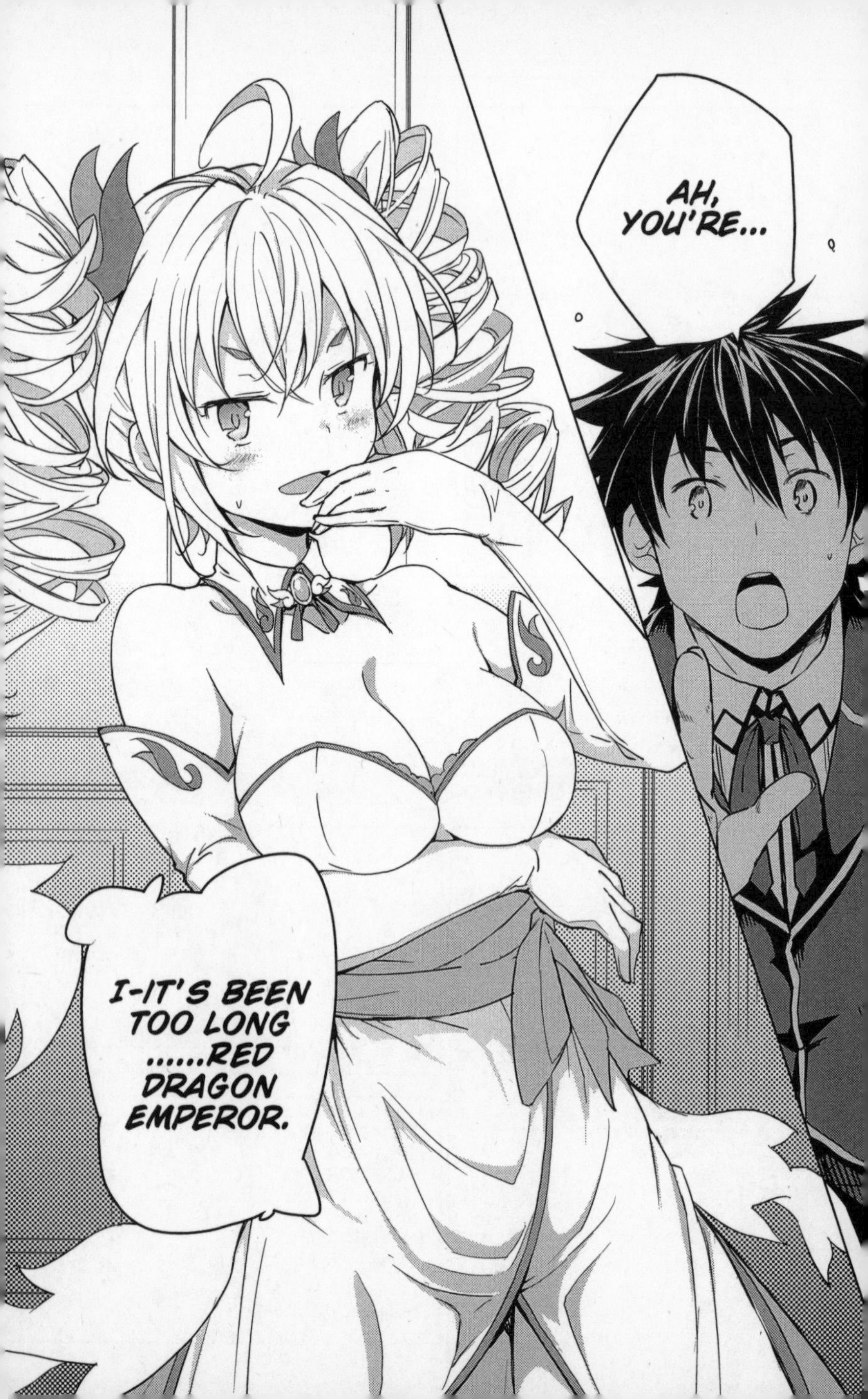
AH, YOU'RE...
I-IT'S BEEN TOO LONG ......RED DRAGON EMPEROR.

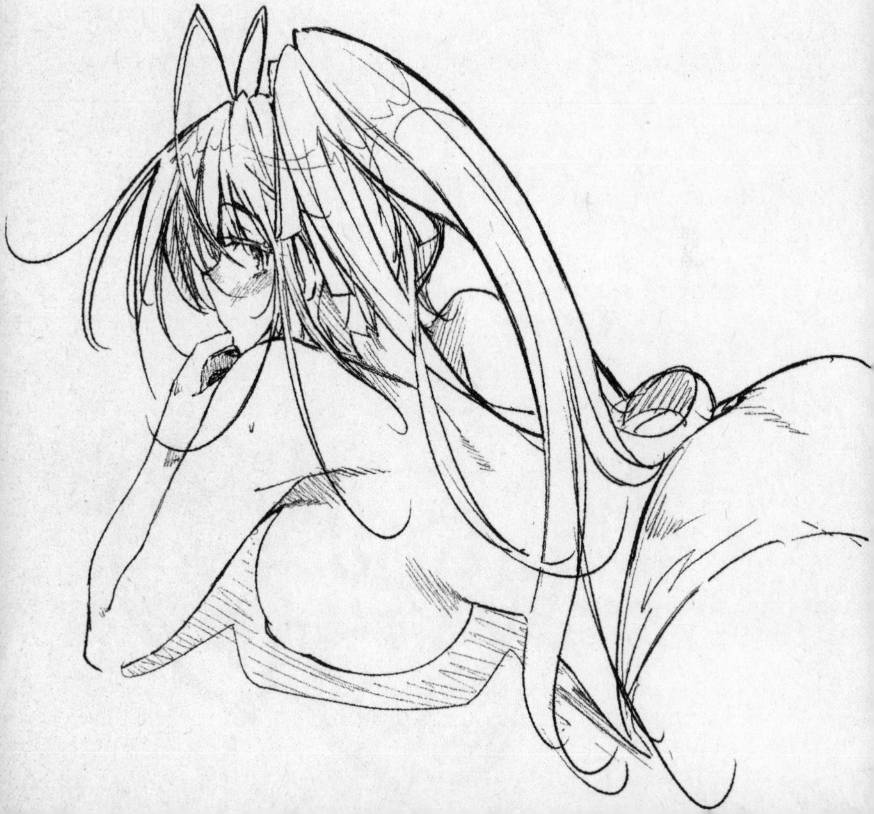

HIGH SCHOOL DxD

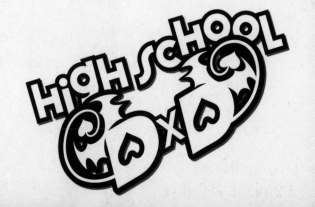

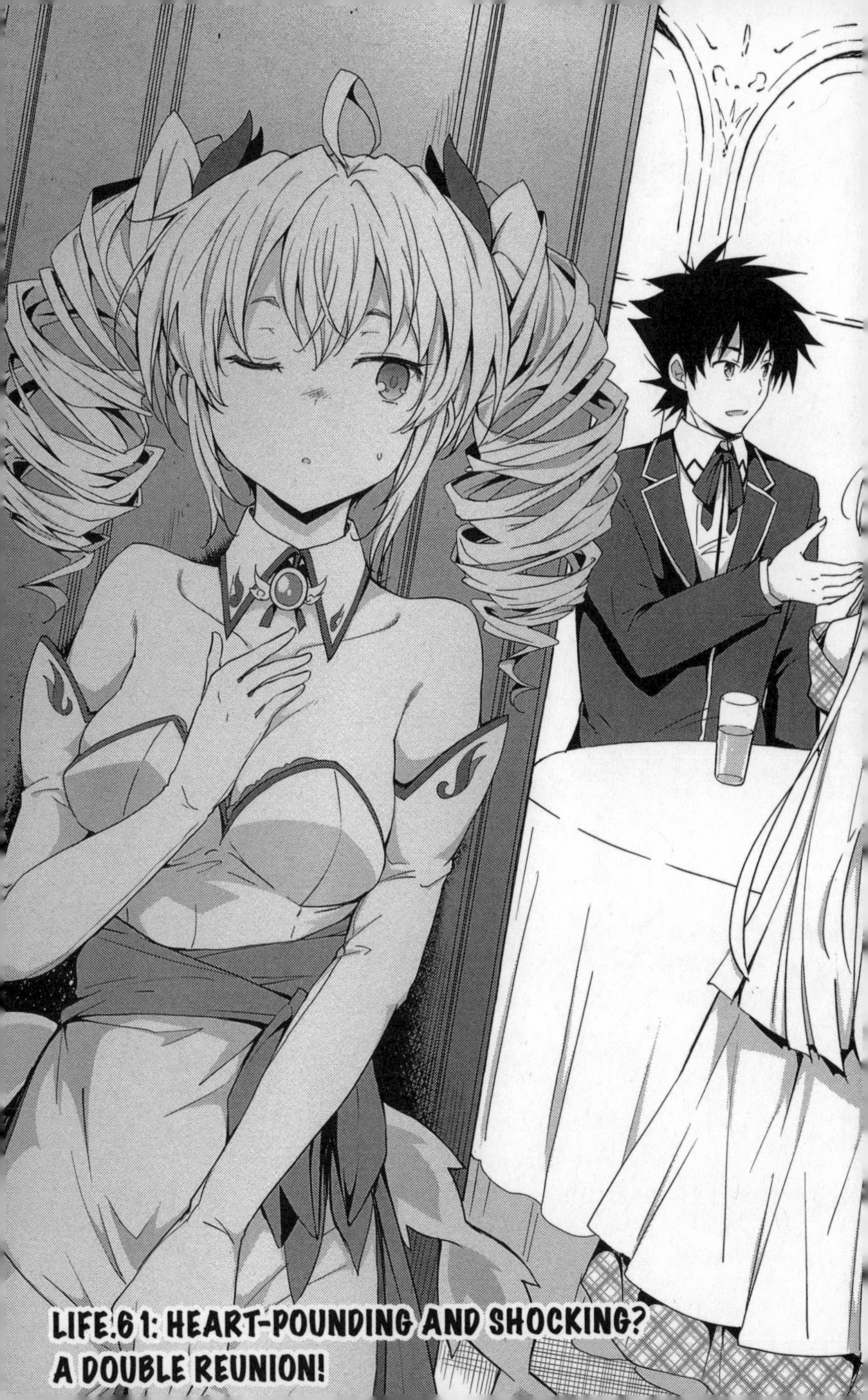

LIFE.61: HEART-POUNDING AND SHOCKING? A DOUBLE REUNION!

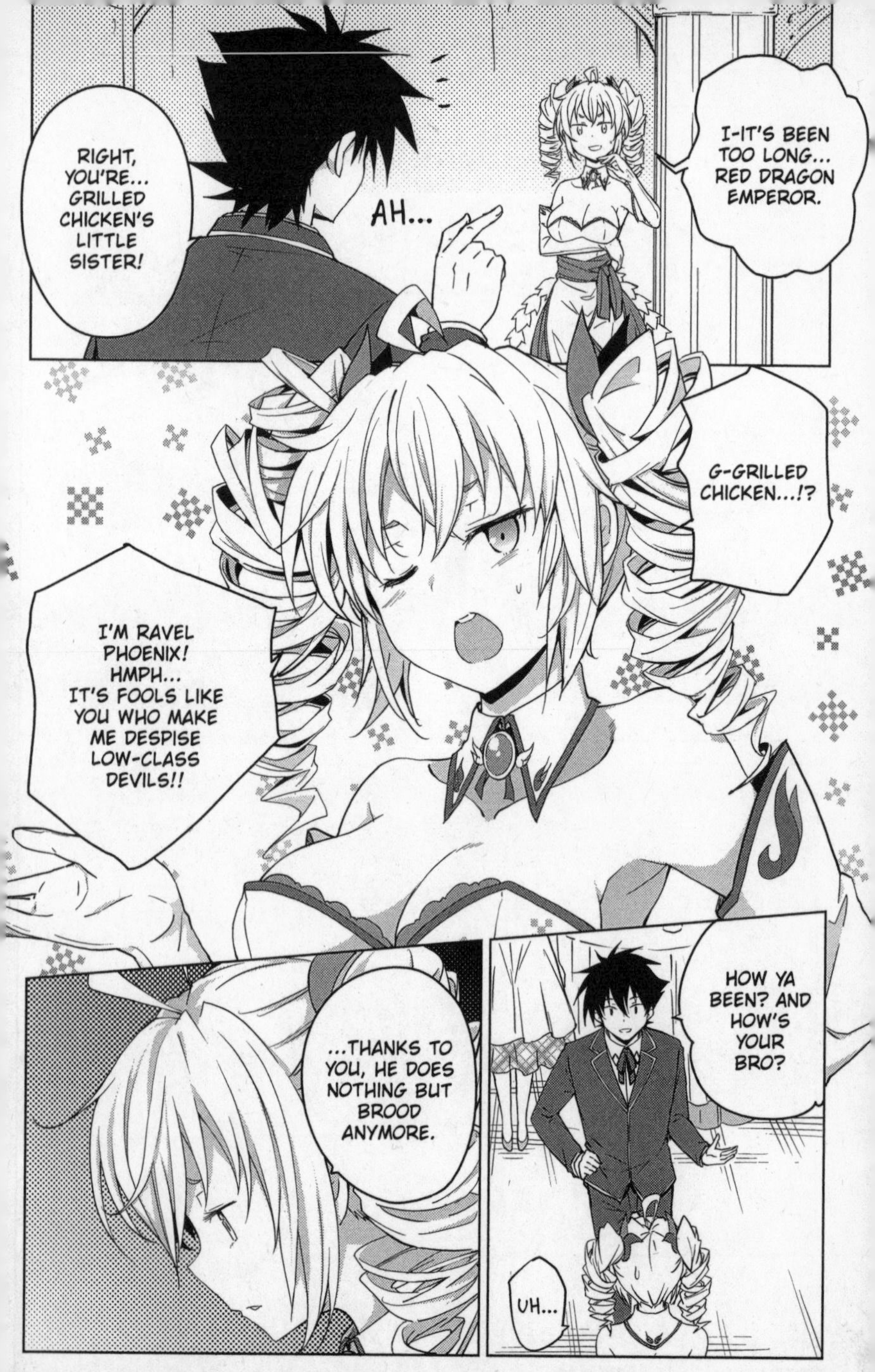
I-IT'S BEEN TOO LONG... RED DRAGON EMPEROR.
AH...
RIGHT, YOU'RE... GRILLED CHICKEN'S LITTLE SISTER!
G-GRILLED CHICKEN...!?
I'M RAVEL PHOENIX! HMPH... IT'S FOOLS LIKE YOU WHO MAKE ME DESPISE LOW-CLASS DEVILS!!
HOW YA BEEN? AND HOW'S YOUR BRO?
UH...
...THANKS TO YOU, HE DOES NOTHING BUT BROOD ANYMORE.

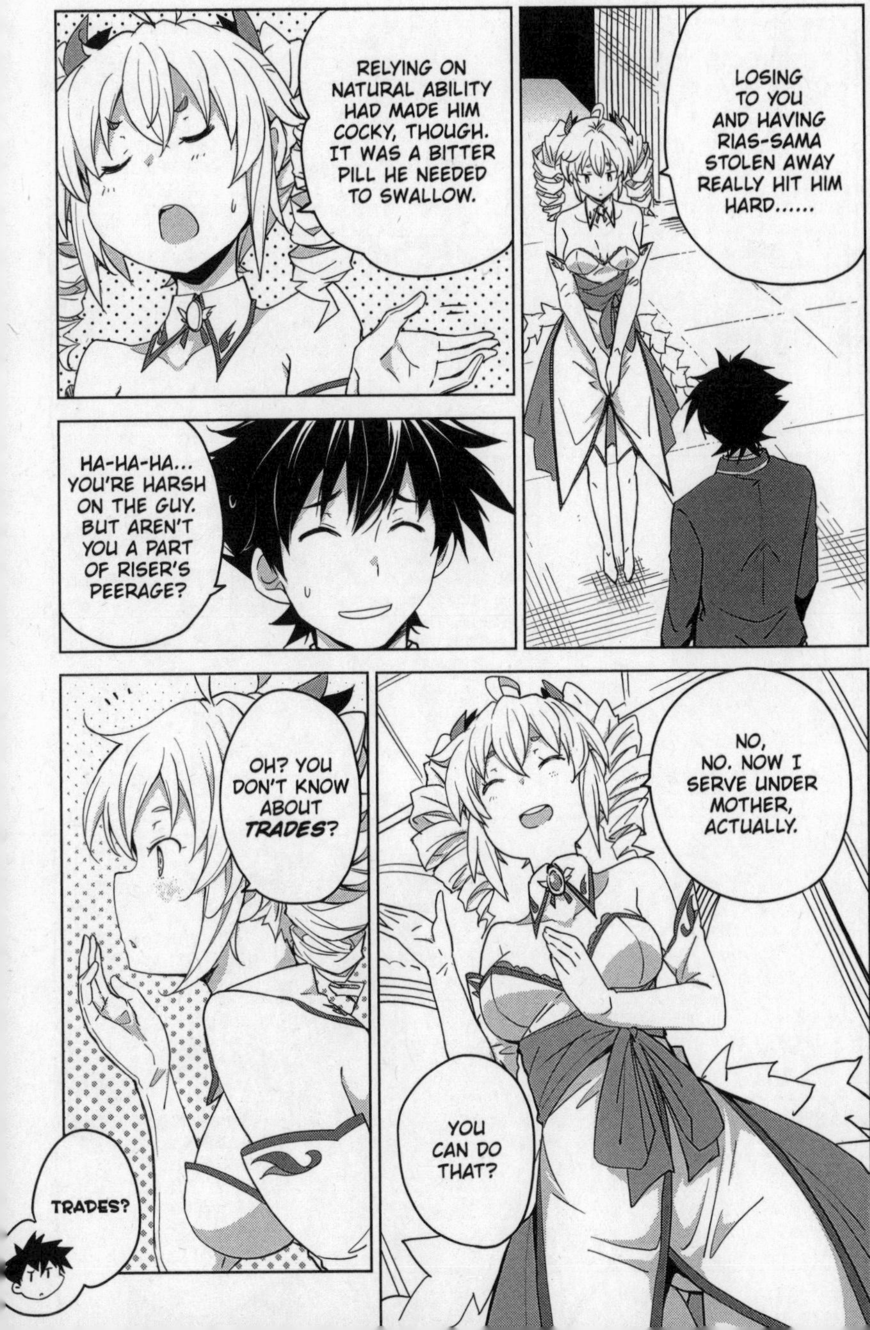
LOSING TO YOU AND HAVING RIAS-SAMA STOLEN AWAY REALLY HIT HIM HARD......
RELYING ON NATURAL ABILITY HAD MADE HIM COCKY, THOUGH. IT WAS A BITTER PILL HE NEEDED TO SWALLOW.
HA-HA-HA... YOU'RE HARSH ON THE GUY. BUT AREN'T YOU A PART OF RISER'S PEERAGE?
NO, NO. NOW I SERVE UNDER MOTHER, ACTUALLY.
YOU CAN DO THAT?
OH? YOU DON'T KNOW ABOUT *TRADES*?
TRADES?

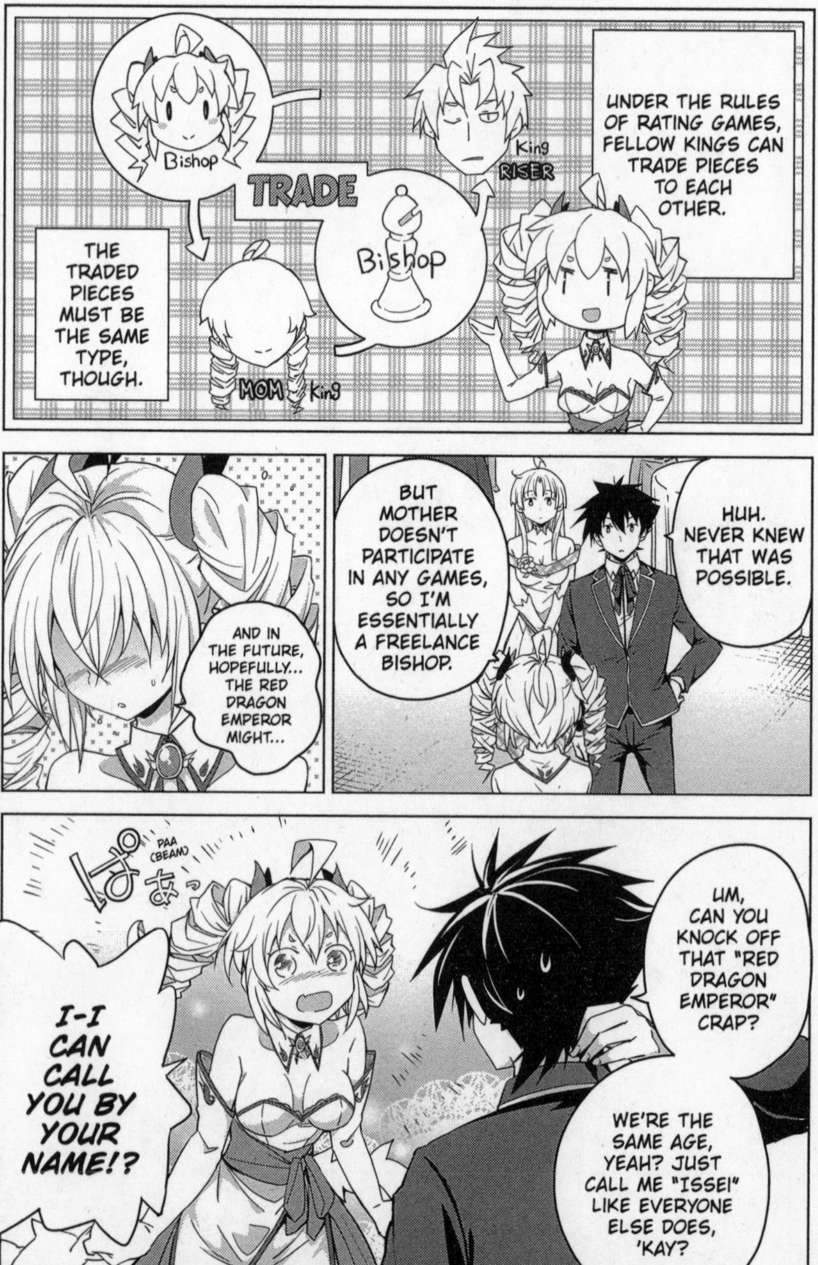

UNDER THE RULES OF RATING GAMES, FELLOW KINGS CAN TRADE PIECES TO EACH OTHER.
King
RISER
Bishop
TRADE
Bishop
THE TRADED PIECES MUST BE THE SAME TYPE, THOUGH.
MOM
King
HUH. NEVER KNEW THAT WAS POSSIBLE.
BUT MOTHER DOESN'T PARTICIPATE IN ANY GAMES, SO I'M ESSENTIALLY A FREELANCE BISHOP.
AND IN THE FUTURE, HOPEFULLY... THE RED DRAGON EMPEROR MIGHT...
UM, CAN YOU KNOCK OFF THAT "RED DRAGON EMPEROR" CRAP?
WE'RE THE SAME AGE, YEAH? JUST CALL ME "ISSEI" LIKE EVERYONE ELSE DOES, 'KAY?
PAA (BEAM)
I-I CAN CALL YOU BY YOUR NAME!?

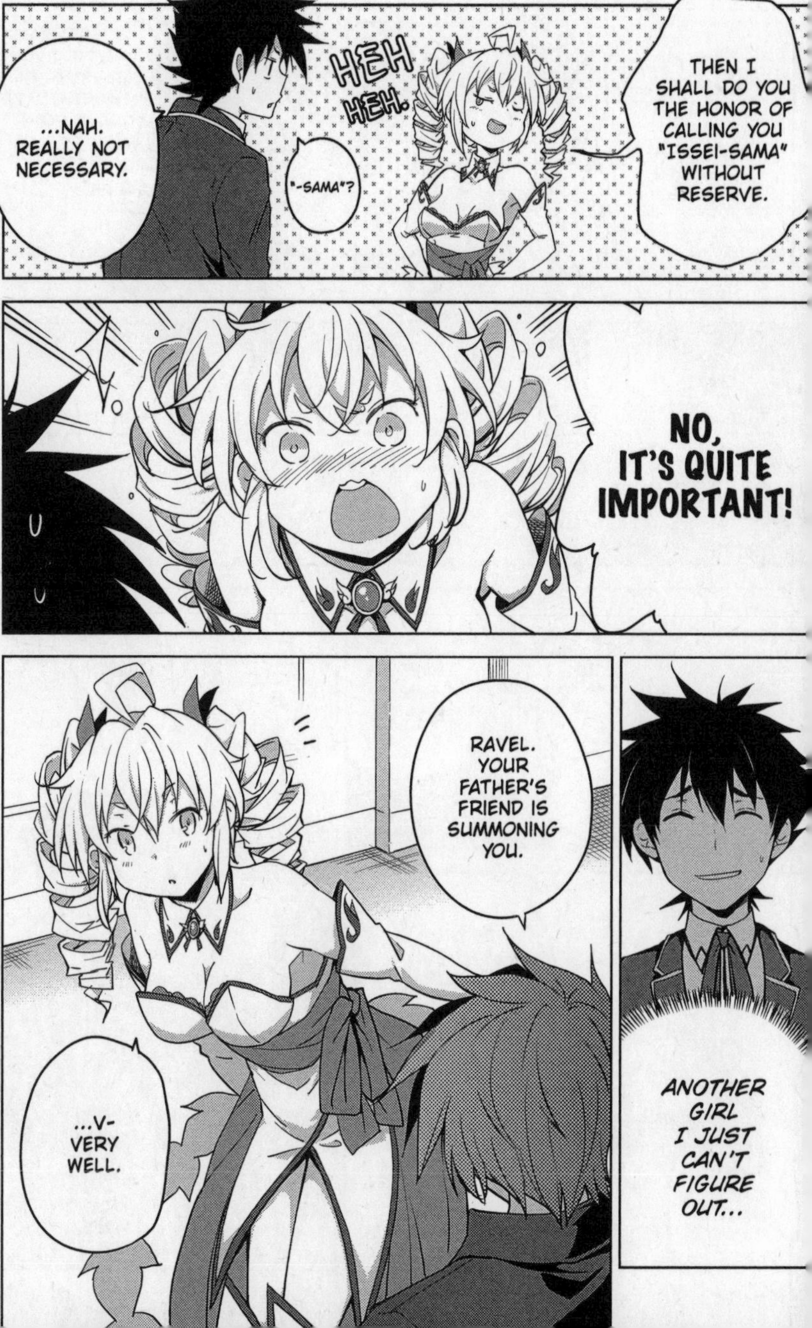
THEN I SHALL DO YOU THE HONOR OF CALLING YOU "ISSEI-SAMA" WITHOUT RESERVE.
HEH HEH.
"-SAMA"?
...NAH. REALLY NOT NECESSARY.
NO, IT'S QUITE IMPORTANT!
ANOTHER GIRL I JUST CAN'T FIGURE OUT...
RAVEL. YOUR FATHER'S FRIEND IS SUMMONING YOU.
...V-VERY WELL.

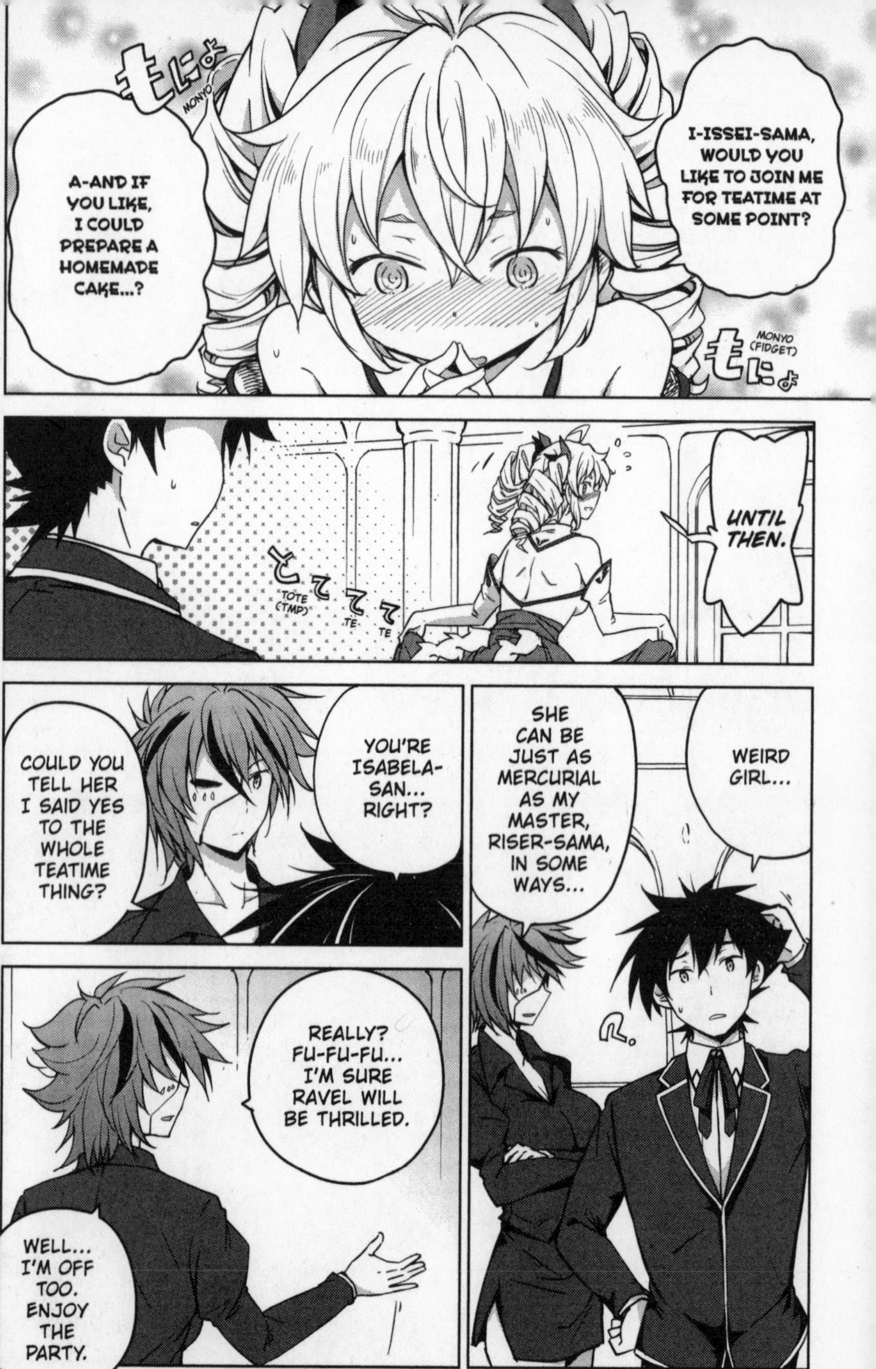

I-ISSEI-SAMA, WOULD YOU LIKE TO JOIN ME FOR TEATIME AT SOME POINT?
MONYO
A-AND IF YOU LIKE, I COULD PREPARE A HOMEMADE CAKE...?
MONYO (FIDGET)
UNTIL THEN.
TOTE (TMP)
TE
TE
WEIRD GIRL...
SHE CAN BE JUST AS MERCURIAL AS MY MASTER, RISER-SAMA, IN SOME WAYS...
YOU'RE ISABELA-SAN... RIGHT?
COULD YOU TELL HER I SAID YES TO THE WHOLE TEATIME THING?
REALLY? FU-FU-FU... I'M SURE RAVEL WILL BE THRILLED.
WELL... I'M OFF TOO. ENJOY THE PARTY.

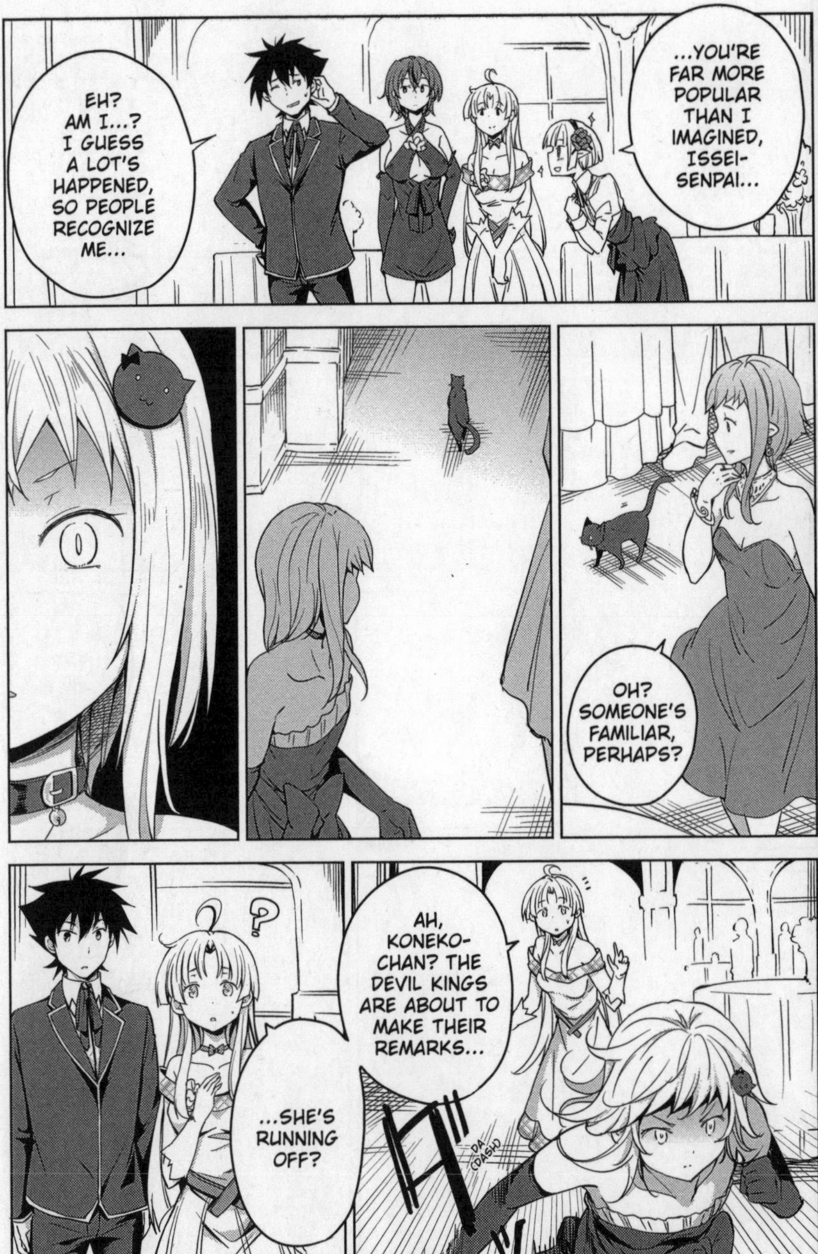
...YOU'RE FAR MORE POPULAR THAN I IMAGINED, ISSEI-SENPAI...
EH? AM I...? I GUESS A LOT'S HAPPENED, SO PEOPLE RECOGNIZE ME...
OH? SOMEONE'S FAMILIAR, PERHAPS?
AH, KONEKO-CHAN? THE DEVIL KINGS ARE ABOUT TO MAKE THEIR REMARKS...
DA (DASH)
?
...SHE'S RUNNING OFF?

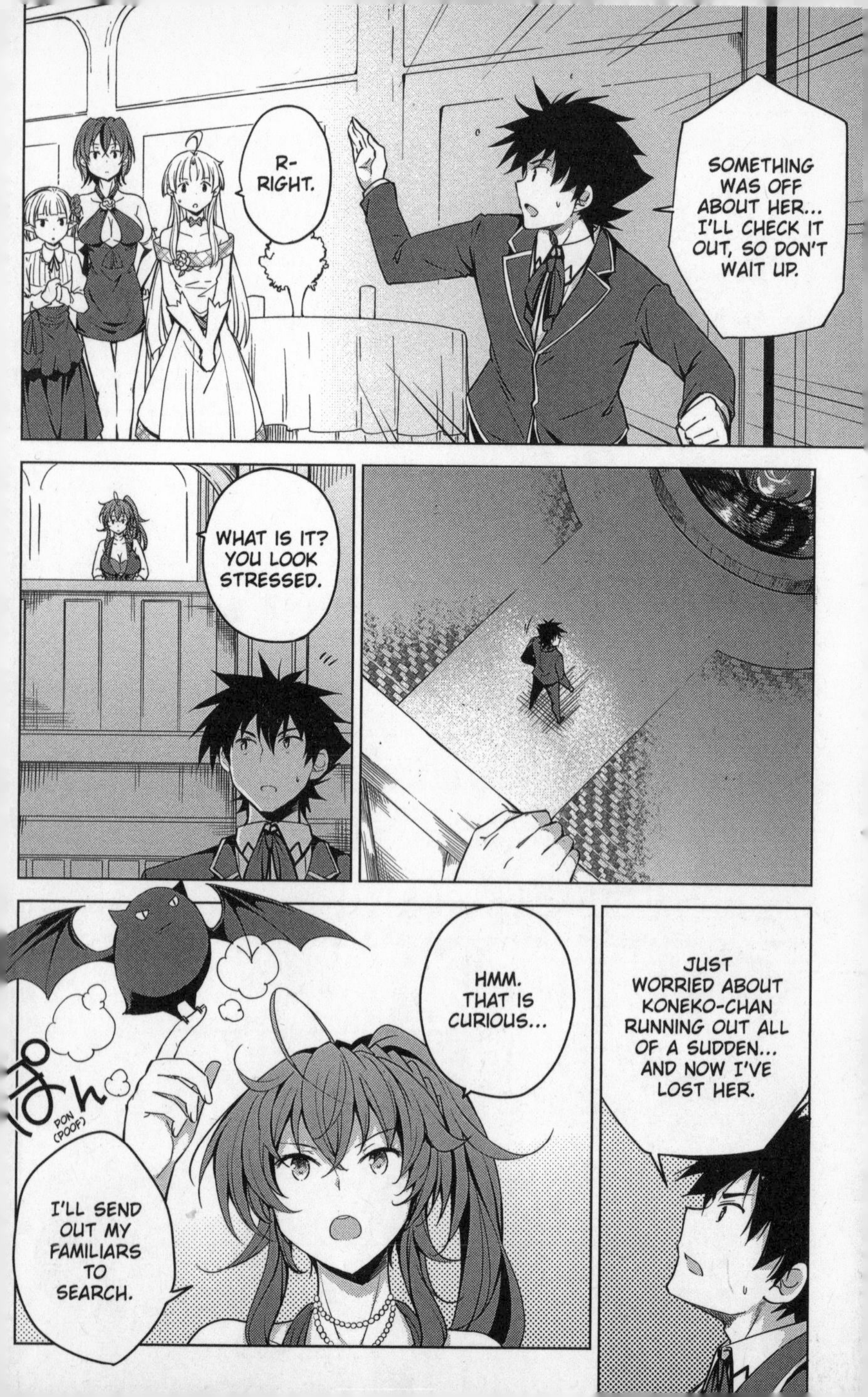
SOMETHING WAS OFF ABOUT HER... I'LL CHECK IT OUT, SO DON'T WAIT UP.
R-RIGHT.
WHAT IS IT? YOU LOOK STRESSED.
JUST WORRIED ABOUT KONEKO-CHAN RUNNING OUT ALL OF A SUDDEN... AND NOW I'VE LOST HER.
HMM. THAT IS CURIOUS...
PON (POOF)
I'LL SEND OUT MY FAMILIARS TO SEARCH.

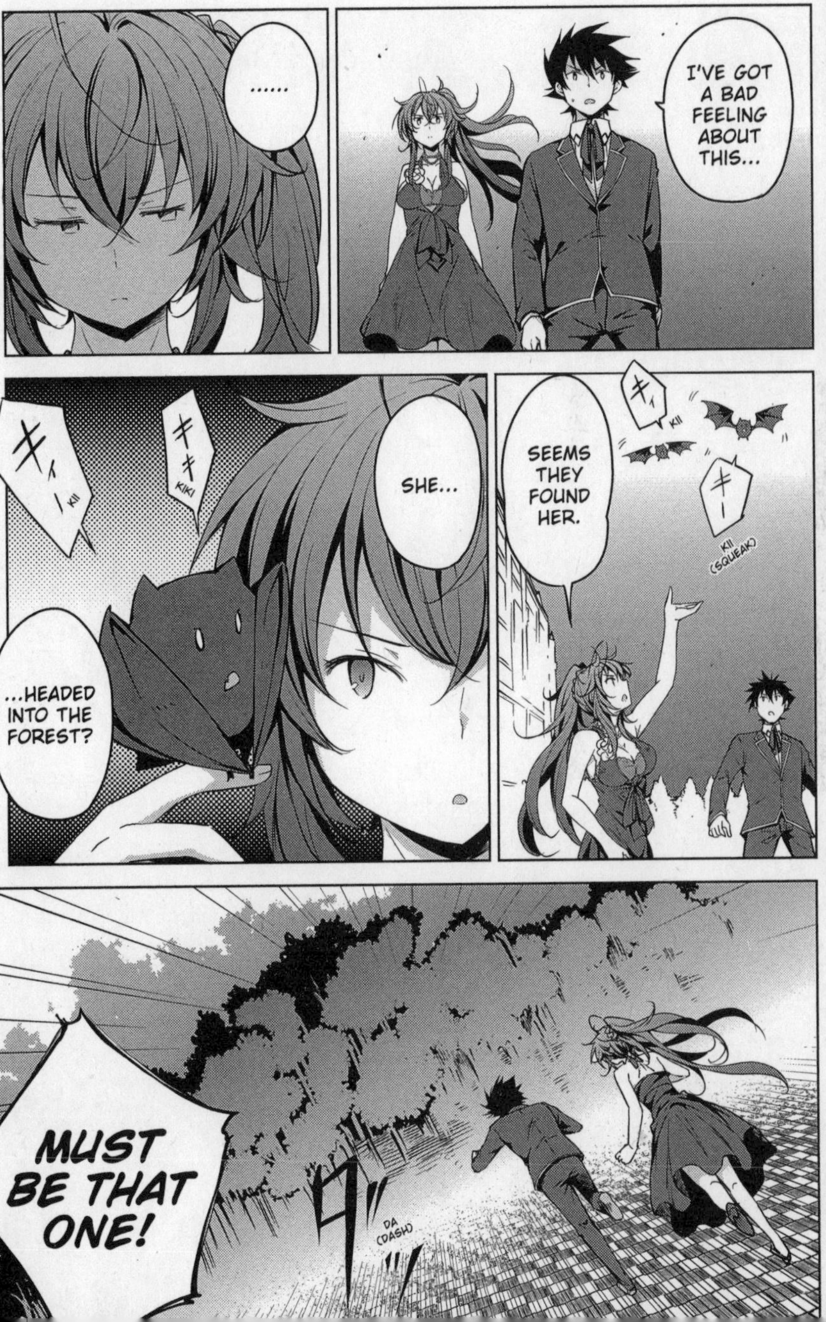
I'VE GOT A BAD FEELING ABOUT THIS...
......
キィ KII
キー KII (SQUEAK)
SEEMS THEY FOUND HER.
SHE...
キキ KIKI
キィー KII
...HEADED INTO THE FOREST?
MUST BE THAT ONE!
DA (DASH)

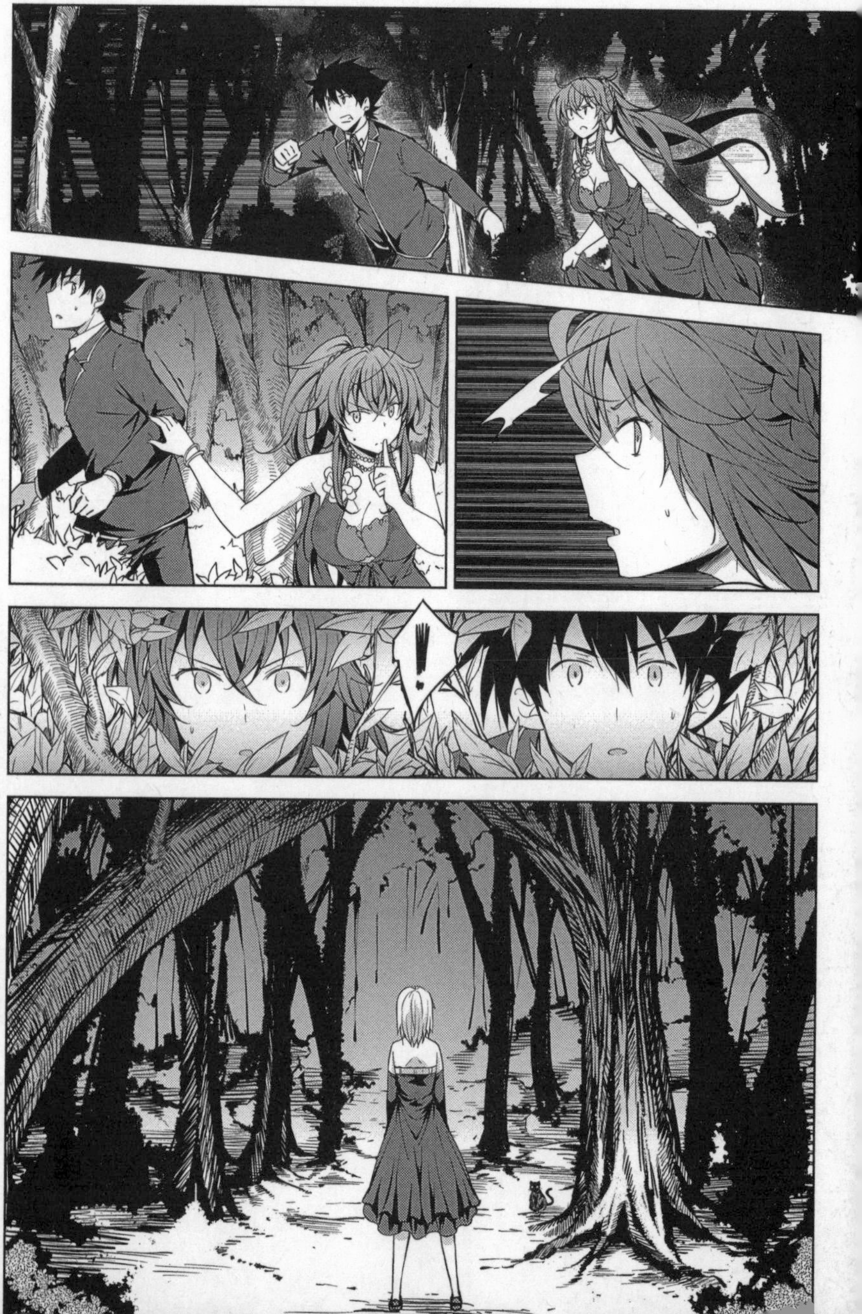
!

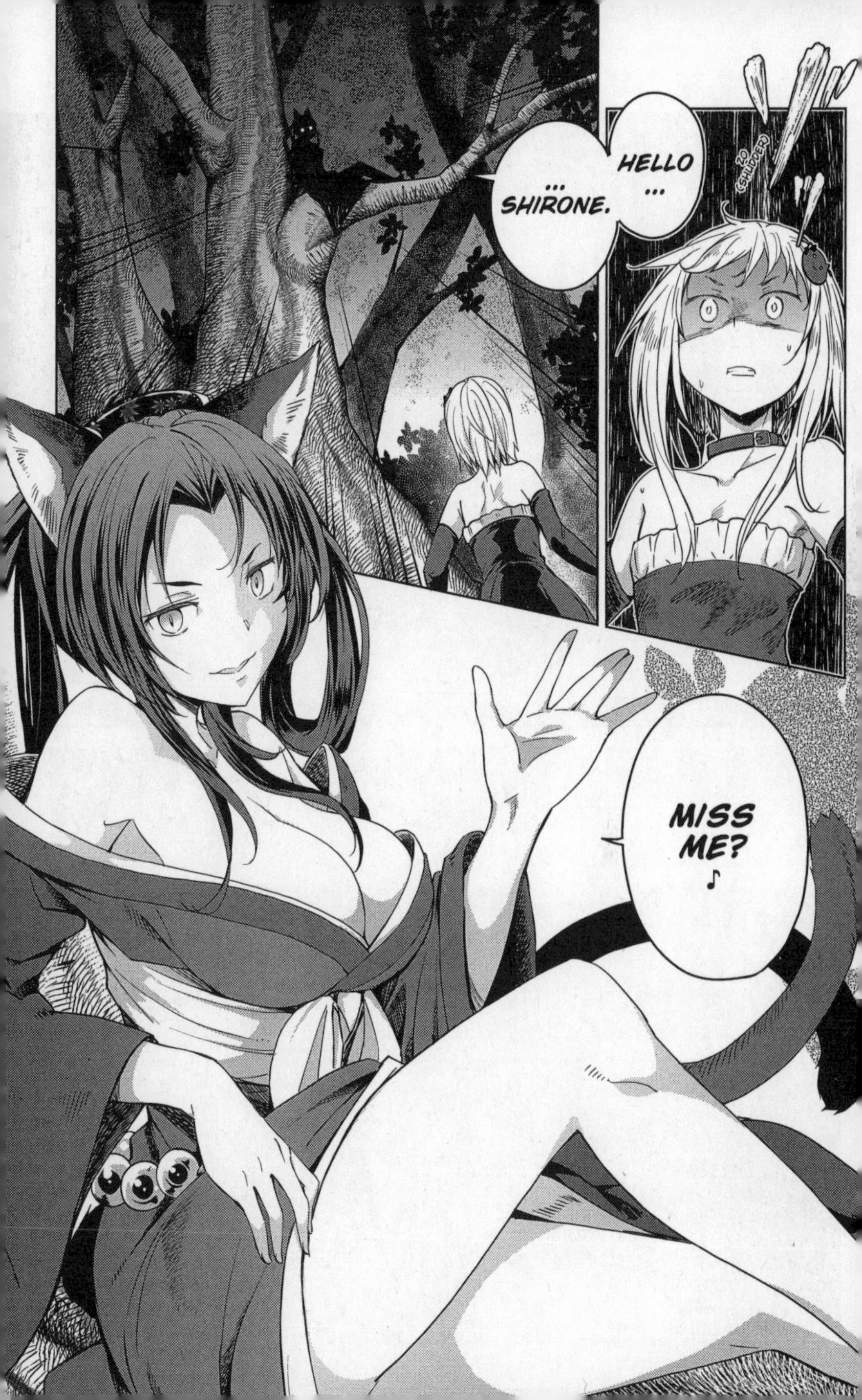
ZO
(SHUDDER)
HELLO... ...SHIRONE.
MISS ME? ♪

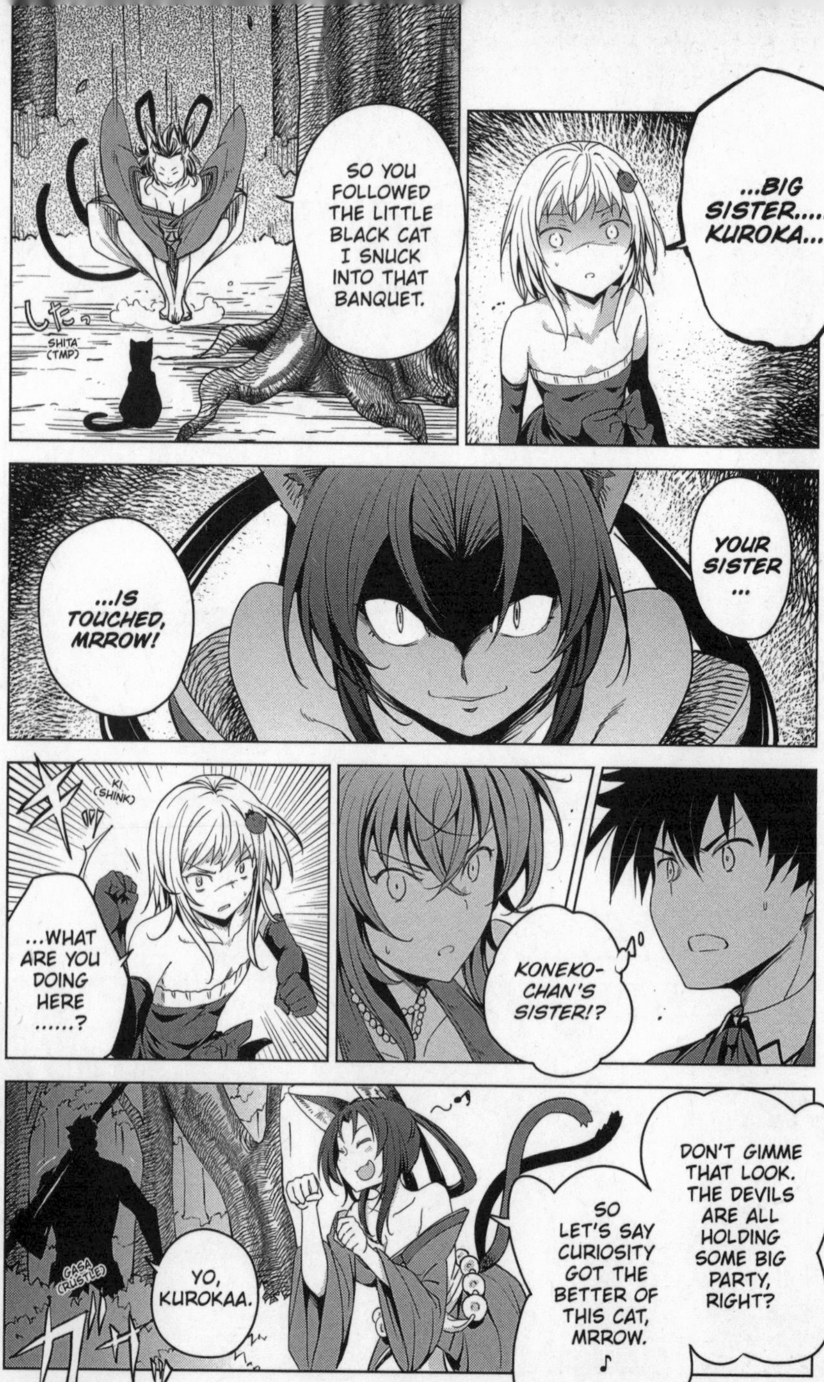
...BIG SISTER...... KUROKA...!
SO YOU FOLLOWED THE LITTLE BLACK CAT I SNUCK INTO THAT BANQUET.
SHITA (TMP)
YOUR SISTER ...
...IS TOUCHED, MRROW!
KONEKO-CHAN'S SISTER!?
KI (SHINK)
...WHAT ARE YOU DOING HERE ......?
DON'T GIMME THAT LOOK. THE DEVILS ARE ALL HOLDING SOME BIG PARTY, RIGHT?
SO LET'S SAY CURIOSITY GOT THE BETTER OF THIS CAT, MRROW. ♪
YO, KUROKAA.
GASA (RUSTLE)

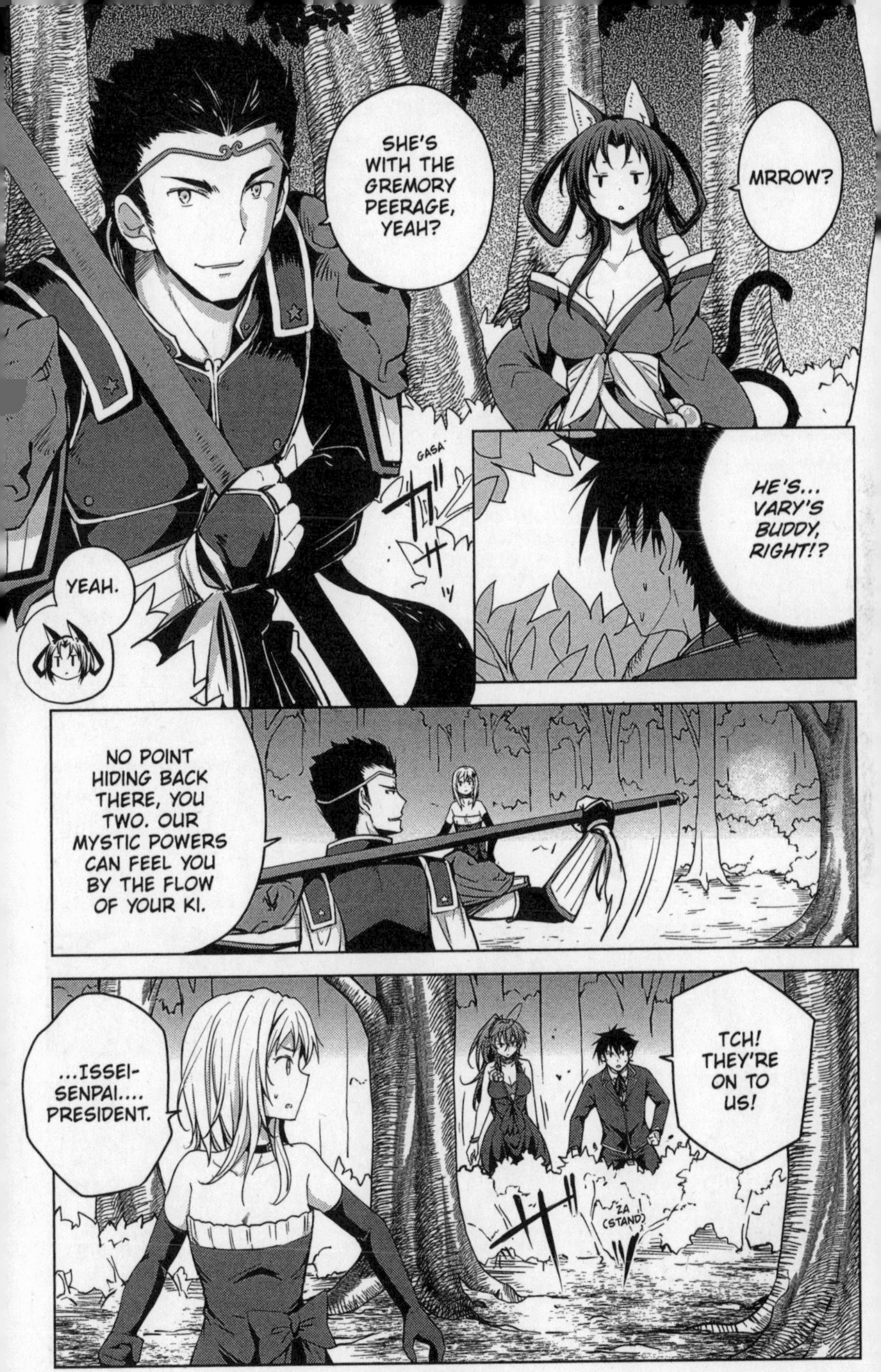
SHE'S WITH THE GREMORY PEERAGE, YEAH?
MRROW?
GASA
HE'S... VARY'S BUDDY, RIGHT!?
YEAH.
NO POINT HIDING BACK THERE, YOU TWO. OUR MYSTIC POWERS CAN FEEL YOU BY THE FLOW OF YOUR KI.
TCH! THEY'RE ON TO US!
ZA (STAND)
...ISSEI-SENPAI.... PRESIDENT.

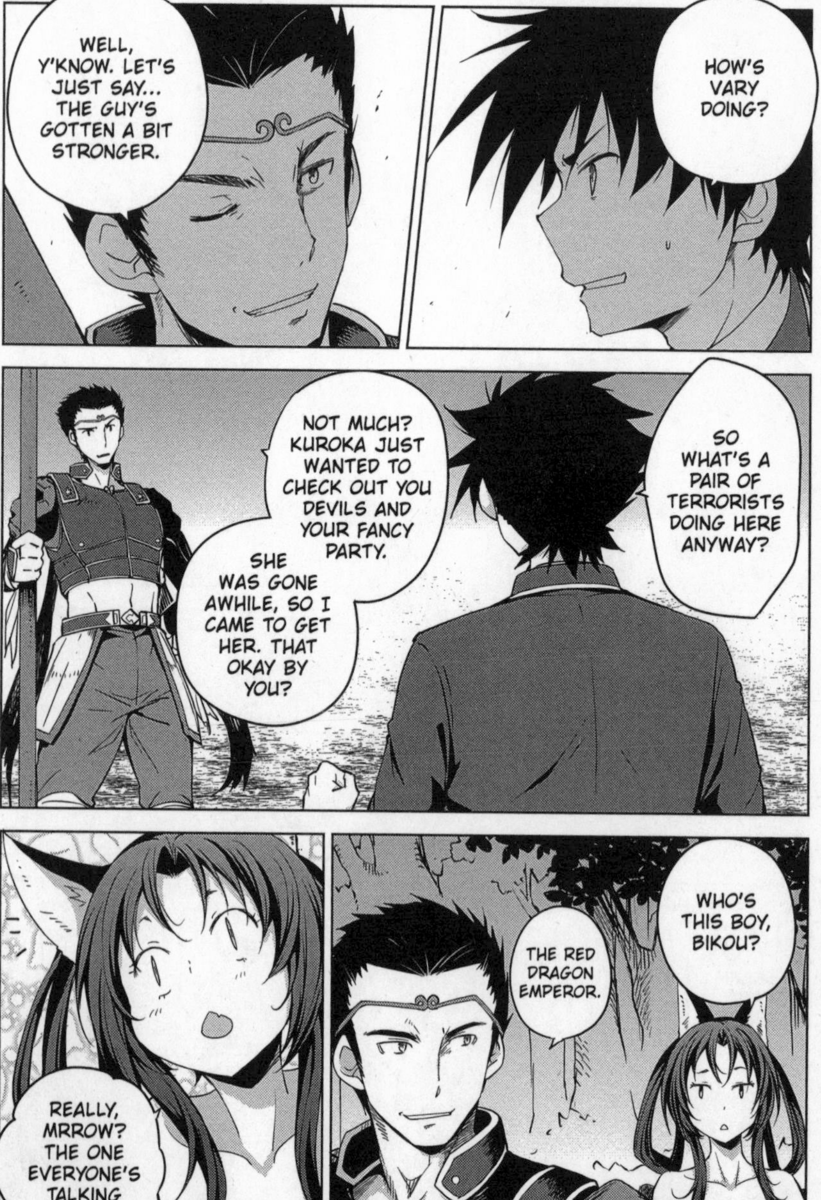
HOW'S VARY DOING?
WELL, Y'KNOW. LET'S JUST SAY... THE GUY'S GOTTEN A BIT STRONGER.
SO WHAT'S A PAIR OF TERRORISTS DOING HERE ANYWAY?
NOT MUCH? KUROKA JUST WANTED TO CHECK OUT YOU DEVILS AND YOUR FANCY PARTY.
SHE WAS GONE AWHILE, SO I CAME TO GET HER. THAT OKAY BY YOU?
WHO'S THIS BOY, BIKOU?
THE RED DRAGON EMPEROR.
REALLY, MRROW? THE ONE EVERYONE'S TALKING ABOUT?

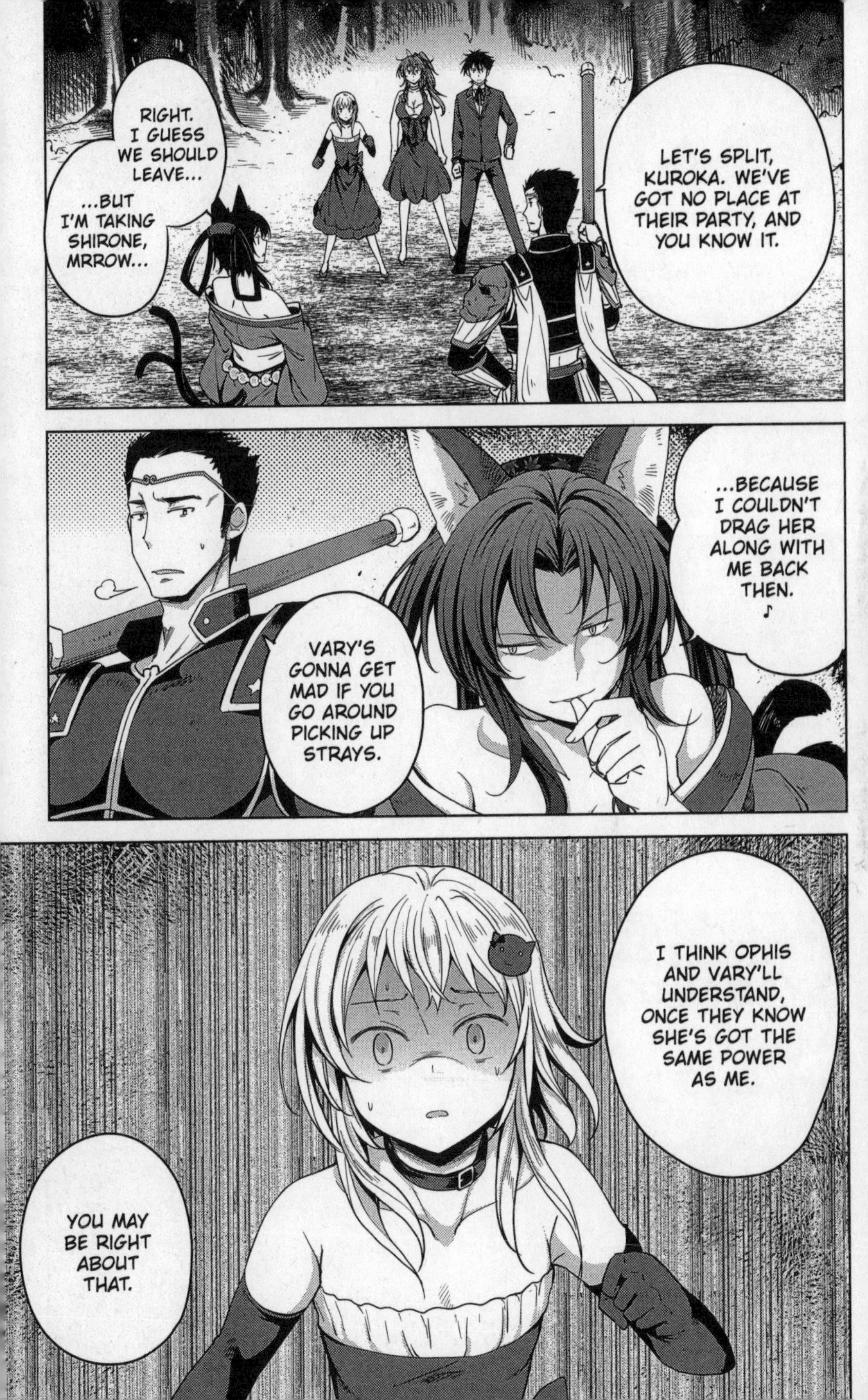
LET'S SPLIT, KUROKA. WE'VE GOT NO PLACE AT THEIR PARTY, AND YOU KNOW IT.
RIGHT. I GUESS WE SHOULD LEAVE...
...BUT I'M TAKING SHIRONE, MRROW...
...BECAUSE I COULDN'T DRAG HER ALONG WITH ME BACK THEN. ♪
VARY'S GONNA GET MAD IF YOU GO AROUND PICKING UP STRAYS.
I THINK OPHIS AND VARY'LL UNDERSTAND, ONCE THEY KNOW SHE'S GOT THE SAME POWER AS ME.
YOU MAY BE RIGHT ABOUT THAT.

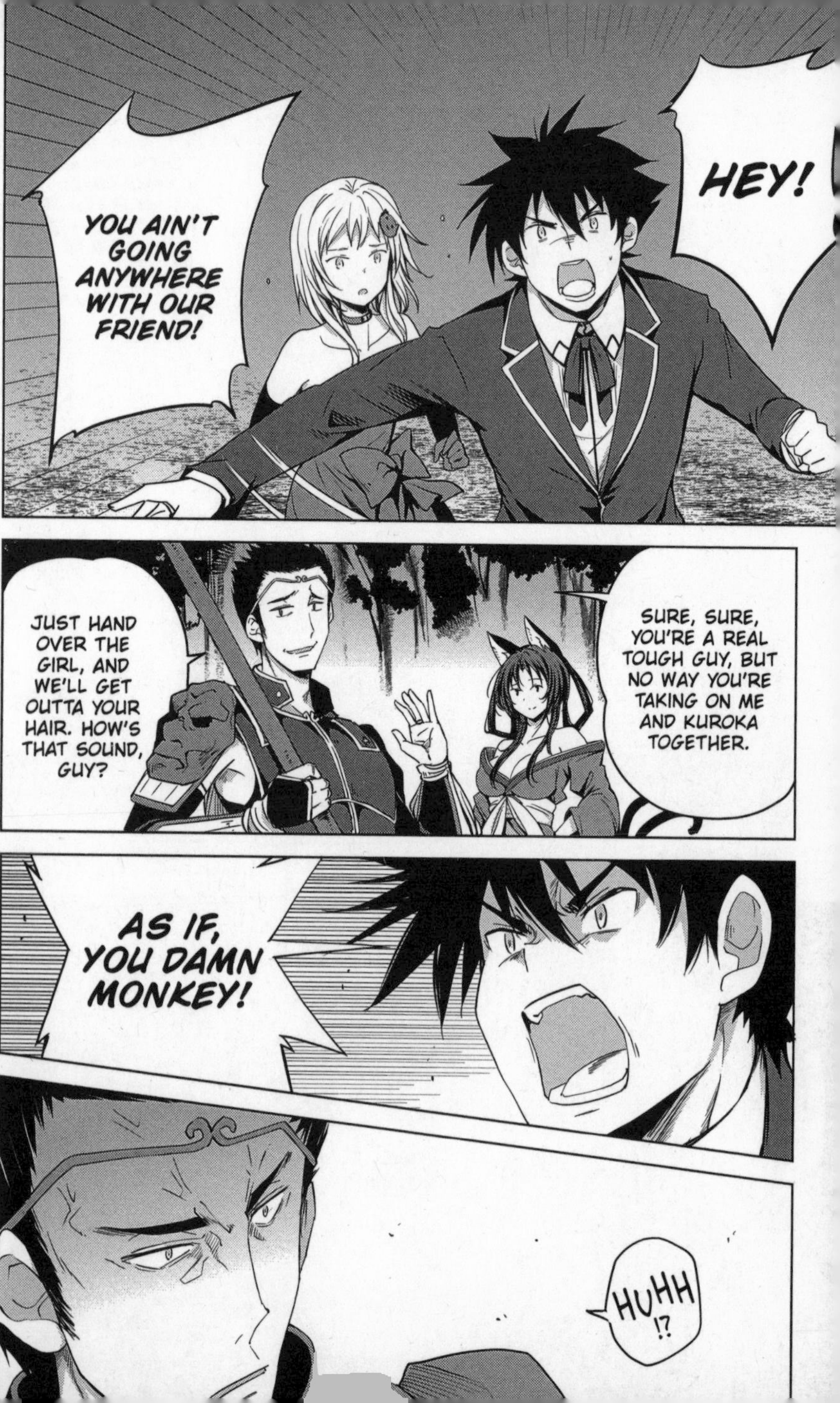
HEY!
YOU AIN'T GOING ANYWHERE WITH OUR FRIEND!
SURE, SURE, YOU'RE A REAL TOUGH GUY, BUT NO WAY YOU'RE TAKING ON ME AND KUROKA TOGETHER.
JUST HAND OVER THE GIRL, AND WE'LL GET OUTTA YOUR HAIR. HOW'S THAT SOUND, GUY?
AS IF, YOU DAMN MONKEY!
HUHH !?

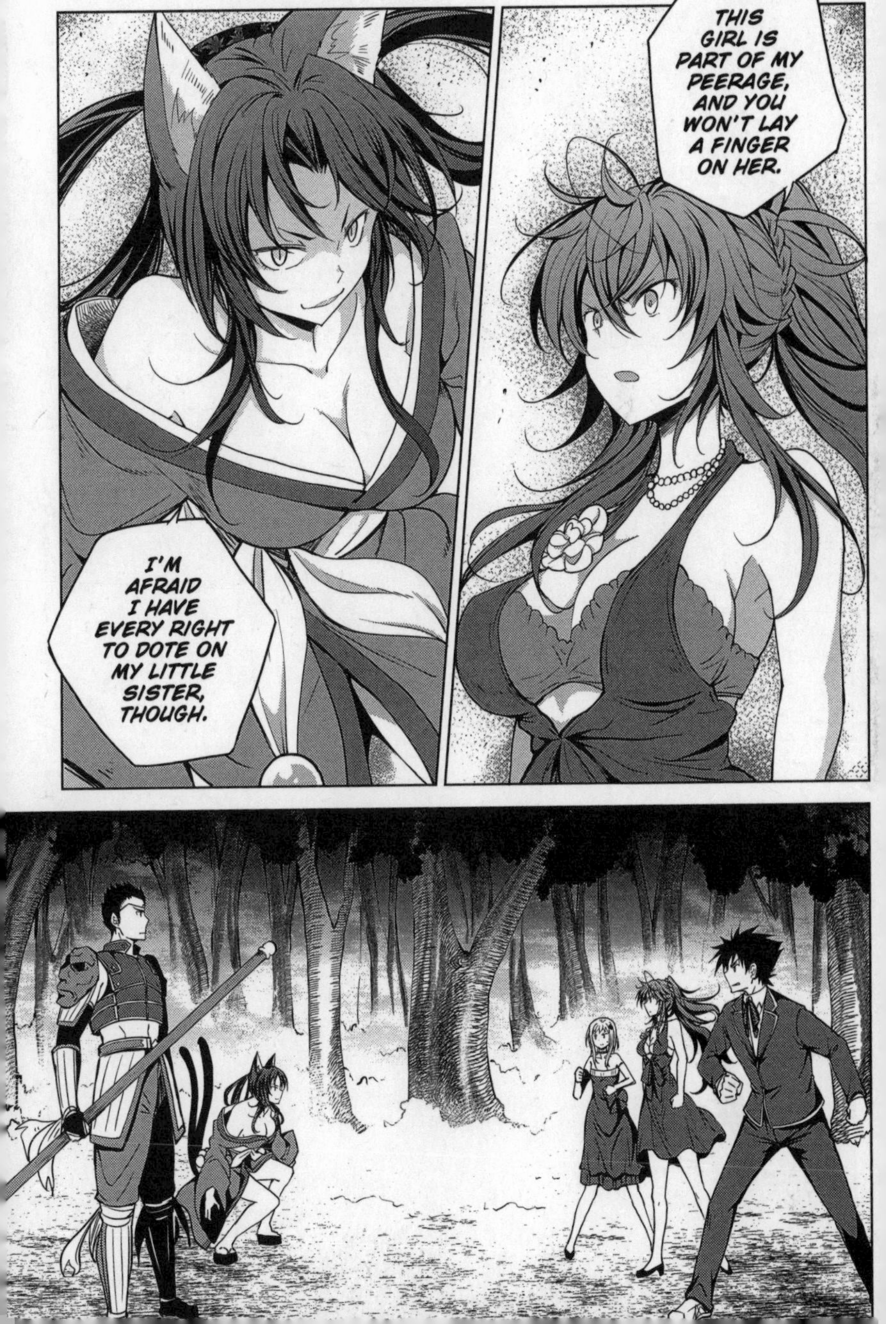
THIS GIRL IS PART OF MY PEERAGE, AND YOU WON'T LAY A FINGER ON HER.
I'M AFRAID I HAVE EVERY RIGHT TO DOTE ON MY LITTLE SISTER, THOUGH.

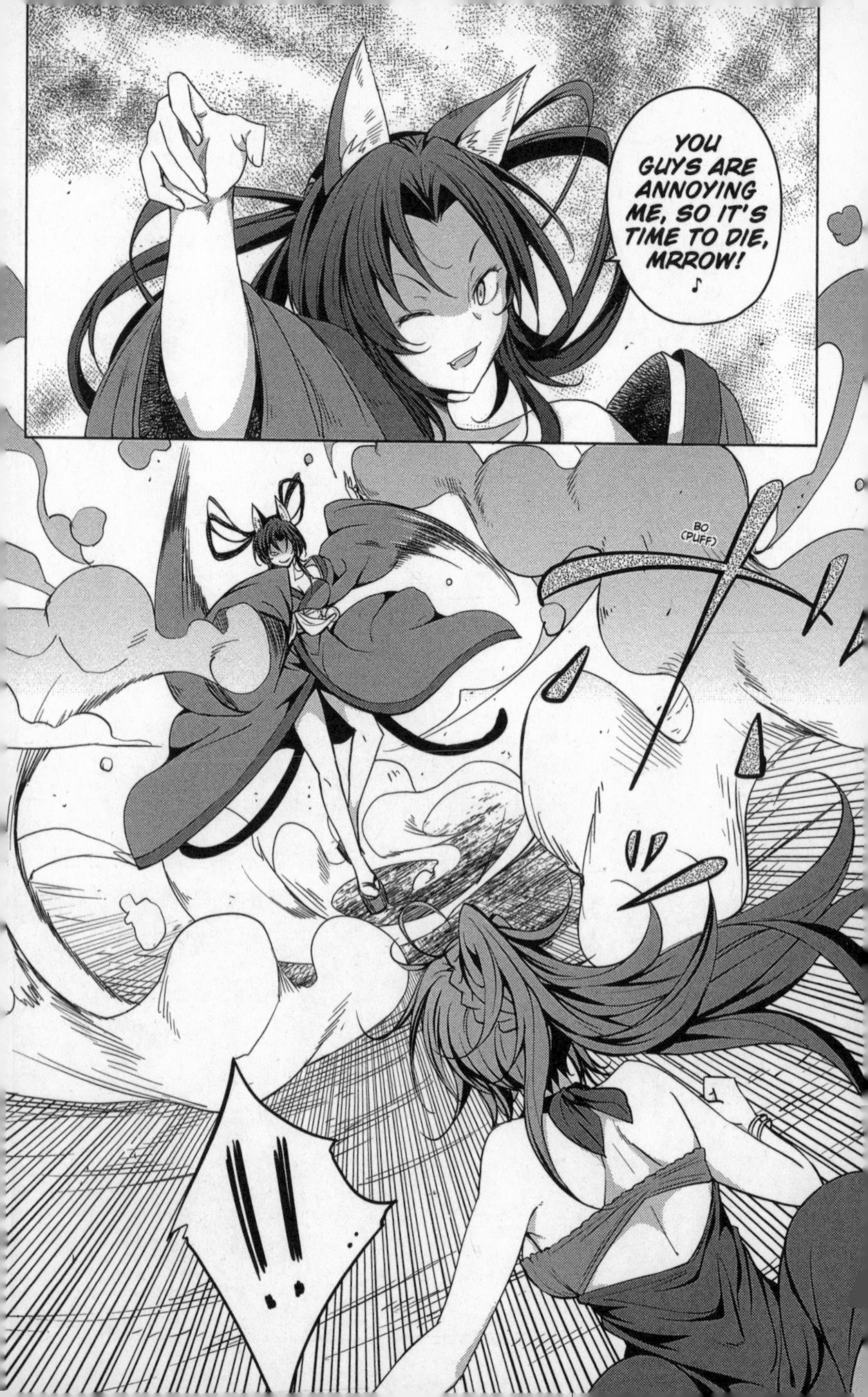
YOU GUYS ARE ANNOYING ME, SO IT'S TIME TO DIE, MRROW! ♪
BO (PUFF)

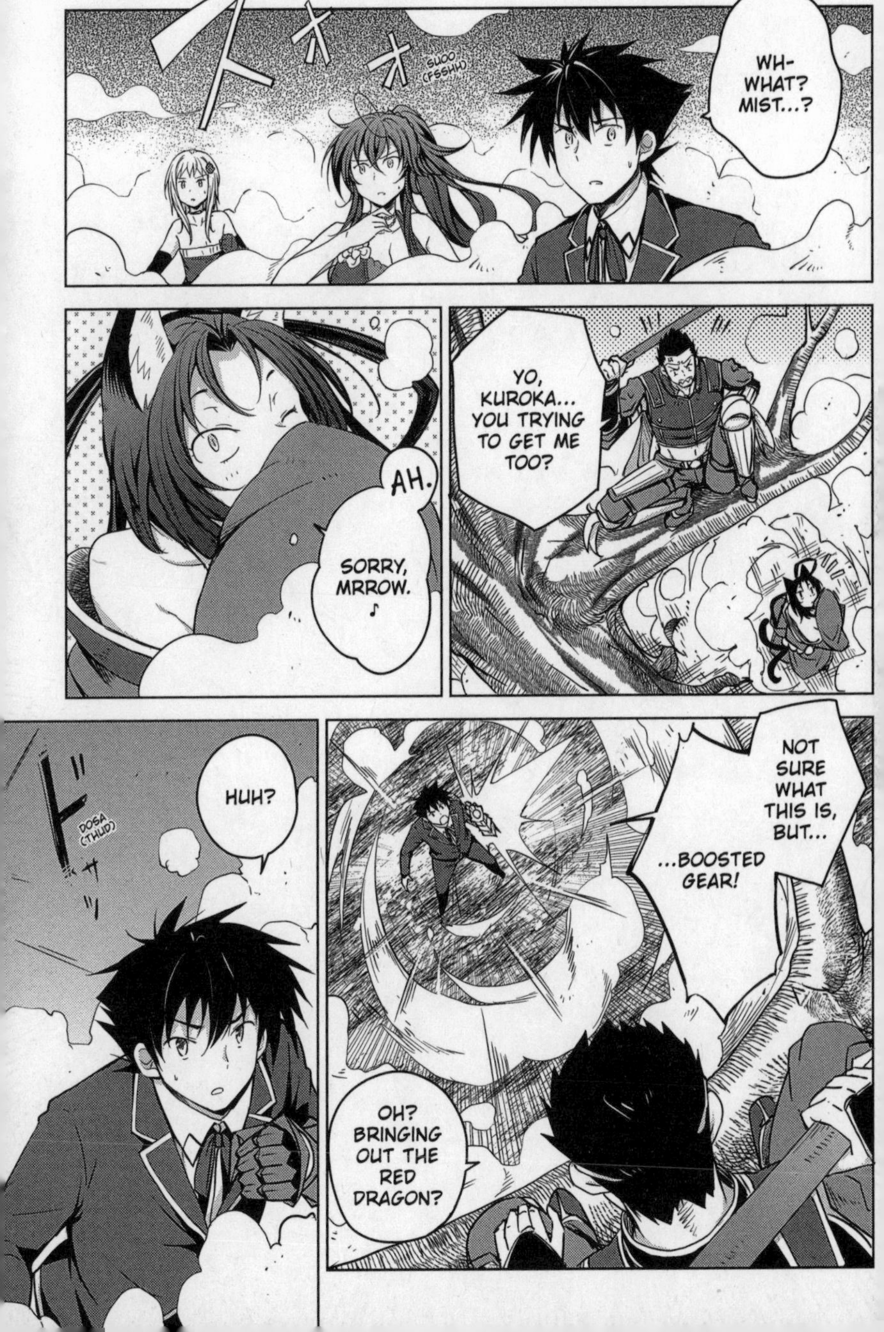
WH-WHAT? MIST...?
SUOO (FSSHH)
YO, KUROKA... YOU TRYING TO GET ME TOO?
AH.
SORRY, MRROW. ♪
NOT SURE WHAT THIS IS, BUT...
...BOOSTED GEAR!
OH? BRINGING OUT THE RED DRAGON?
HUH?
DOSA (THUD)

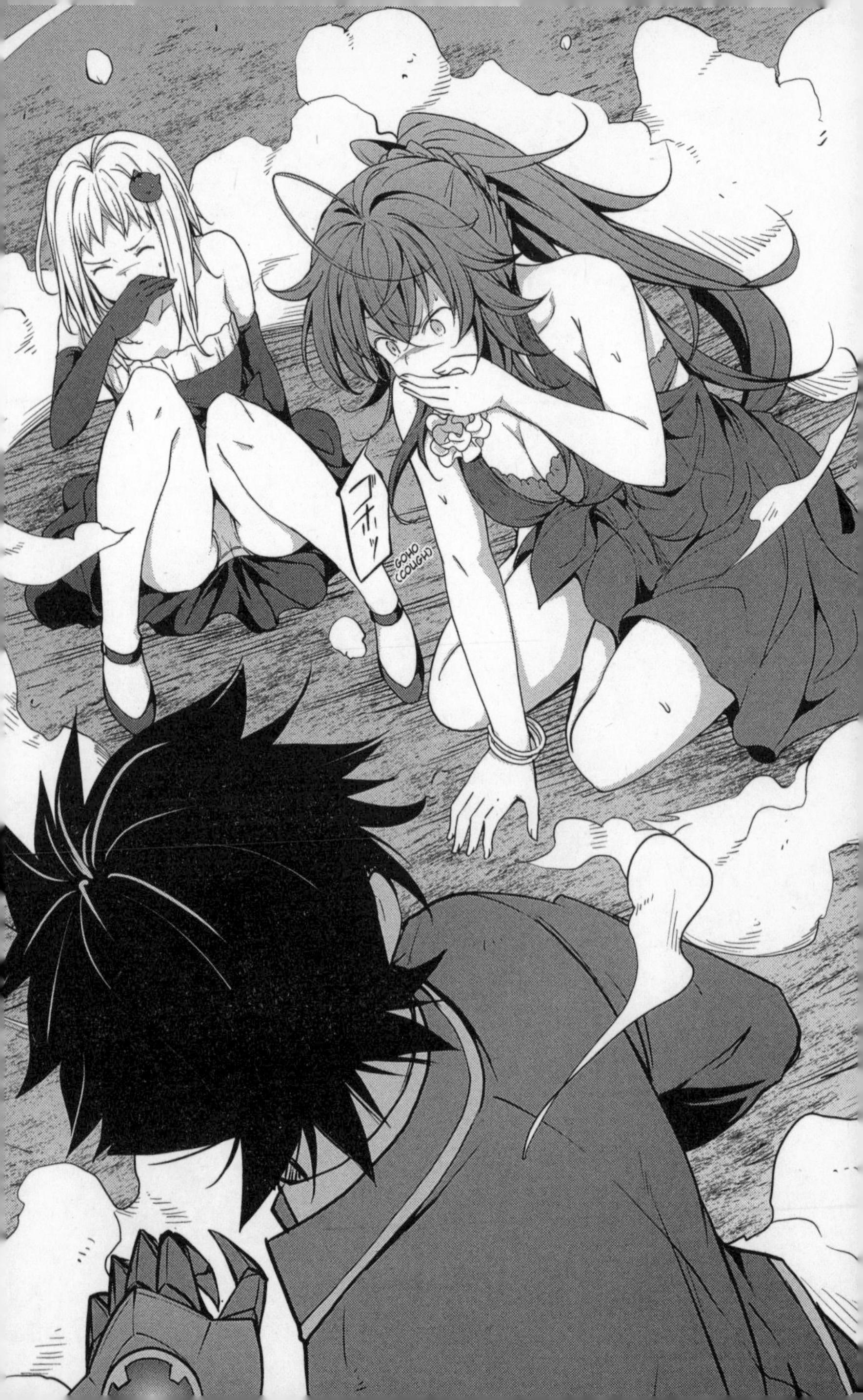
ゴホッ
GOHO (COUGH)

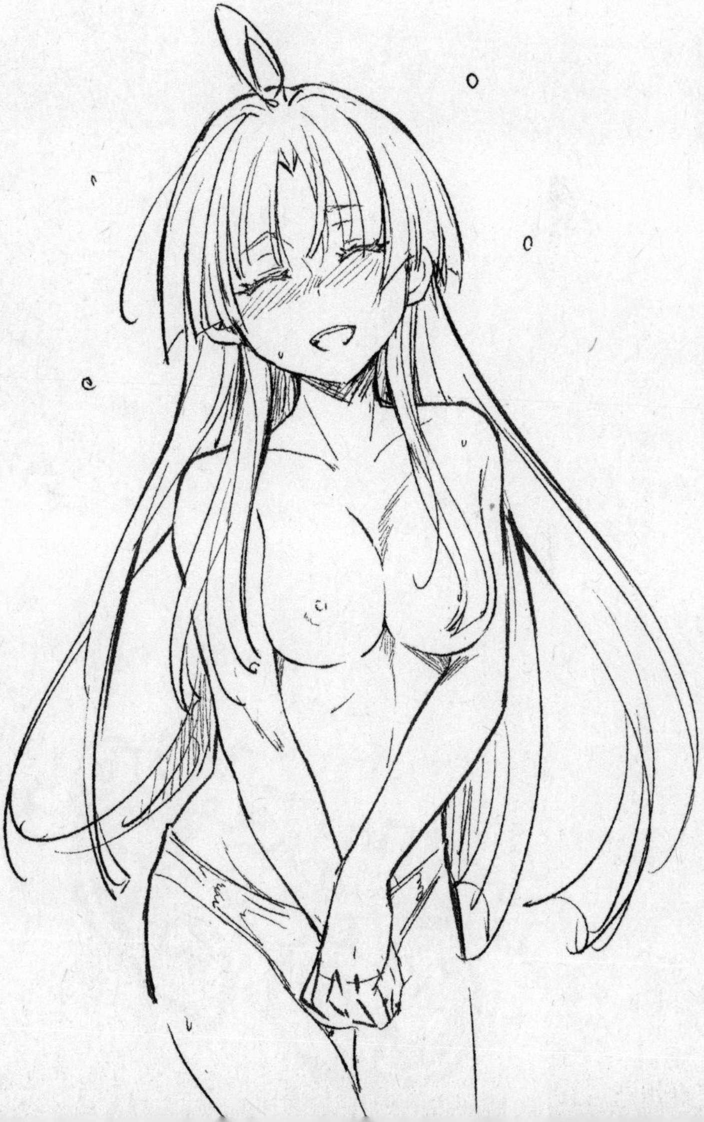

HIGH SCHOOL DxD

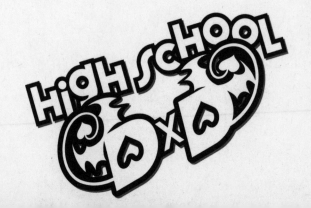

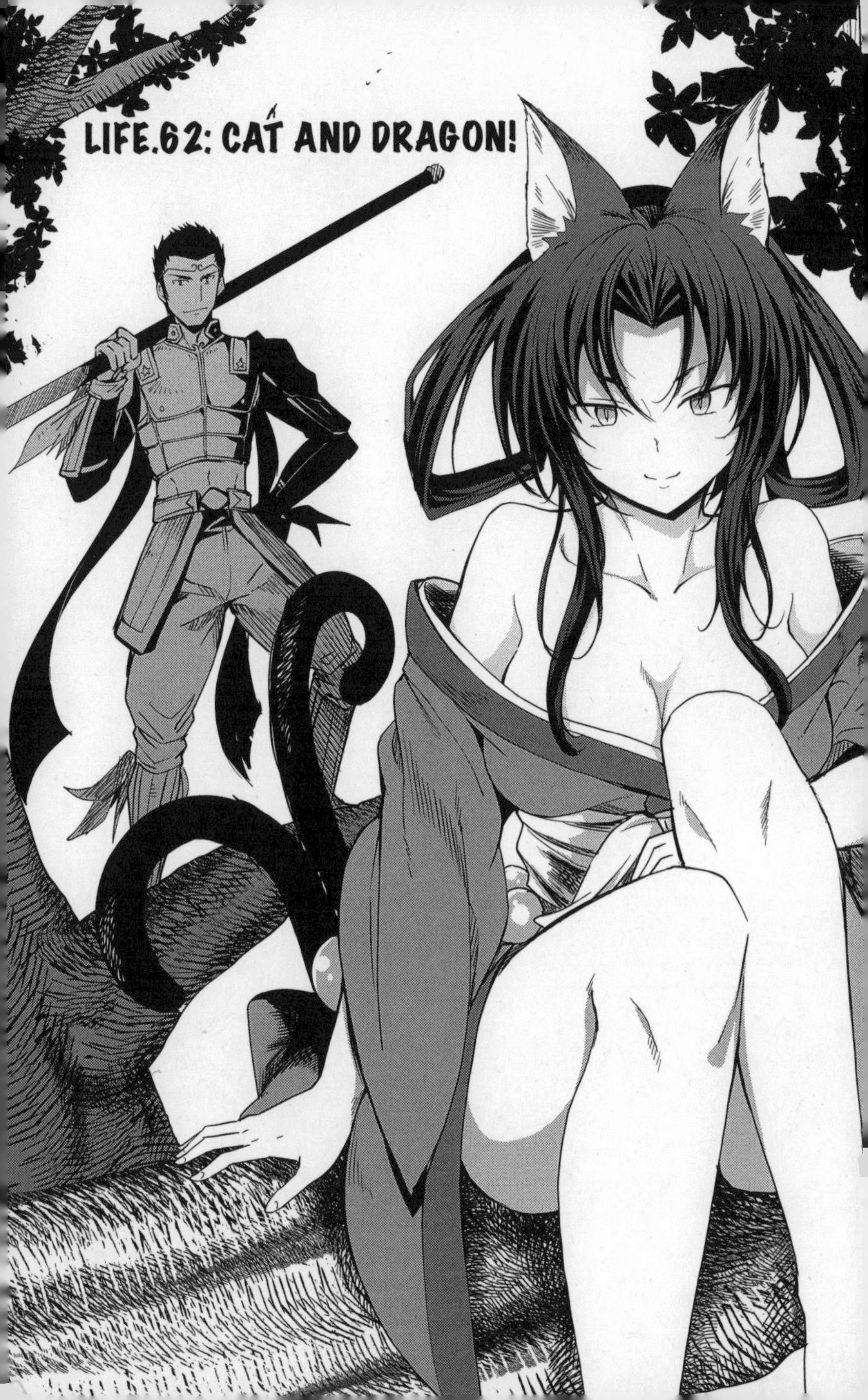
LIFE.62: CAT AND DRAGON!

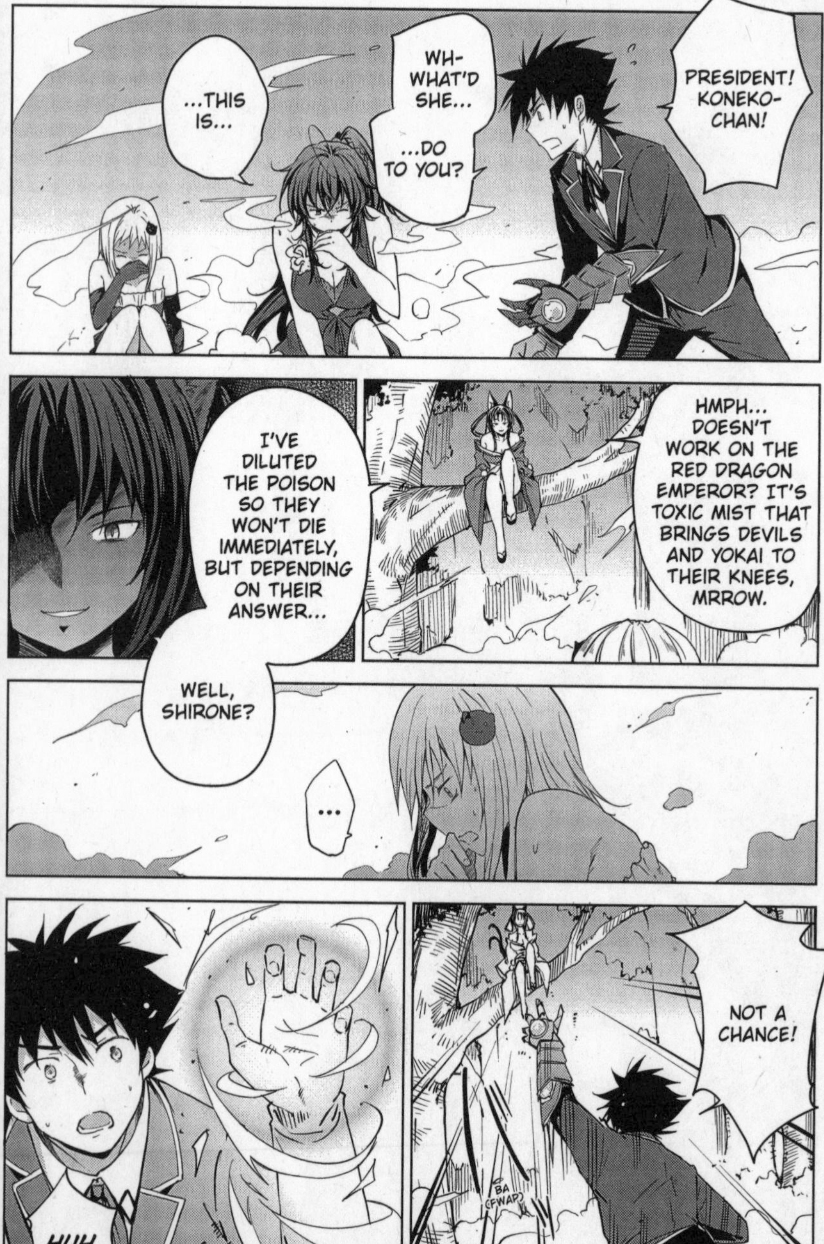
PRESIDENT! KONEKO-CHAN!
WH- WHAT'D SHE...
...DO TO YOU?
...THIS IS...
HMPH... DOESN'T WORK ON THE RED DRAGON EMPEROR? IT'S TOXIC MIST THAT BRINGS DEVILS AND YOKAI TO THEIR KNEES, MRROW.
I'VE DILUTED THE POISON SO THEY WON'T DIE IMMEDIATELY, BUT DEPENDING ON THEIR ANSWER...
WELL, SHIRONE?
...
NOT A CHANCE!
BA (FWAP)
HUH ...!?

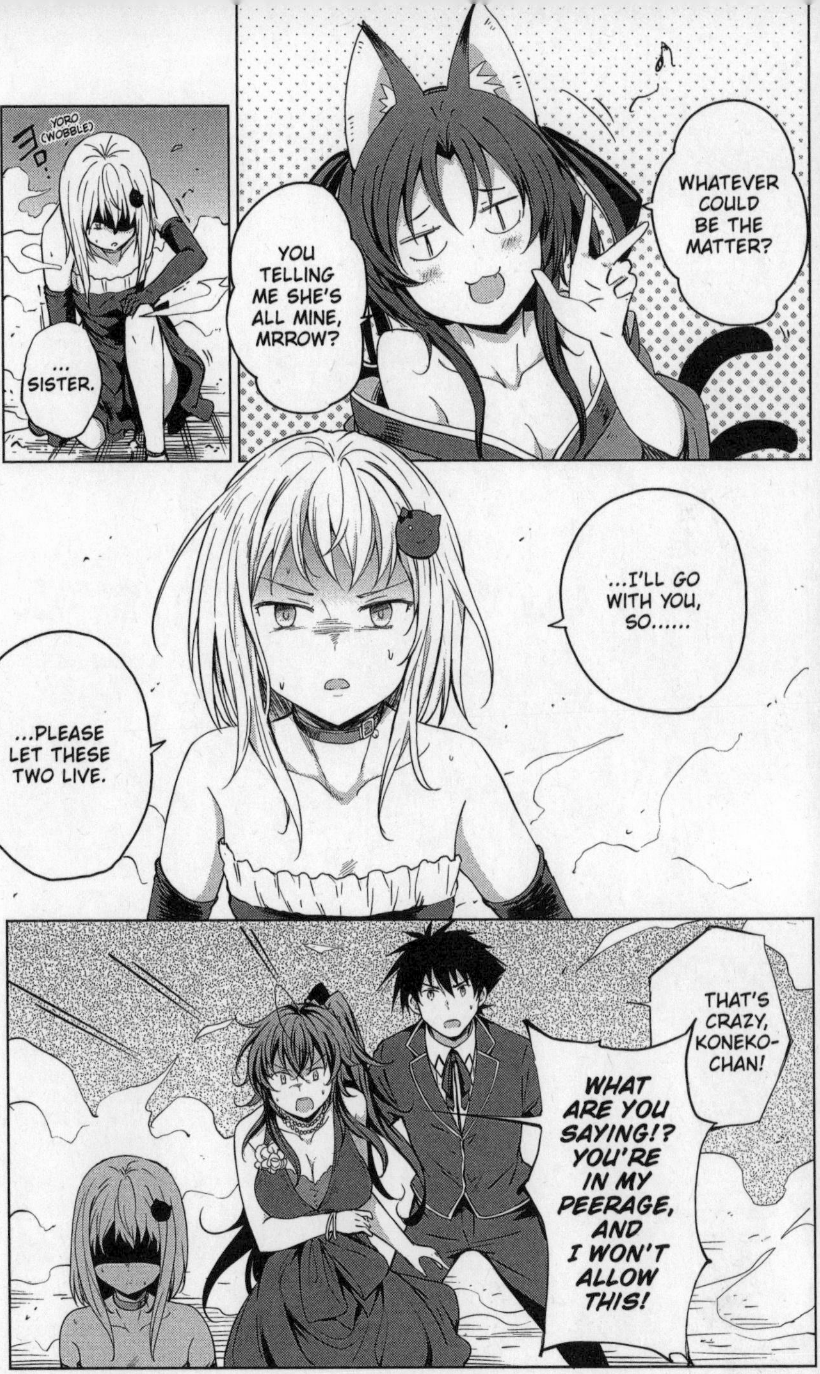
WHATEVER COULD BE THE MATTER?
YOU TELLING ME SHE'S ALL MINE, MRROW?
ヨロ
YORO (WOBBLE)
...SISTER.
...I'LL GO WITH YOU, SO......
...PLEASE LET THESE TWO LIVE.
THAT'S CRAZY, KONEKO-CHAN!
WHAT ARE YOU SAYING!? YOU'RE IN MY PEERAGE, AND I WON'T ALLOW THIS!

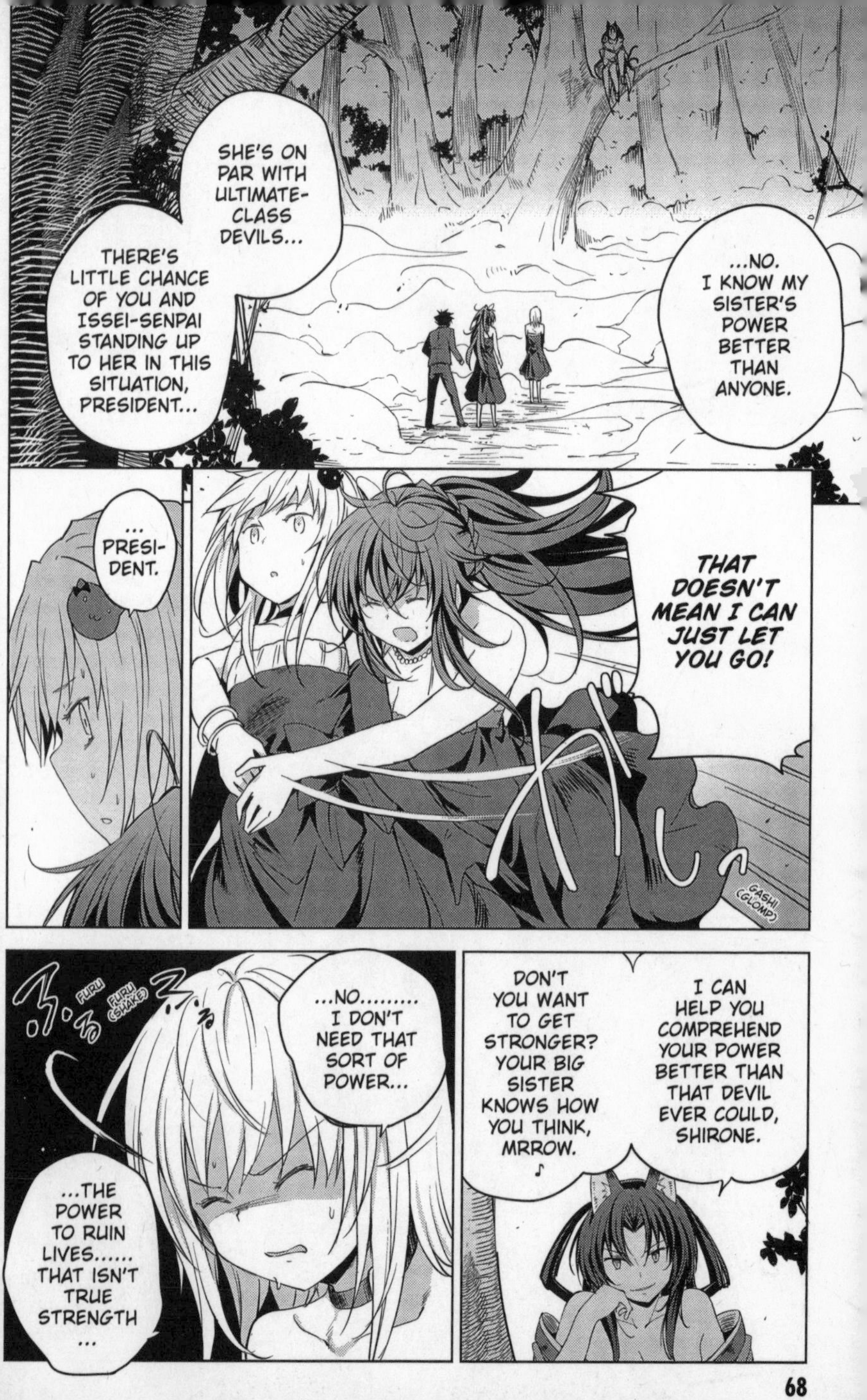
...NO. I KNOW MY SISTER'S POWER BETTER THAN ANYONE.
SHE'S ON PAR WITH ULTIMATE-CLASS DEVILS...
THERE'S LITTLE CHANCE OF YOU AND ISSEI-SENPAI STANDING UP TO HER IN THIS SITUATION, PRESIDENT...
THAT DOESN'T MEAN I CAN JUST LET YOU GO!
GASHI (GLOMP)
... PRESI-DENT.
I CAN HELP YOU COMPREHEND YOUR POWER BETTER THAN THAT DEVIL EVER COULD, SHIRONE.
DON'T YOU WANT TO GET STRONGER? YOUR BIG SISTER KNOWS HOW YOU THINK, MRROW. ♪
FURU FURU (SHAKE)
...NO......... I DON'T NEED THAT SORT OF POWER...
...THE POWER TO RUIN LIVES...... THAT ISN'T TRUE STRENGTH ...

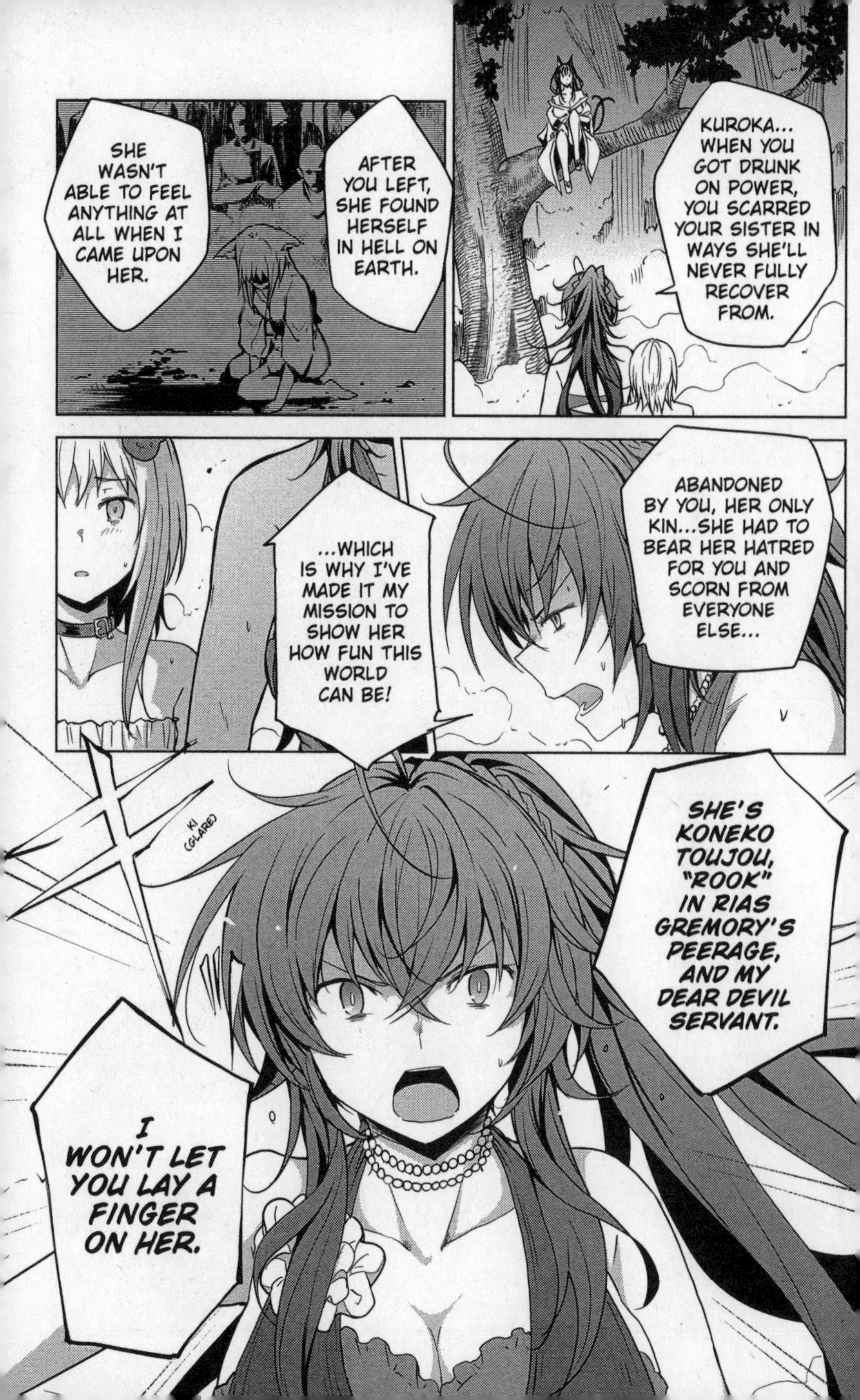
KUROKA... WHEN YOU GOT DRUNK ON POWER, YOU SCARRED YOUR SISTER IN WAYS SHE'LL NEVER FULLY RECOVER FROM.
AFTER YOU LEFT, SHE FOUND HERSELF IN HELL ON EARTH.
SHE WASN'T ABLE TO FEEL ANYTHING AT ALL WHEN I CAME UPON HER.
ABANDONED BY YOU, HER ONLY KIN...SHE HAD TO BEAR HER HATRED FOR YOU AND SCORN FROM EVERYONE ELSE...
...WHICH IS WHY I'VE MADE IT MY MISSION TO SHOW HER HOW FUN THIS WORLD CAN BE!
SHE'S KONEKO TOUJOU, "ROOK" IN RIAS GREMORY'S PEERAGE, AND MY DEAR DEVIL SERVANT.
KI (GLARE)
I WON'T LET YOU LAY A FINGER ON HER.

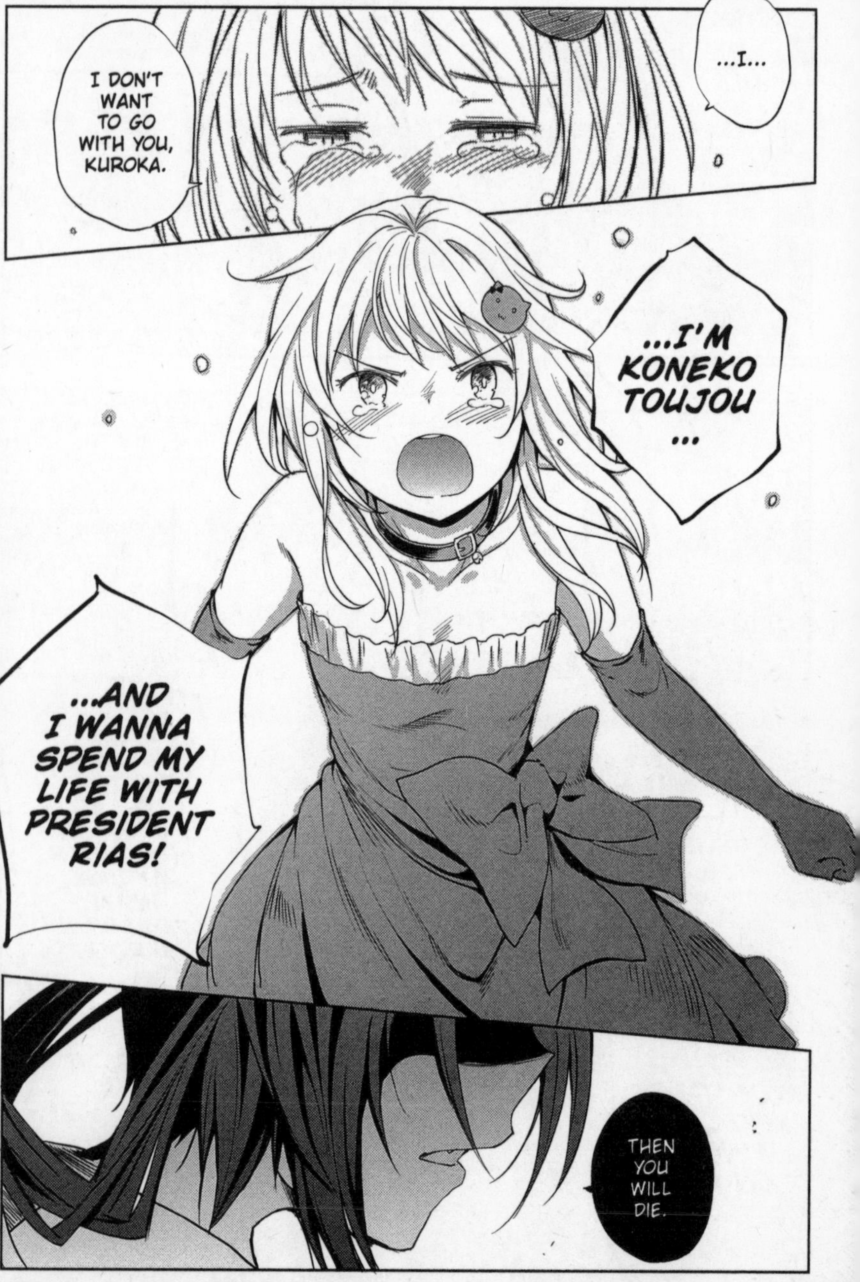
...I...
I DON'T WANT TO GO WITH YOU, KUROKA.
...I'M KONEKO TOUJOU...
...AND I WANNA SPEND MY LIFE WITH PRESIDENT RIAS!
THEN YOU WILL DIE.

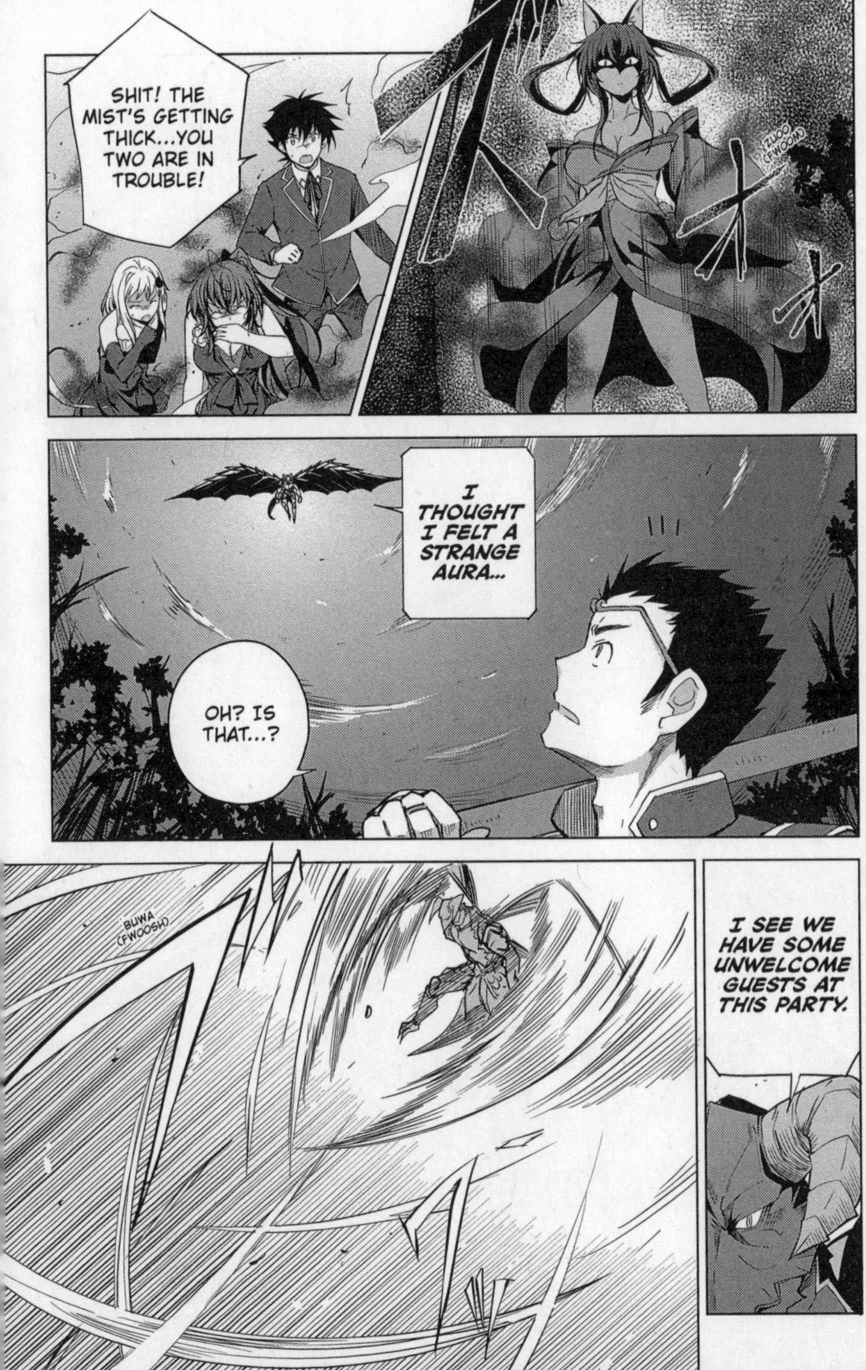
ZUOO (FWOOM)
SHIT! THE MIST'S GETTING THICK...YOU TWO ARE IN TROUBLE!
I THOUGHT I FELT A STRANGE AURA...
OH? IS THAT...?
I SEE WE HAVE SOME UNWELCOME GUESTS AT THIS PARTY.
BUWA (FWOOSH)

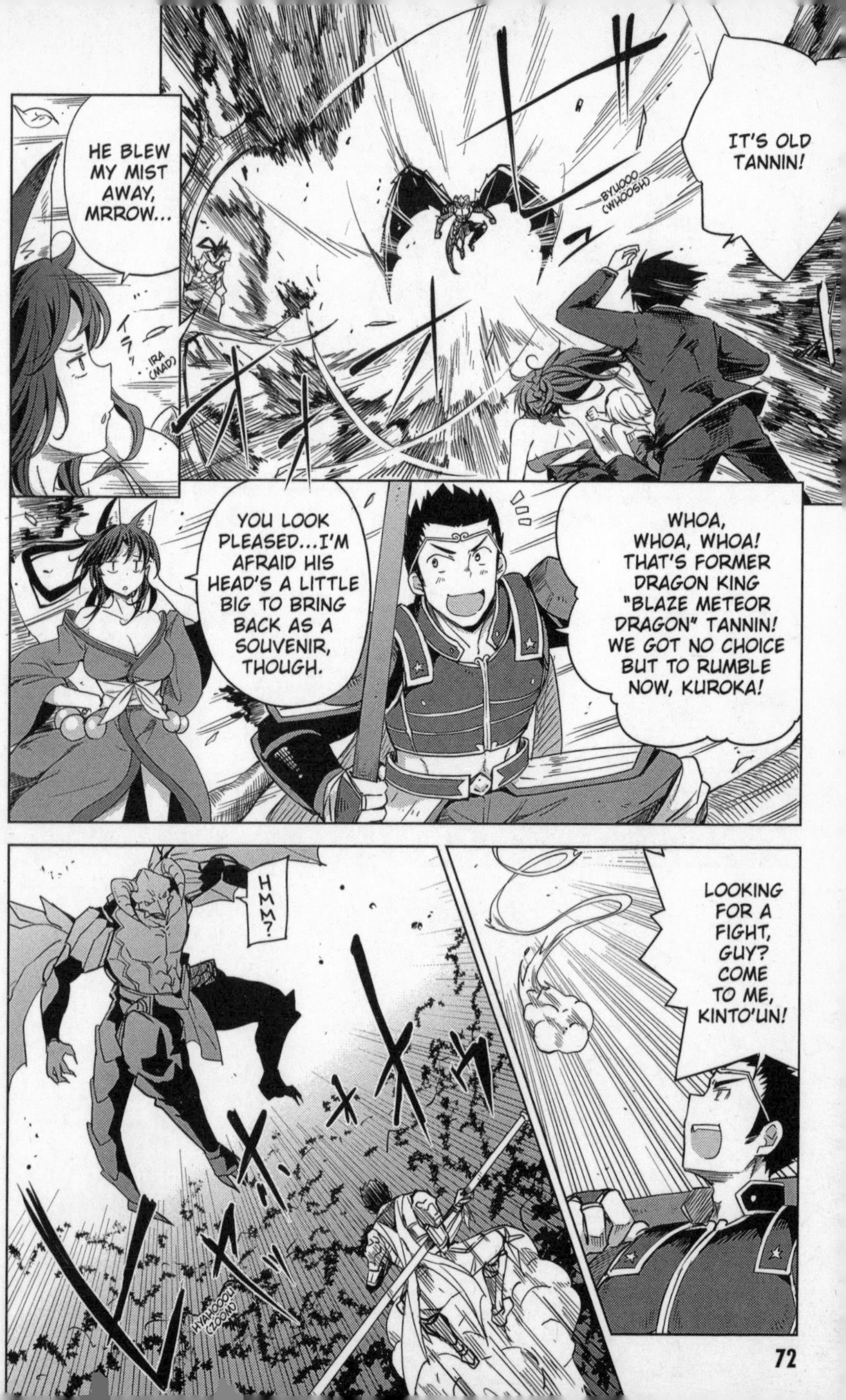
IT'S OLD TANNIN!
BYUOOO (WHOOSH)
HE BLEW MY MIST AWAY, MRROW...
IRA (MAD)
WHOA, WHOA, WHOA! THAT'S FORMER DRAGON KING "BLAZE METEOR DRAGON" TANNIN! WE GOT NO CHOICE BUT TO RUMBLE NOW, KUROKA!
YOU LOOK PLEASED...I'M AFRAID HIS HEAD'S A LITTLE BIG TO BRING BACK AS A SOUVENIR, THOUGH.
LOOKING FOR A FIGHT, GUY? COME TO ME, KINTO'UN!
HMM?
HYAHOOOU (ZOOM)

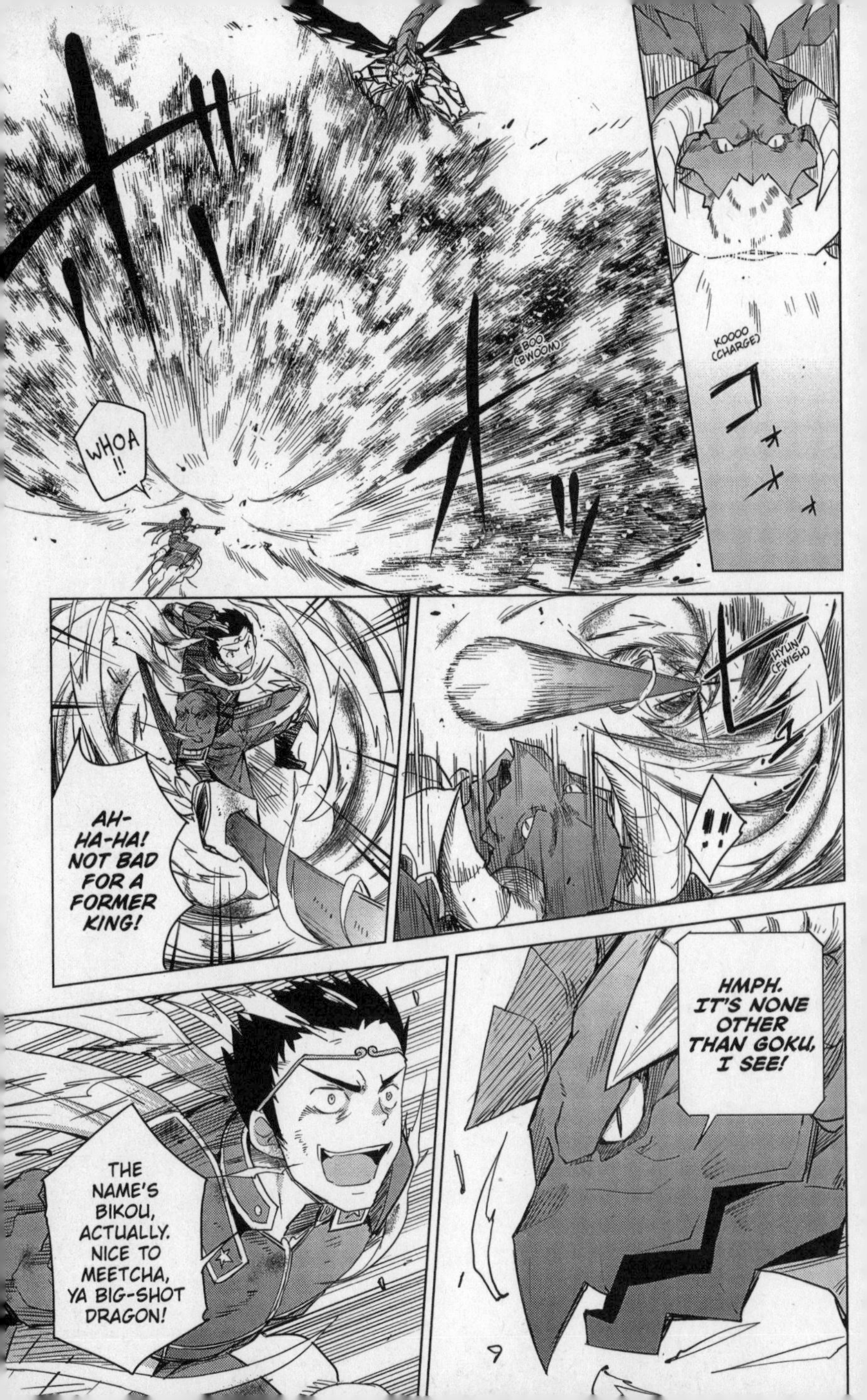
KOOOO (CHARGE)
BOO (BWOOM)
WHOA !!
HYUN (FWISH)
!!
AH-HA-HA! NOT BAD FOR A FORMER KING!
HMPH. IT'S NONE OTHER THAN GOKU, I SEE!
THE NAME'S BIKOU, ACTUALLY. NICE TO MEETCHA, YA BIG-SHOT DRAGON!

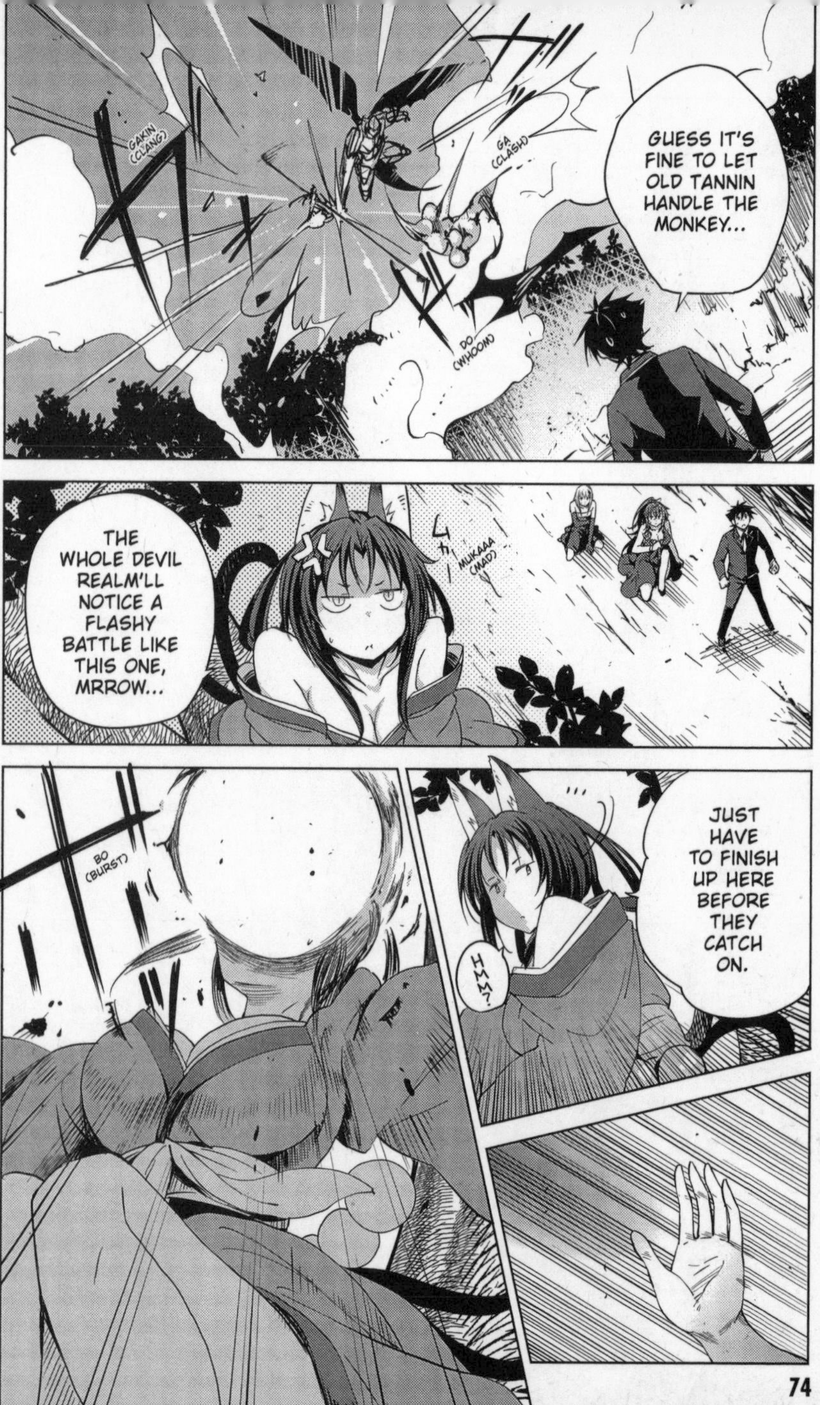
GUESS IT'S FINE TO LET OLD TANNIN HANDLE THE MONKEY...
GA (CLASH)
GAKIN (CLANG)
DO (WHOOM)
MUKAAA (MAD)
THE WHOLE DEVIL REALM'LL NOTICE A FLASHY BATTLE LIKE THIS ONE, MRROW...
JUST HAVE TO FINISH UP HERE BEFORE THEY CATCH ON.
HMM?
BO (BURST)

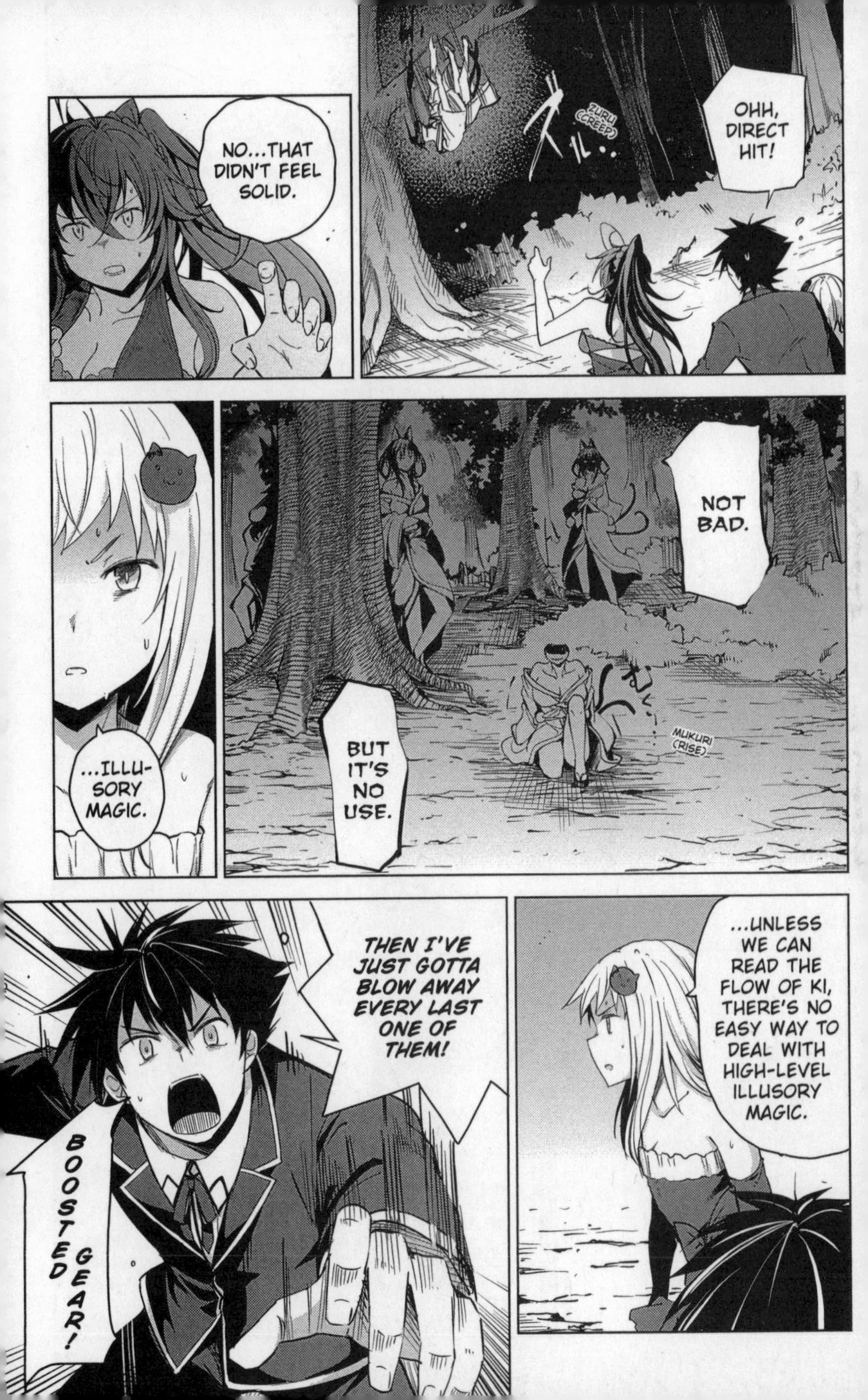
OHH, DIRECT HIT!
ZURU (CREEP)
NO...THAT DIDN'T FEEL SOLID.
NOT BAD.
MUKURI (RISE)
BUT IT'S NO USE.
...ILLUSORY MAGIC.
...UNLESS WE CAN READ THE FLOW OF KI, THERE'S NO EASY WAY TO DEAL WITH HIGH-LEVEL ILLUSORY MAGIC.
THEN I'VE JUST GOTTA BLOW AWAY EVERY LAST ONE OF THEM!
BOOSTED GEAR!

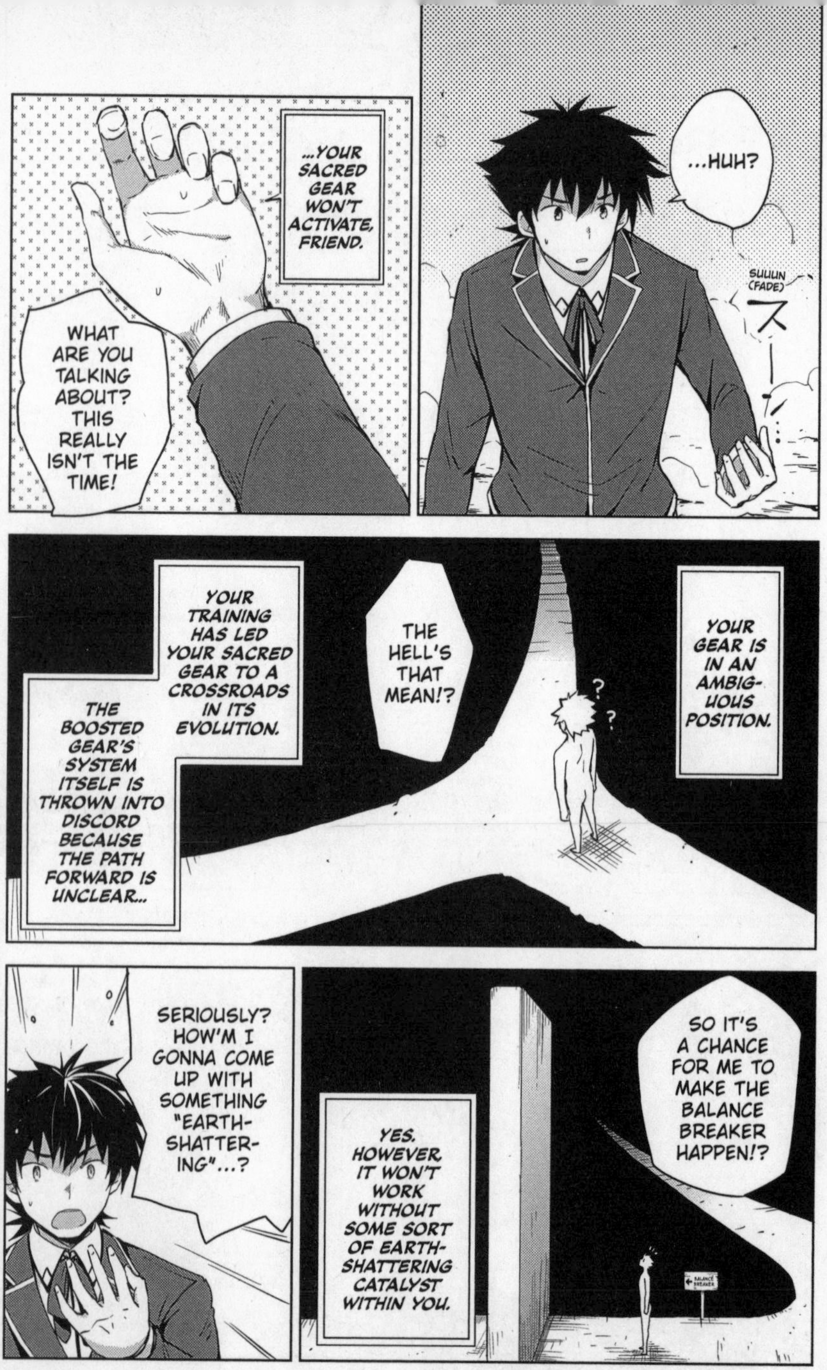
...HUH?
SUUUN (FADE)
スー
...YOUR SACRED GEAR WON'T ACTIVATE, FRIEND.
WHAT ARE YOU TALKING ABOUT? THIS REALLY ISN'T THE TIME!
YOUR GEAR IS IN AN AMBIG-UOUS POSITION.
THE HELL'S THAT MEAN!?
YOUR TRAINING HAS LED YOUR SACRED GEAR TO A CROSSROADS IN ITS EVOLUTION.
THE BOOSTED GEAR'S SYSTEM ITSELF IS THROWN INTO DISCORD BECAUSE THE PATH FORWARD IS UNCLEAR...
SO IT'S A CHANCE FOR ME TO MAKE THE BALANCE BREAKER HAPPEN!?
YES. HOWEVER IT WON'T WORK WITHOUT SOME SORT OF EARTH-SHATTERING CATALYST WITHIN YOU.
BALANCE BREAKER
SERIOUSLY? HOW'M I GONNA COME UP WITH SOMETHING "EARTH-SHATTER-ING"...?

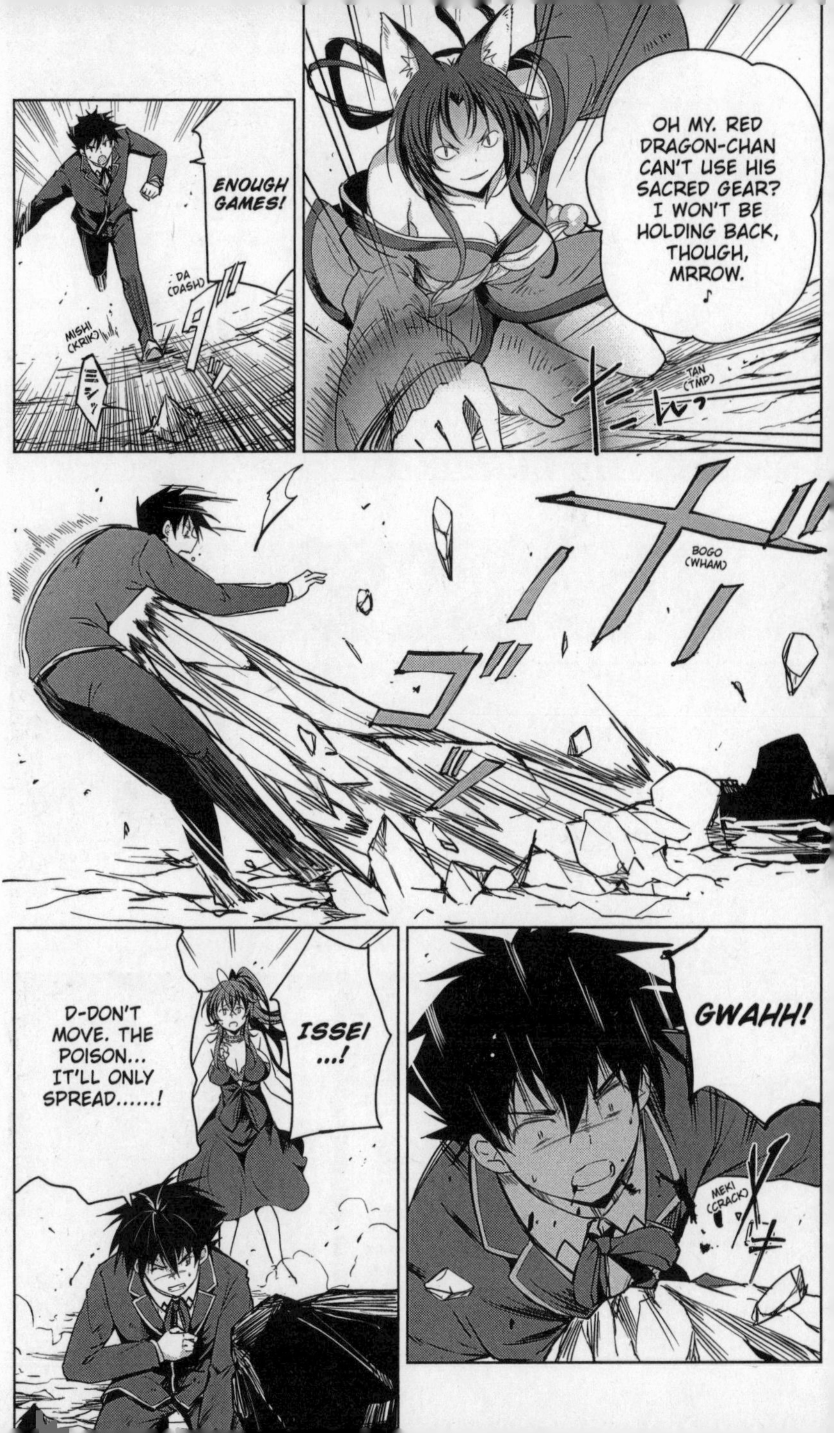
OH MY. RED DRAGON-CHAN CAN'T USE HIS SACRED GEAR? I WON'T BE HOLDING BACK, THOUGH, MRROW. ♪
TAN (TMP)
ENOUGH GAMES!
DA (DASH)
MISHI (KRIK)
BOGO (WHAM)
GWAHH!
MEKI (CRACK)
ISSEI ...!
D-DON'T MOVE. THE POISON... IT'LL ONLY SPREAD......!

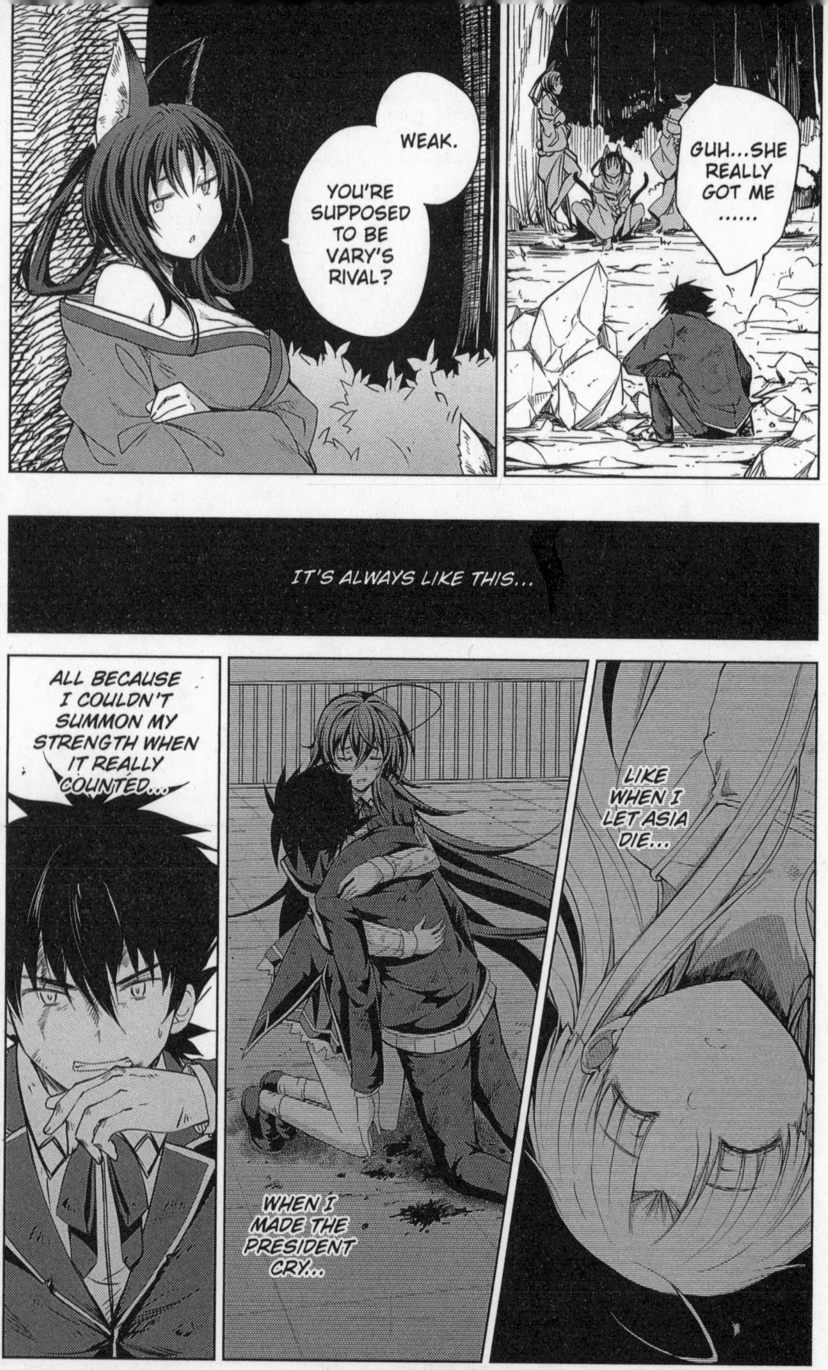
GUH...SHE REALLY GOT ME ......
WEAK.
YOU'RE SUPPOSED TO BE VARY'S RIVAL?
IT'S ALWAYS LIKE THIS...
LIKE WHEN I LET ASIA DIE...
WHEN I MADE THE PRESIDENT CRY...
ALL BECAUSE I COULDN'T SUMMON MY STRENGTH WHEN IT REALLY COUNTED...

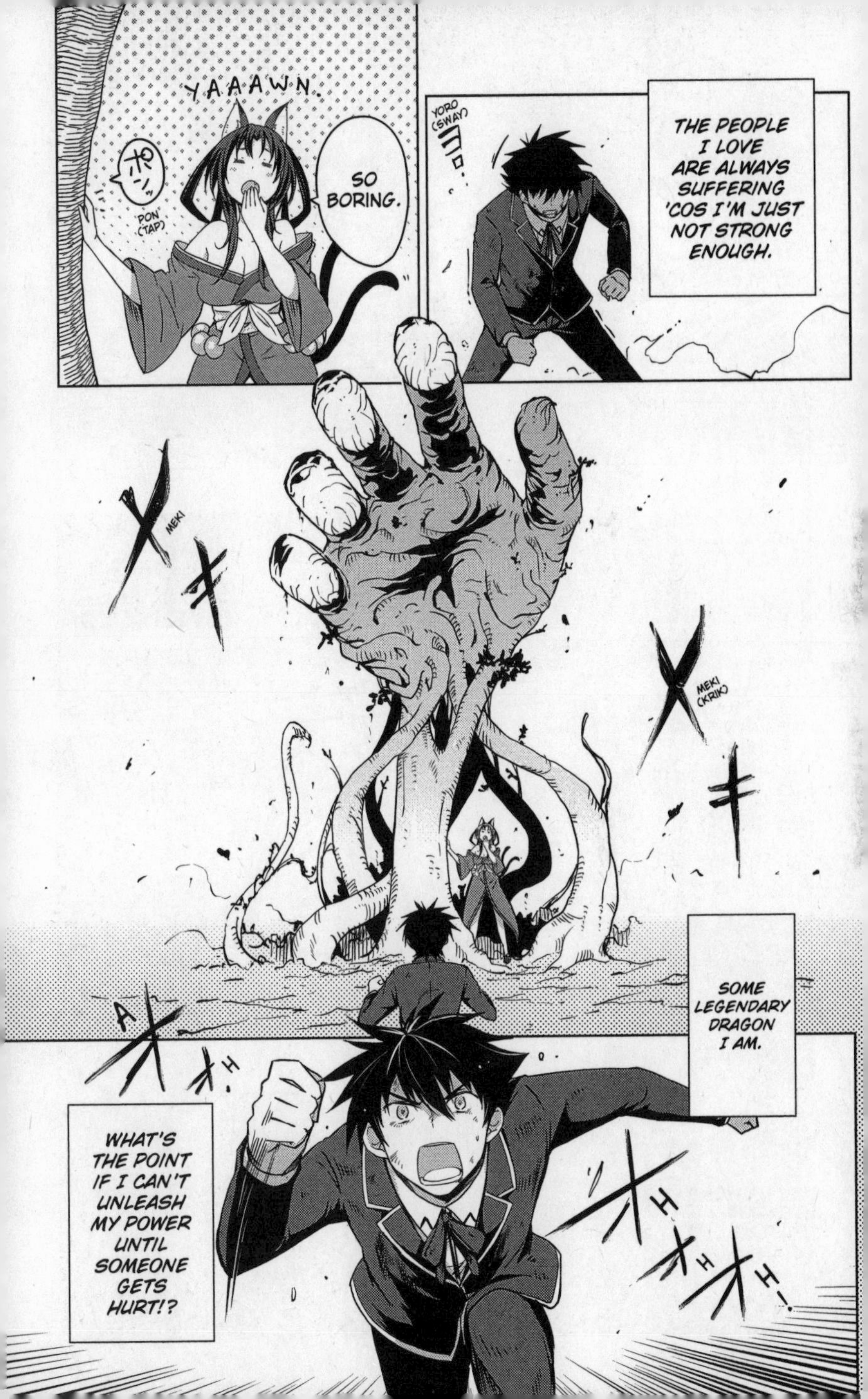

THE PEOPLE I LOVE ARE ALWAYS SUFFERING 'COS I'M JUST NOT STRONG ENOUGH.
YORO (SWAY)
YAAAWN.
SO BORING.
PON (TAP)
MEKI (KRIK)
MEKI
SOME LEGENDARY DRAGON I AM.
AAAAAH!
WHAT'S THE POINT IF I CAN'T UNLEASH MY POWER UNTIL SOMEONE GETS HURT!?

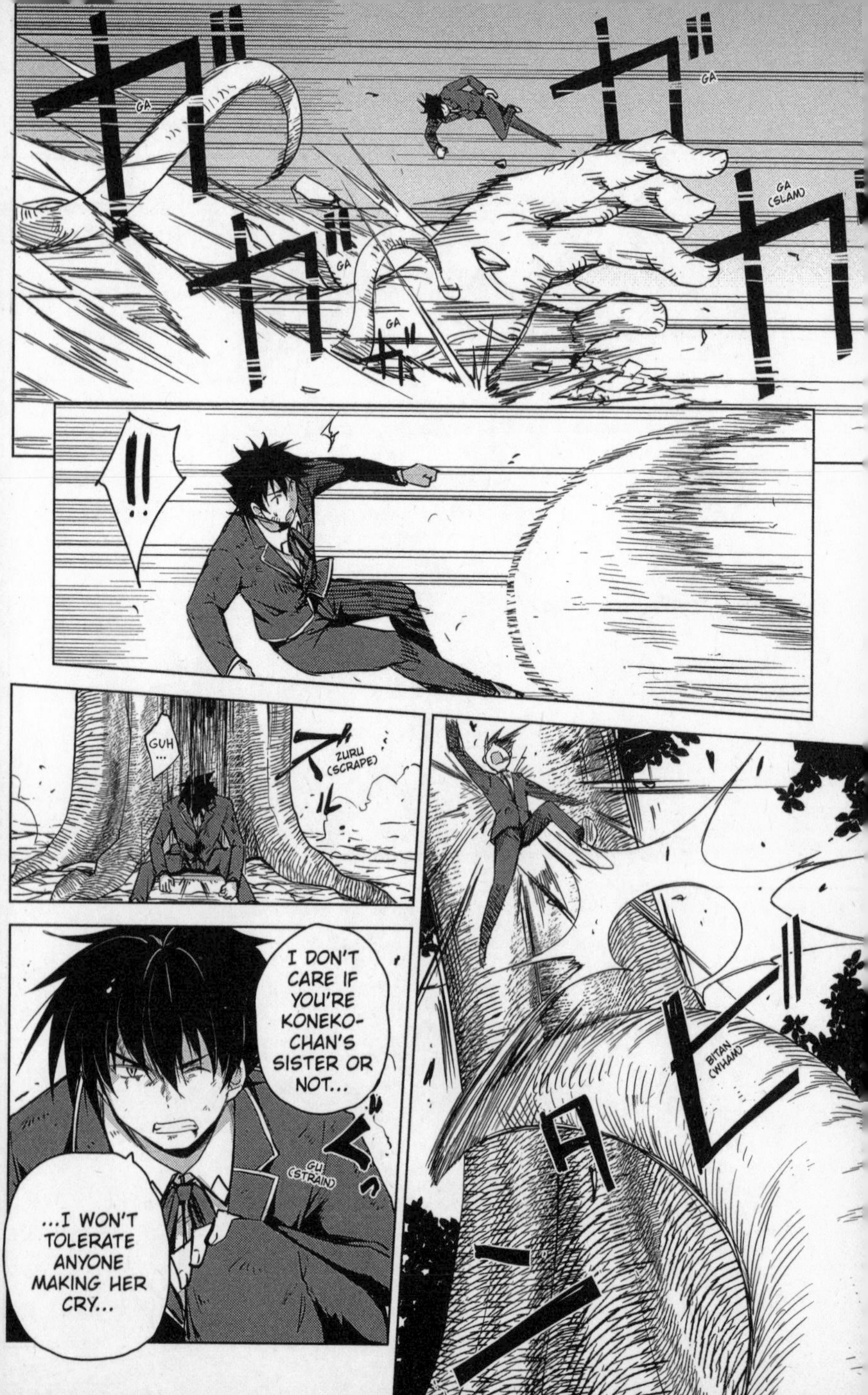
GA (SLAM)
GA
GA
GA
GA
!!
BITAN (WHAM)
ZURU (SCRAPE)
GUH...
I DON'T CARE IF YOU'RE KONEKO-CHAN'S SISTER OR NOT...
GU (STRAIN)
...I WON'T TOLERATE ANYONE MAKING HER CRY...

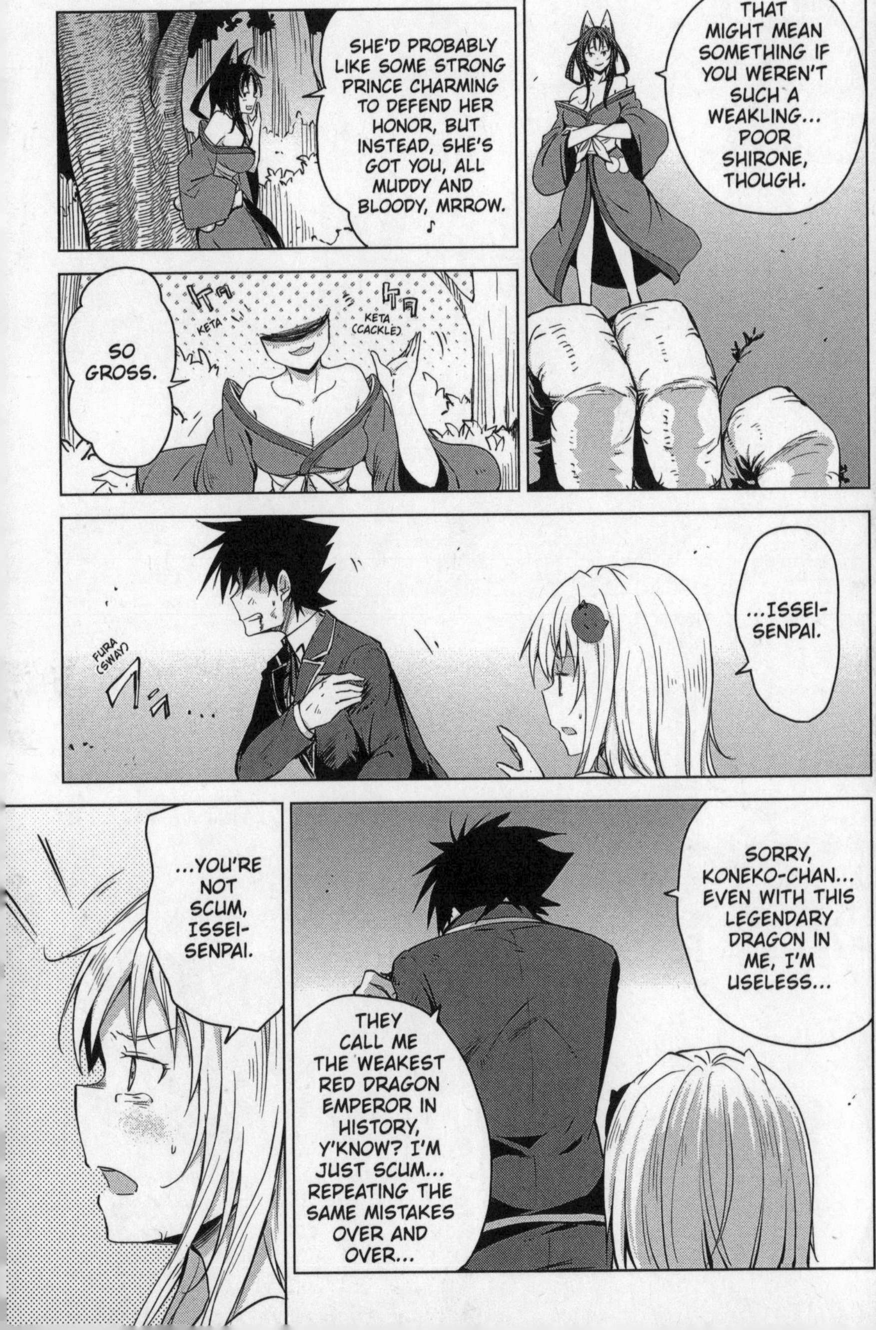
THAT MIGHT MEAN SOMETHING IF YOU WEREN'T SUCH A WEAKLING... POOR SHIRONE, THOUGH.
SHE'D PROBABLY LIKE SOME STRONG PRINCE CHARMING TO DEFEND HER HONOR, BUT INSTEAD, SHE'S GOT YOU, ALL MUDDY AND BLOODY, MRROW. ♪
KETA (CACKLE)
KETA
SO GROSS.
...ISSEI-SENPAI.
FURA (SWAY)
SORRY, KONEKO-CHAN... EVEN WITH THIS LEGENDARY DRAGON IN ME, I'M USELESS...
THEY CALL ME THE WEAKEST RED DRAGON EMPEROR IN HISTORY, Y'KNOW? I'M JUST SCUM... REPEATING THE SAME MISTAKES OVER AND OVER...
...YOU'RE NOT SCUM, ISSEI-SENPAI.

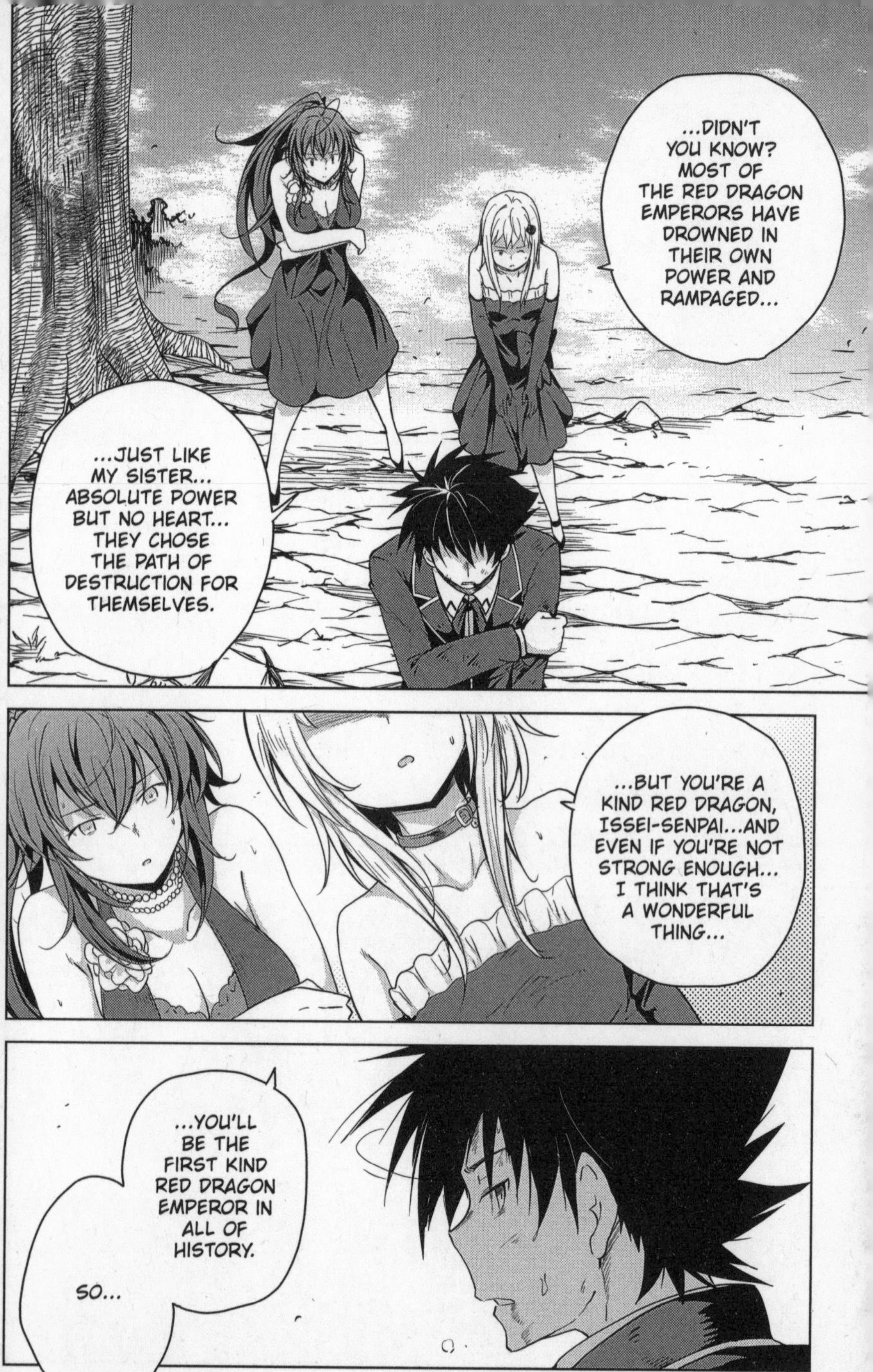
...DIDN'T YOU KNOW? MOST OF THE RED DRAGON EMPERORS HAVE DROWNED IN THEIR OWN POWER AND RAMPAGED...
...JUST LIKE MY SISTER... ABSOLUTE POWER BUT NO HEART... THEY CHOSE THE PATH OF DESTRUCTION FOR THEMSELVES.
...BUT YOU'RE A KIND RED DRAGON, ISSEI-SENPAI...AND EVEN IF YOU'RE NOT STRONG ENOUGH... I THINK THAT'S A WONDERFUL THING...
...YOU'LL BE THE FIRST KIND RED DRAGON EMPEROR IN ALL OF HISTORY.
SO...

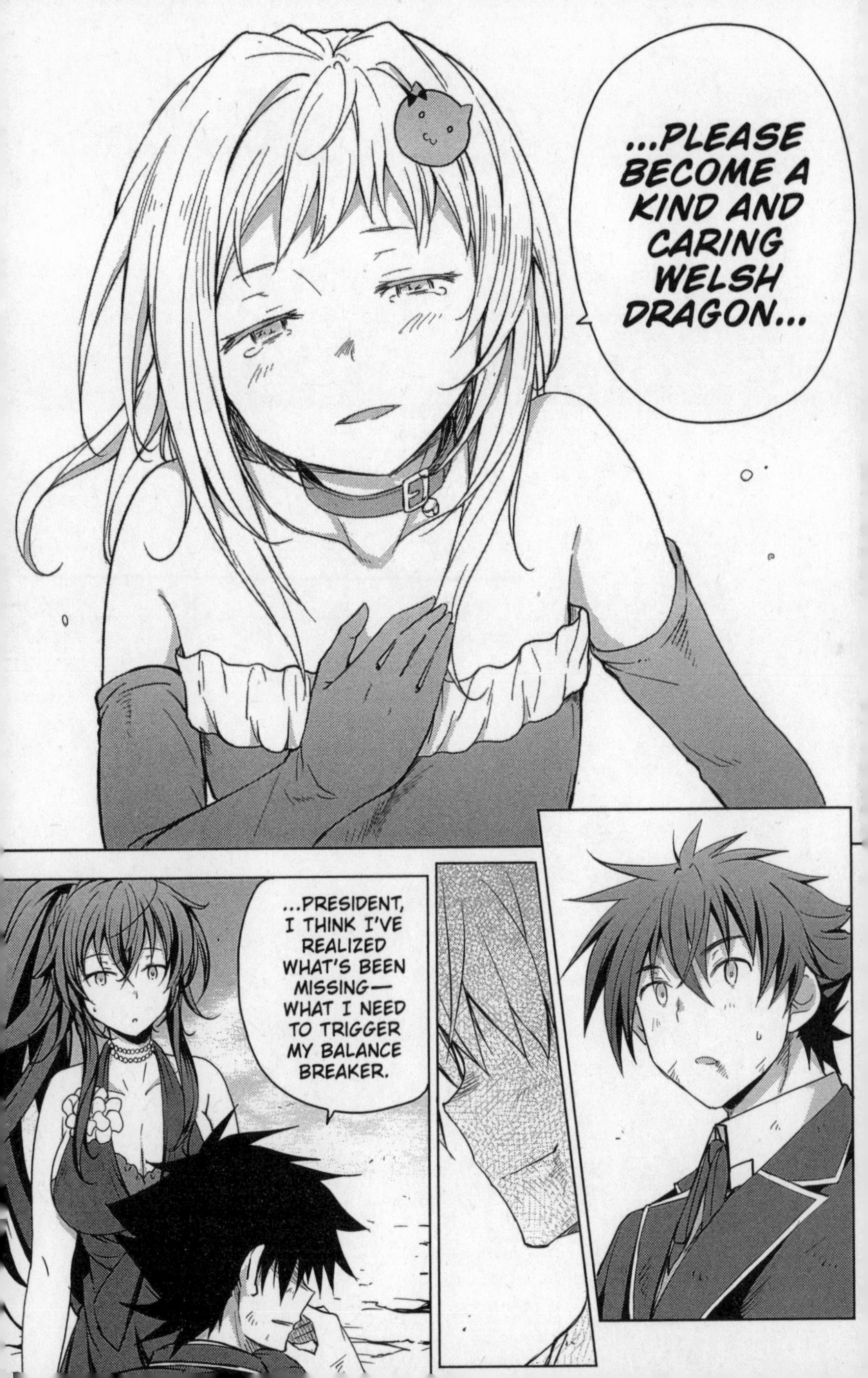
...PLEASE BECOME A KIND AND CARING WELSH DRAGON...
...PRESIDENT, I THINK I'VE REALIZED WHAT'S BEEN MISSING—WHAT I NEED TO TRIGGER MY BALANCE BREAKER.

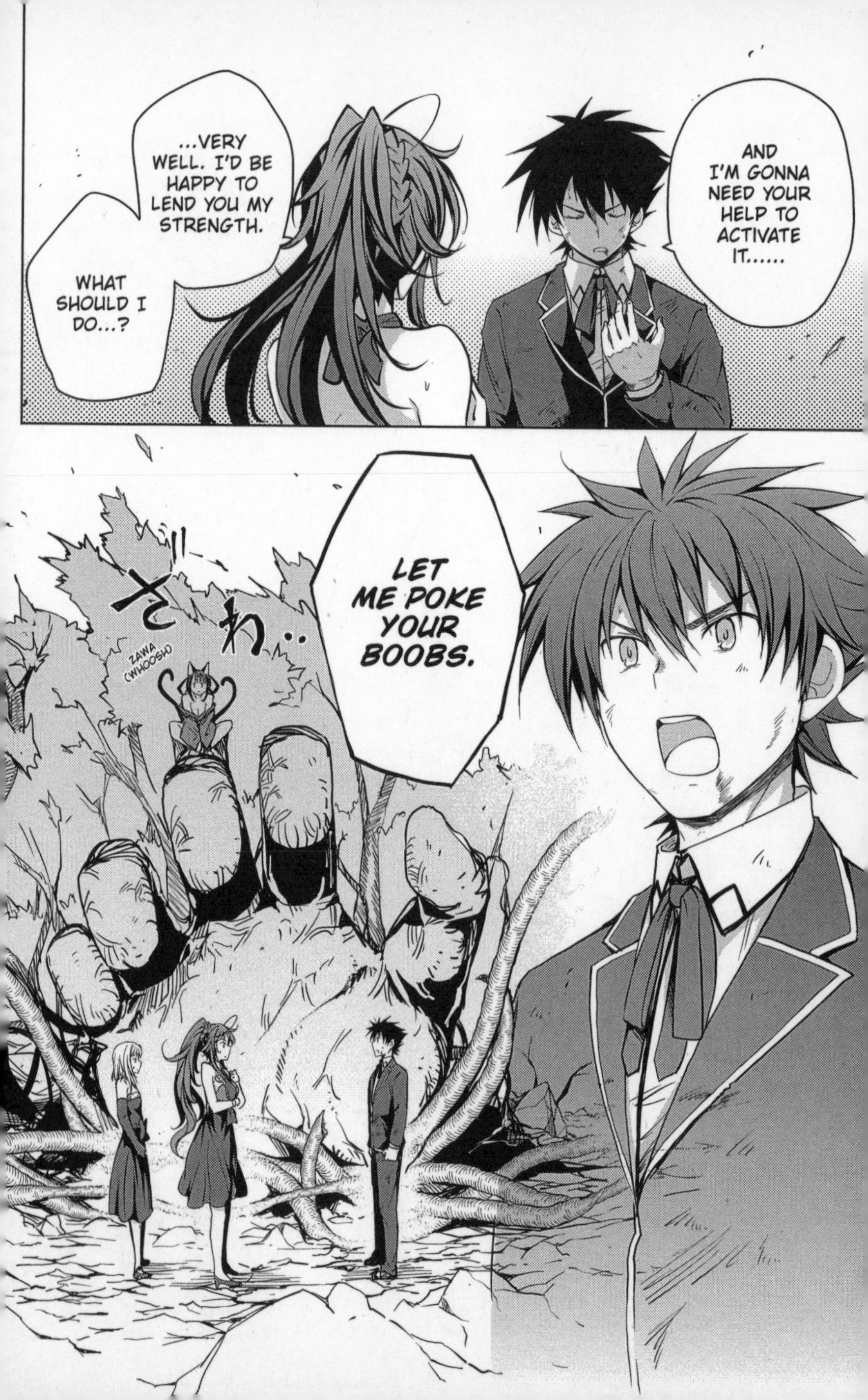
AND I'M GONNA NEED YOUR HELP TO ACTIVATE IT......
...VERY WELL. I'D BE HAPPY TO LEND YOU MY STRENGTH.
WHAT SHOULD I DO...?
LET ME POKE YOUR BOOBS.
ざわ..
ZAWA (WHOOSH)

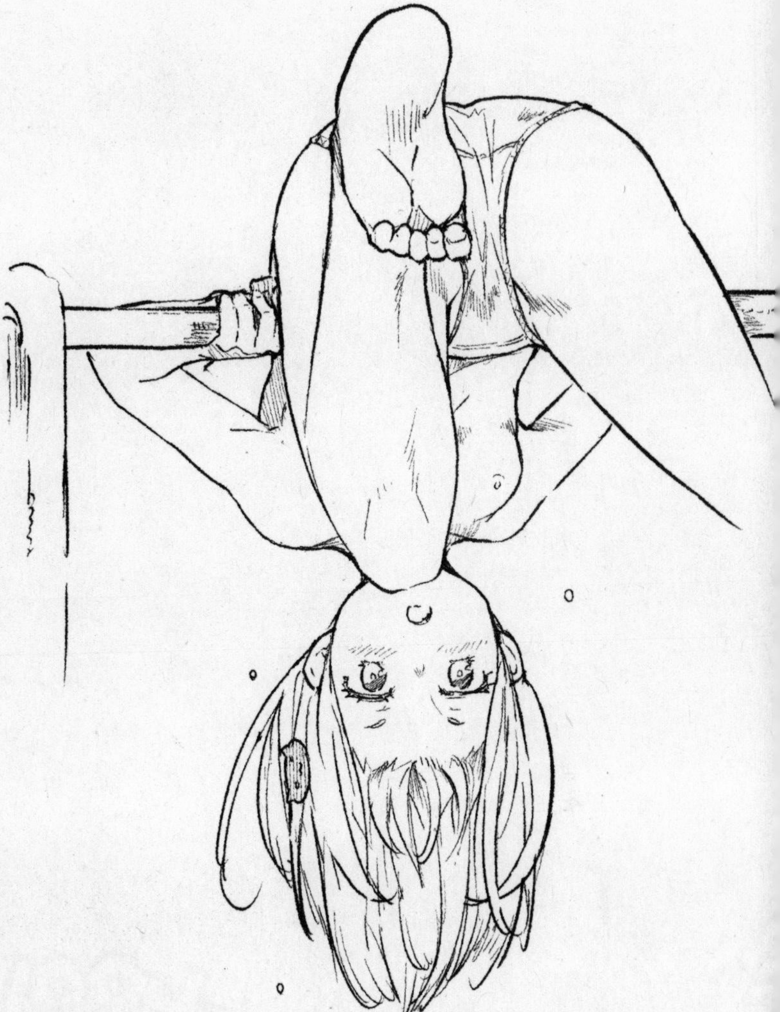

HIGH SCHOOL DxD

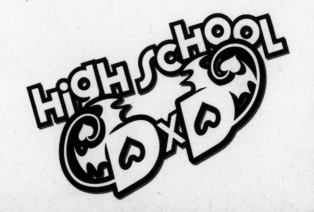

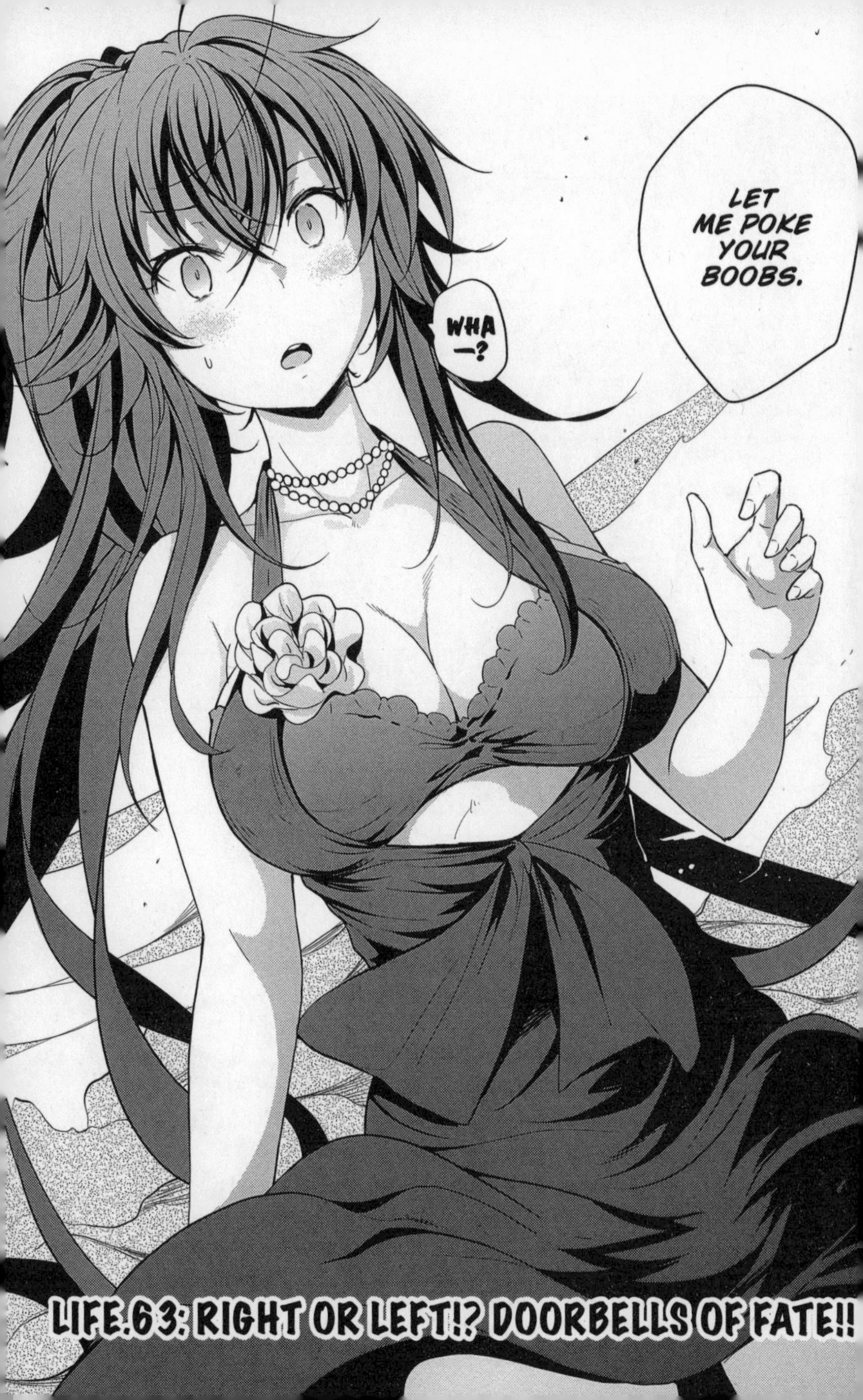
LET ME POKE YOUR BOOBS.
WHA—?

LIFE.63: RIGHT OR LEFT!? DOORBELLS OF FATE!!

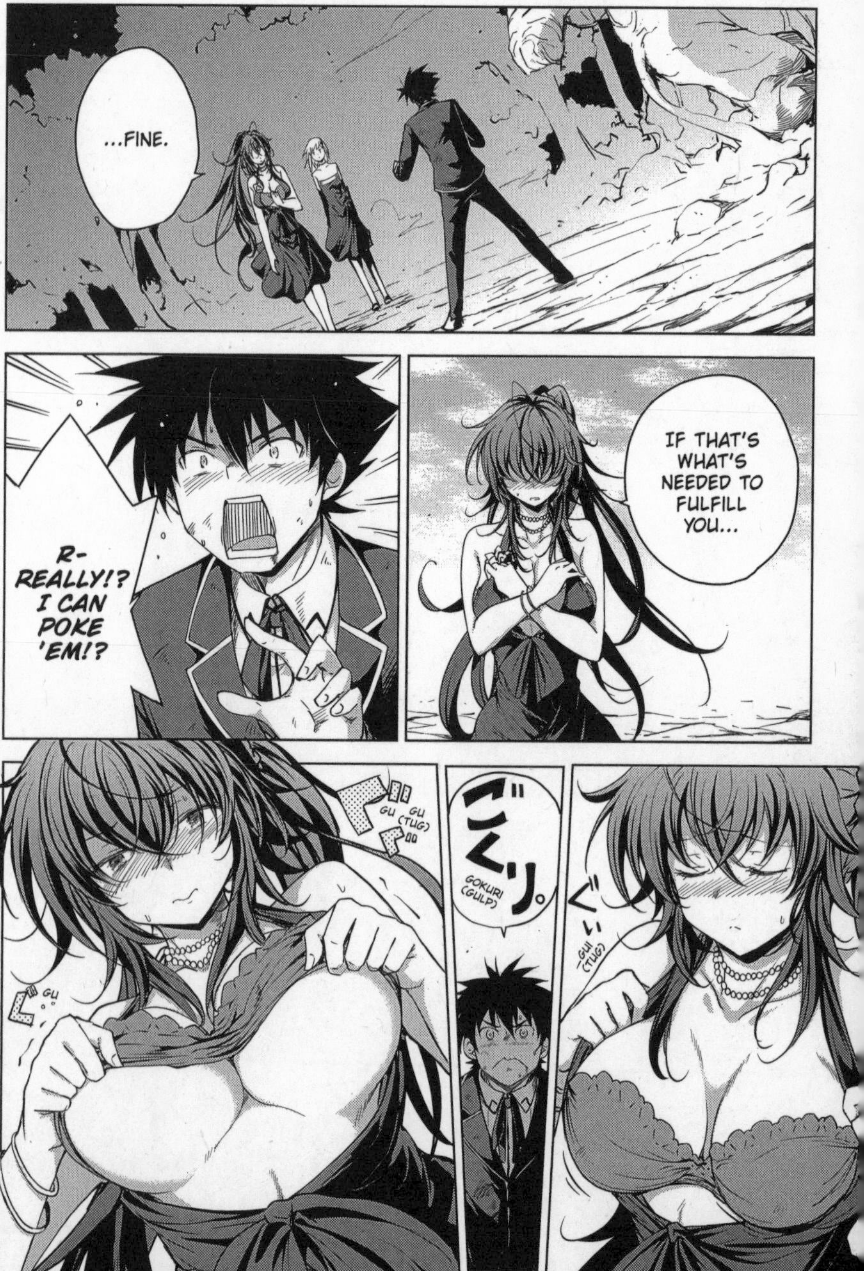
...FINE.
IF THAT'S WHAT'S NEEDED TO FULFILL YOU...
R-REALLY!? I CAN POKE 'EM!?
ぐい
GUI (TUG)
ごくり。
GOKURI (GULP)
GU GU (TUG)
GU

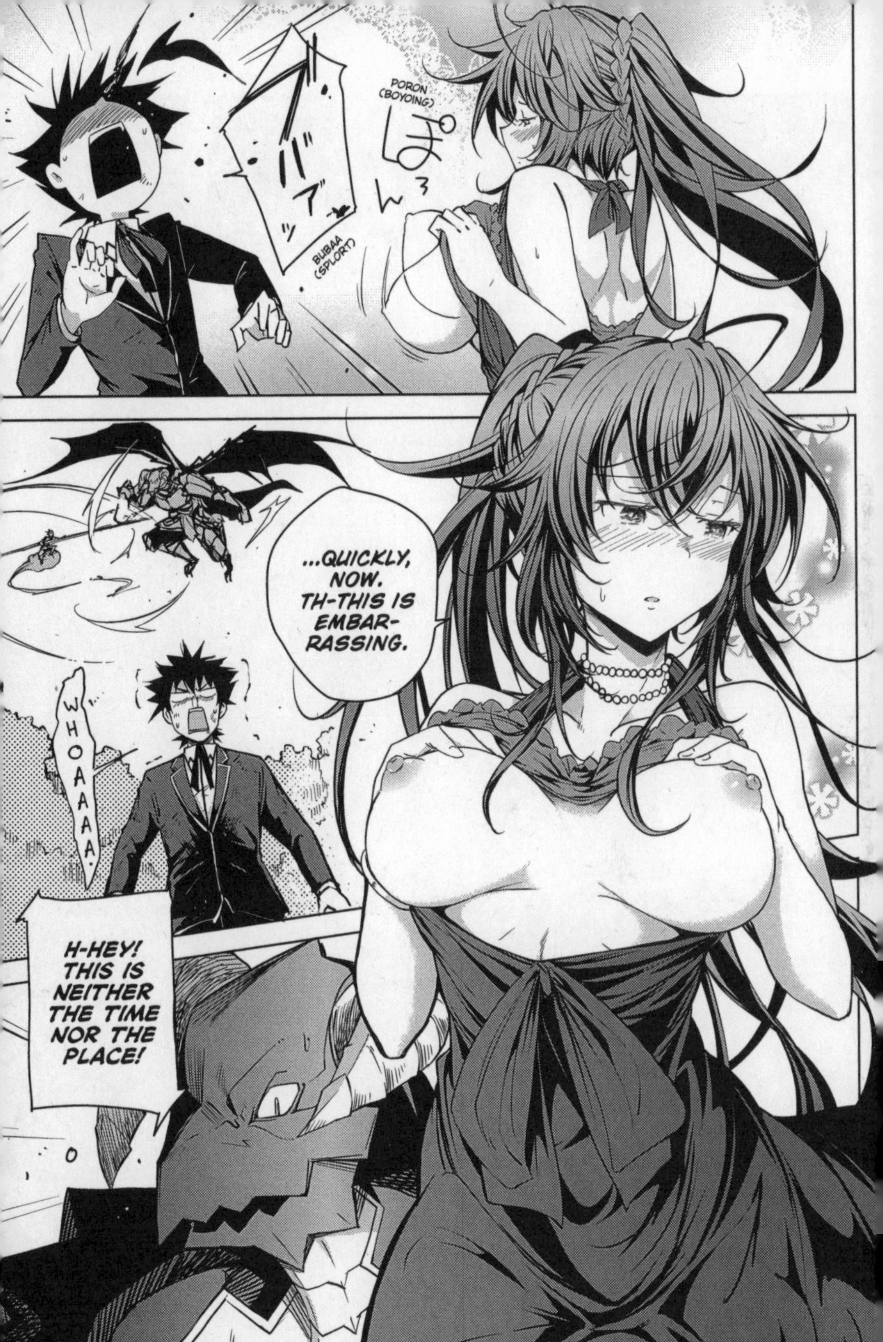
ぽろん
PORON (BOYOING)
ブバアッ
BUBAA (SPLORT)
...QUICKLY, NOW. TH-THIS IS EMBARRASSING.
WHOAAAAA
H-HEY! THIS IS NEITHER THE TIME NOR THE PLACE!

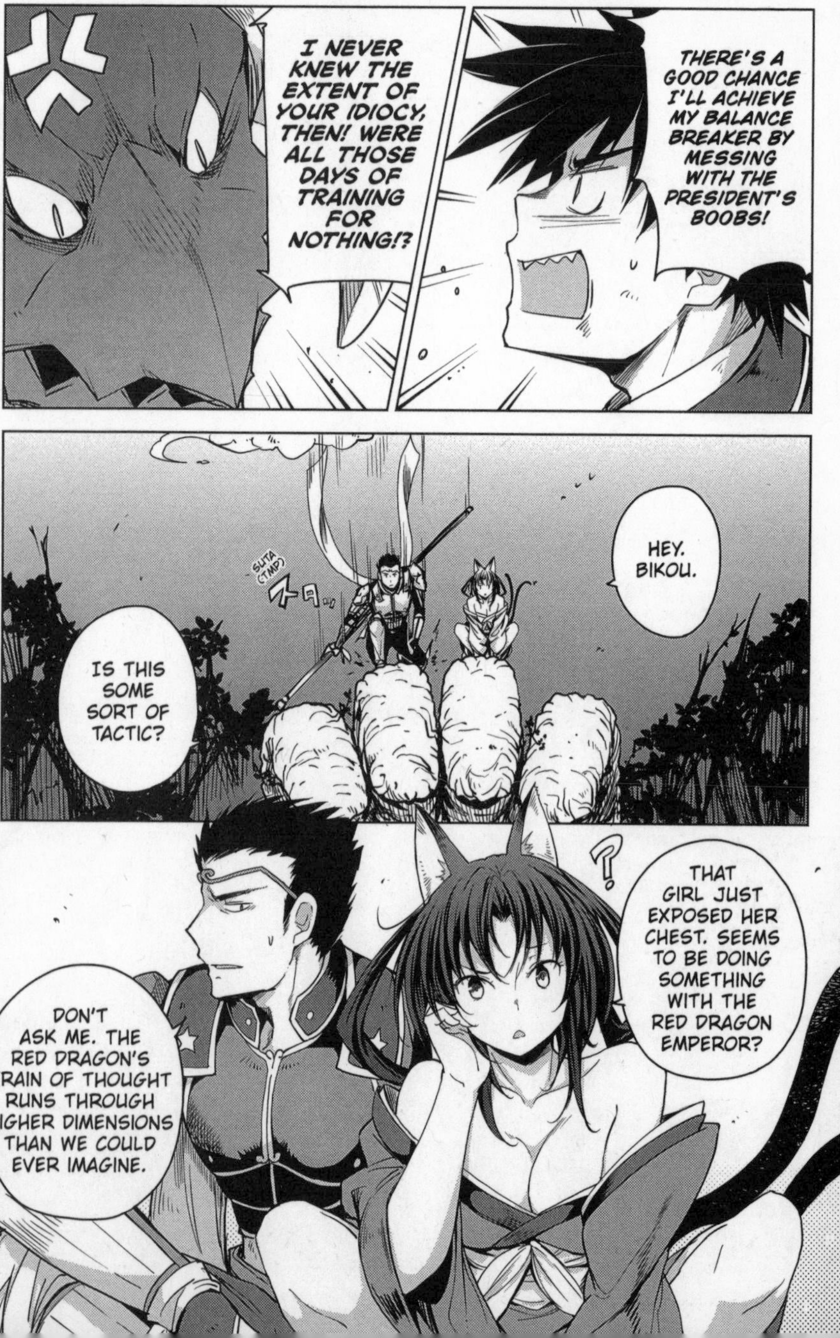
THERE'S A GOOD CHANCE I'LL ACHIEVE MY BALANCE BREAKER BY MESSING WITH THE PRESIDENT'S BOOBS!
I NEVER KNEW THE EXTENT OF YOUR IDIOCY, THEN! WERE ALL THOSE DAYS OF TRAINING FOR NOTHING!?
HEY. BIKOU.
SUTA (TMP)
IS THIS SOME SORT OF TACTIC?
?
THAT GIRL JUST EXPOSED HER CHEST. SEEMS TO BE DOING SOMETHING WITH THE RED DRAGON EMPEROR?
DON'T ASK ME. THE RED DRAGON'S TRAIN OF THOUGHT RUNS THROUGH HIGHER DIMENSIONS THAN WE COULD EVER IMAGINE.

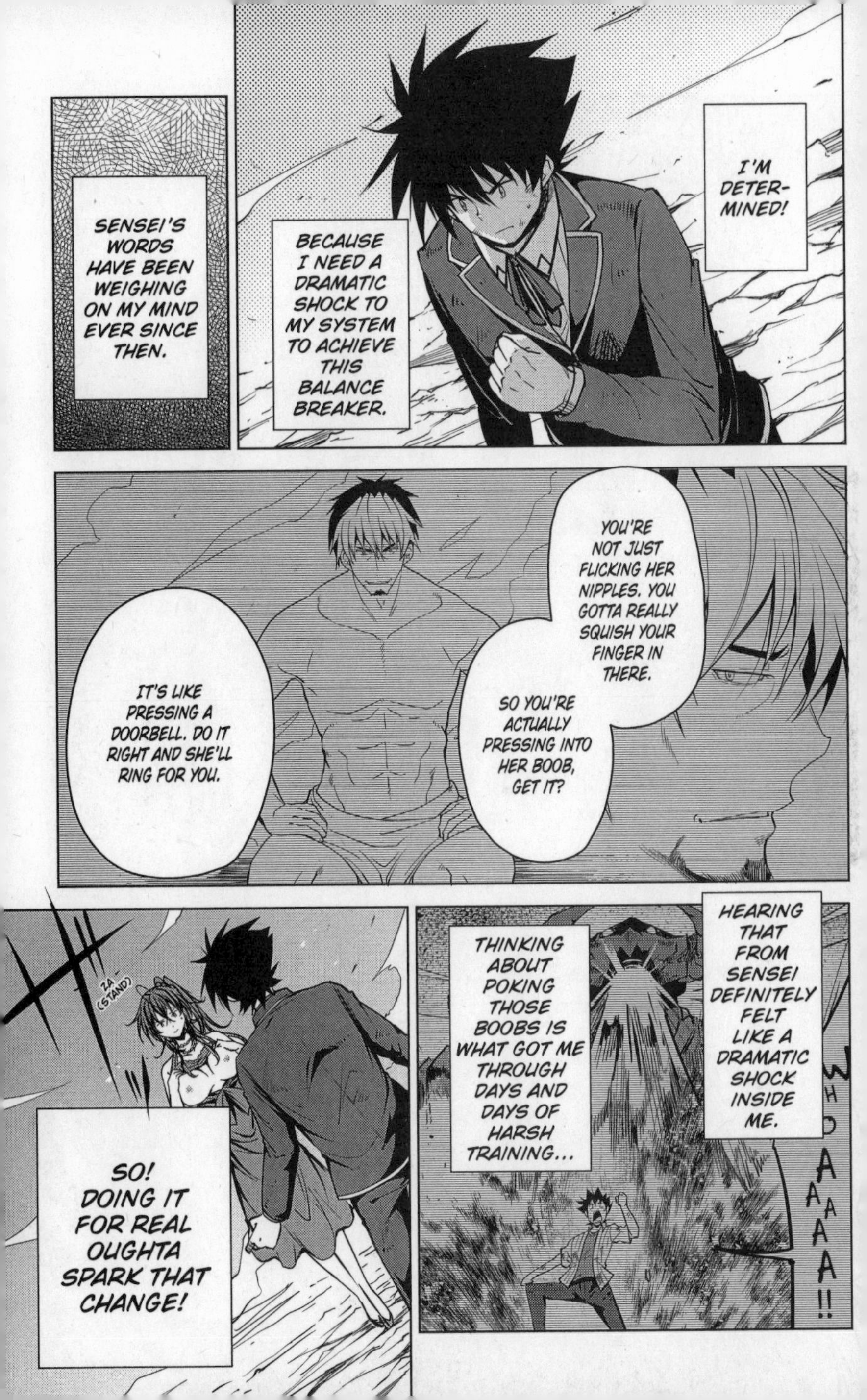
I'M DETER-MINED!
BECAUSE I NEED A DRAMATIC SHOCK TO MY SYSTEM TO ACHIEVE THIS BALANCE BREAKER.
SENSEI'S WORDS HAVE BEEN WEIGHING ON MY MIND EVER SINCE THEN.
YOU'RE NOT JUST FLICKING HER NIPPLES. YOU GOTTA REALLY SQUISH YOUR FINGER IN THERE.
SO YOU'RE ACTUALLY PRESSING INTO HER BOOB, GET IT?
IT'S LIKE PRESSING A DOORBELL. DO IT RIGHT AND SHE'LL RING FOR YOU.
HEARING THAT FROM SENSEI DEFINITELY FELT LIKE A DRAMATIC SHOCK INSIDE ME.
WHOAAAAAA!!
THINKING ABOUT POKING THOSE BOOBS IS WHAT GOT ME THROUGH DAYS AND DAYS OF HARSH TRAINING...
ZA (STAND)
SO! DOING IT FOR REAL OUGHTA SPARK THAT CHANGE!

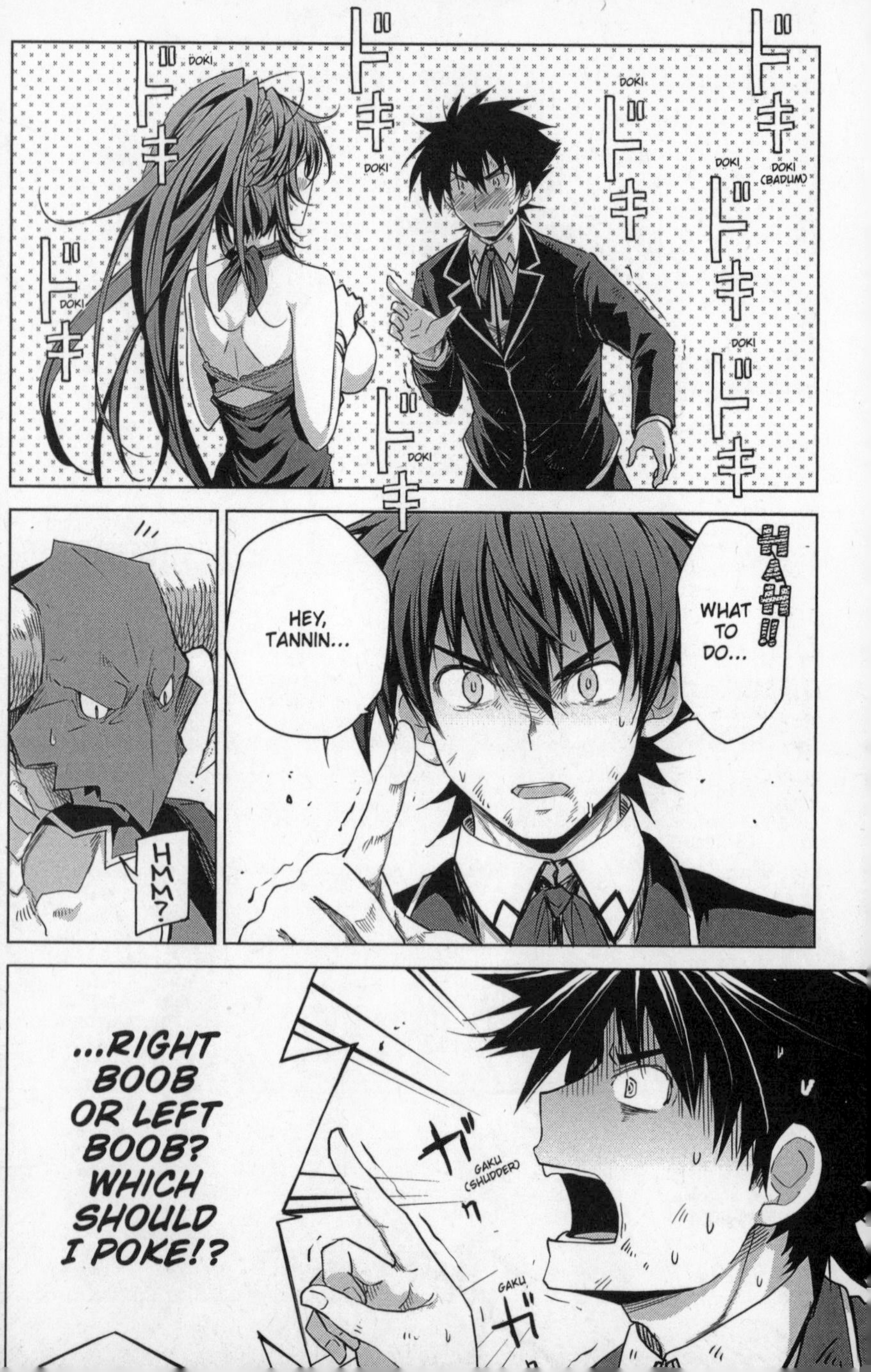
DOKI (BADUM)
DOKI
DOKI
DOKI
DOKI
DOKI
DOKI
DOKI
WHAT TO DO...
HEY, TANNIN...
HMM?
...RIGHT BOOB OR LEFT BOOB? WHICH SHOULD I POKE!?
GAKU (SHUDDER)
GAKU

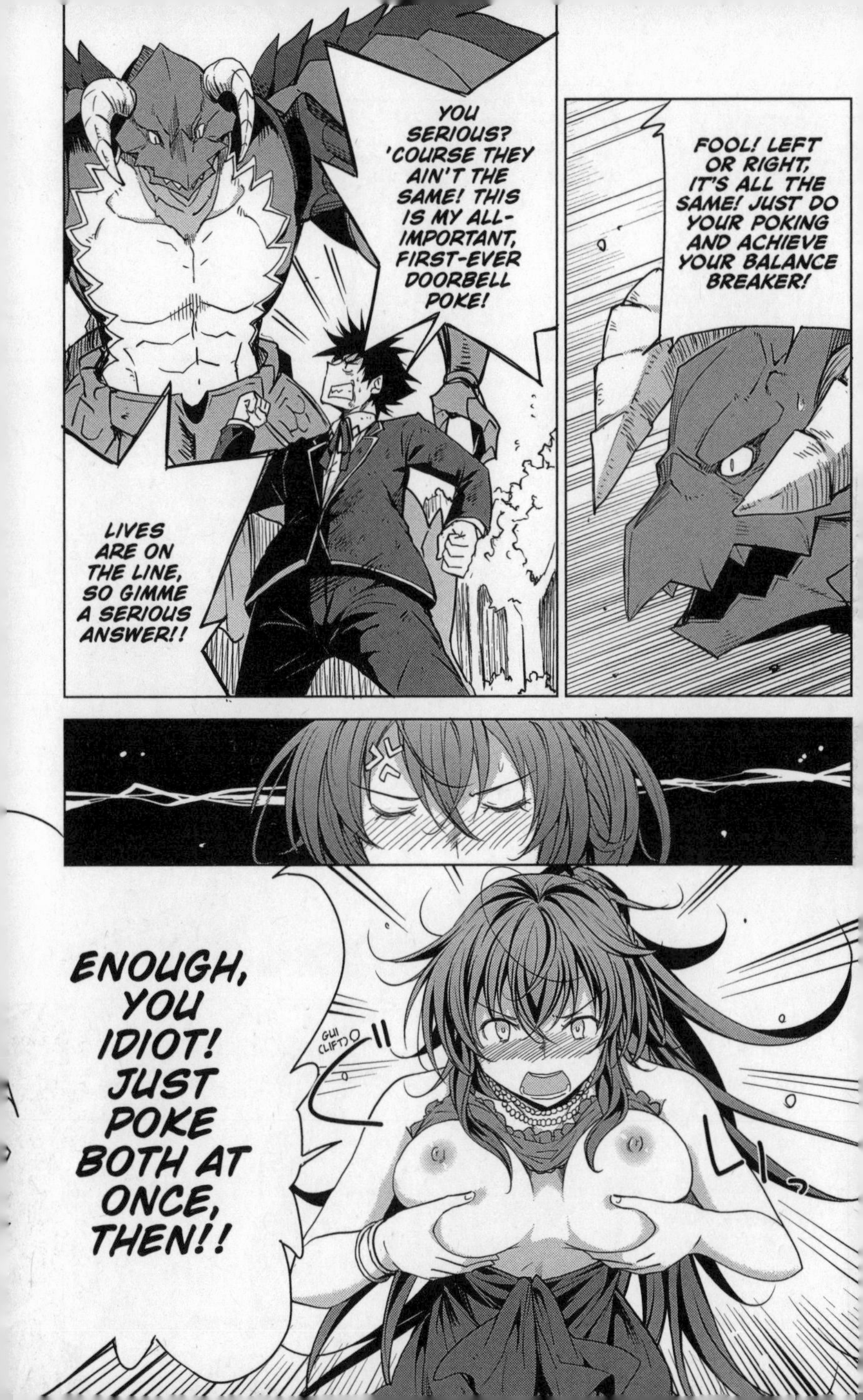
FOOL! LEFT OR RIGHT, IT'S ALL THE SAME! JUST DO YOUR POKING AND ACHIEVE YOUR BALANCE BREAKER!
YOU SERIOUS? 'COURSE THEY AIN'T THE SAME! THIS IS MY ALL-IMPORTANT, FIRST-EVER DOORBELL POKE!
LIVES ARE ON THE LINE, SO GIMME A SERIOUS ANSWER!!
GUI (LIFT)
ENOUGH, YOU IDIOT! JUST POKE BOTH AT ONCE, THEN!!

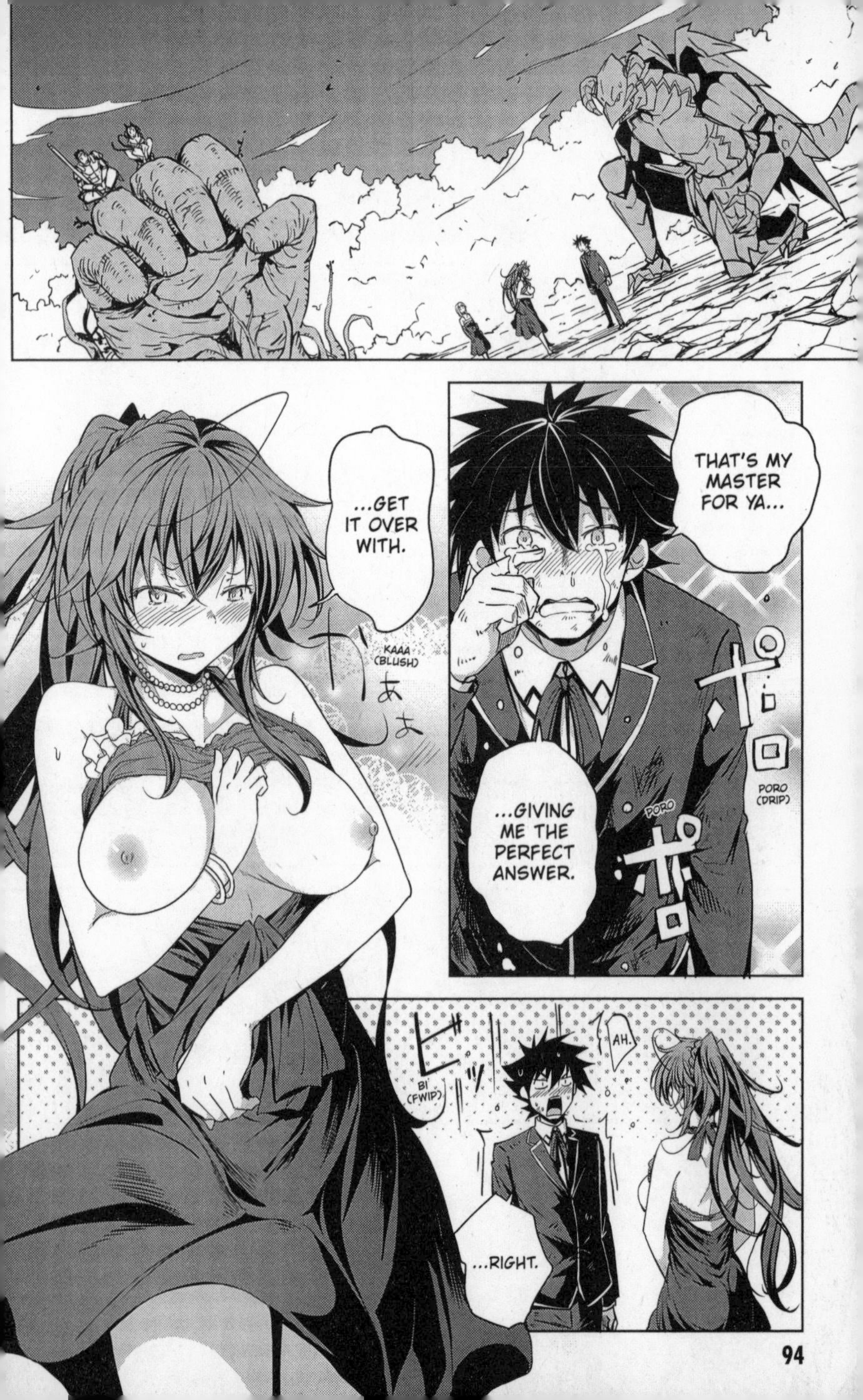
THAT'S MY MASTER FOR YA...
...GIVING ME THE PERFECT ANSWER.
PORO (DRIP)
PORO
...GET IT OVER WITH.
KAAA (BLUSH)
AH.
BI (FWIP)
...RIGHT.

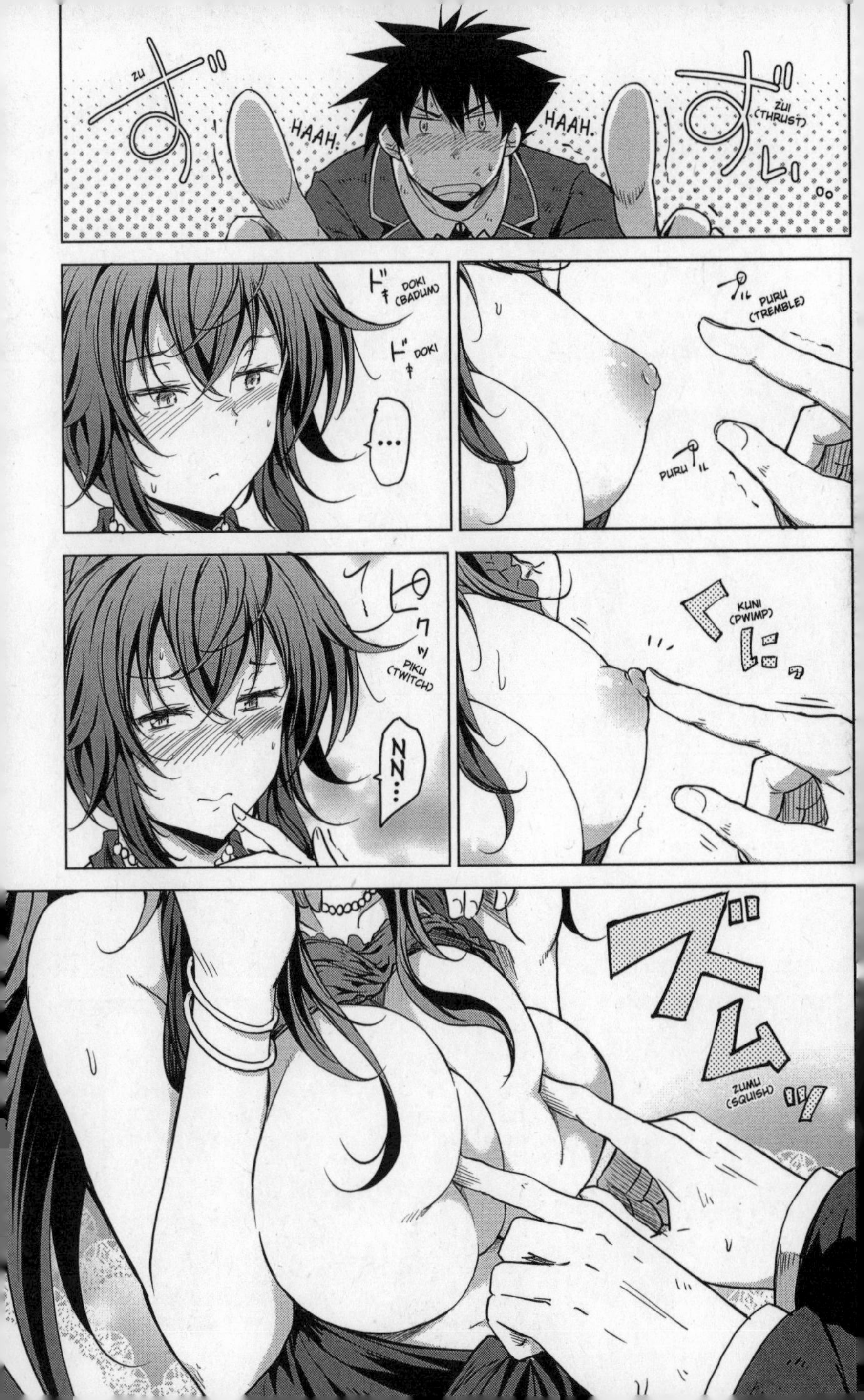
ZUI (THRUST)
HAAH.
HAAH.
ZU
PURU (TREMBLE)
PURU
DOKI (BADUM)
DOKI
...
KUNI (PWIMP)
PIKU (TWITCH)
NN...
ZUMU (SQUISH)

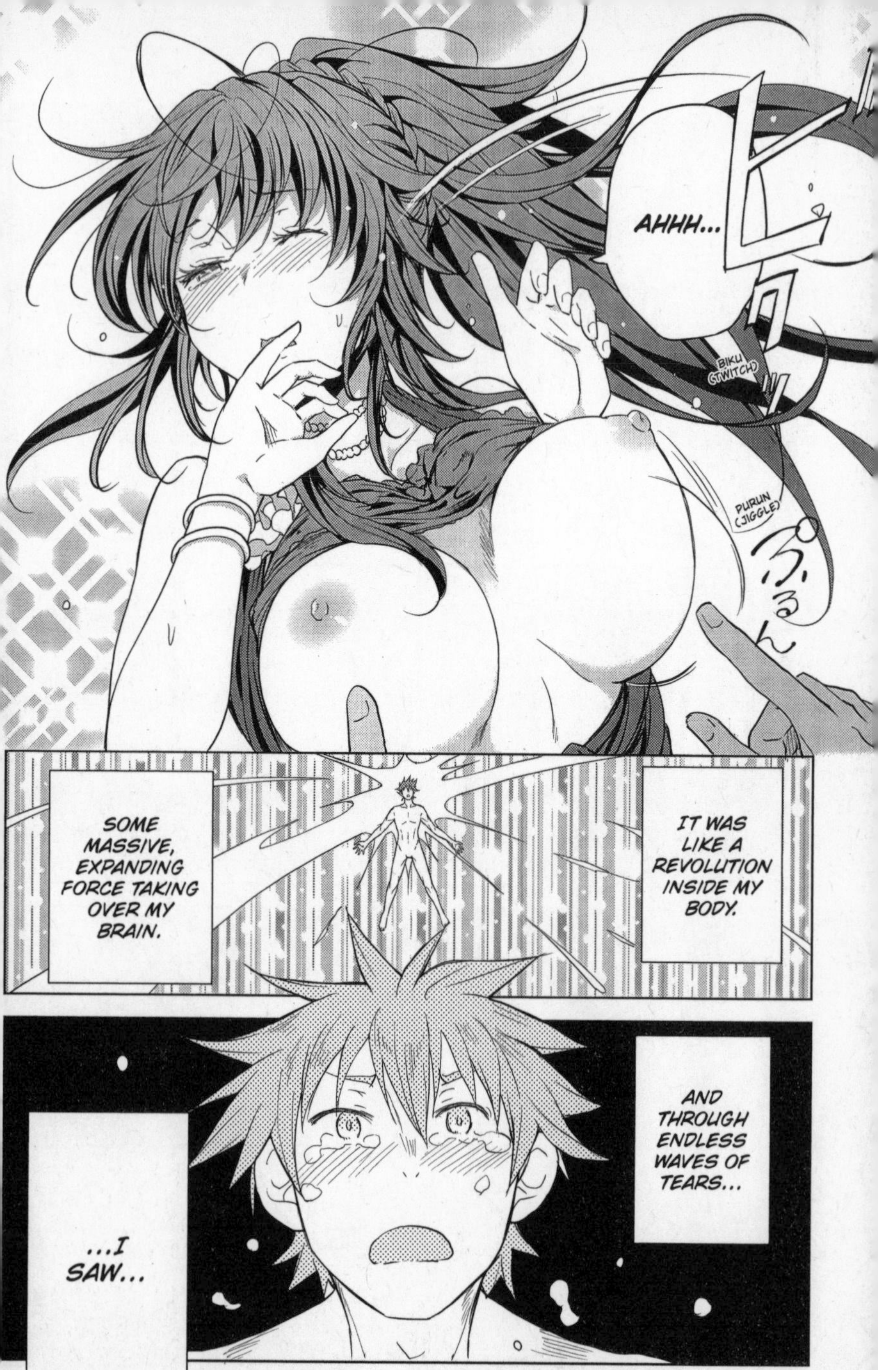
AHHH...
ビクッ
BIKU (TWITCH)
ぷるん
PURUN (JIGGLE)
IT WAS LIKE A REVOLUTION INSIDE MY BODY.
SOME MASSIVE, EXPANDING FORCE TAKING OVER MY BRAIN.
AND THROUGH ENDLESS WAVES OF TEARS...
...I SAW...

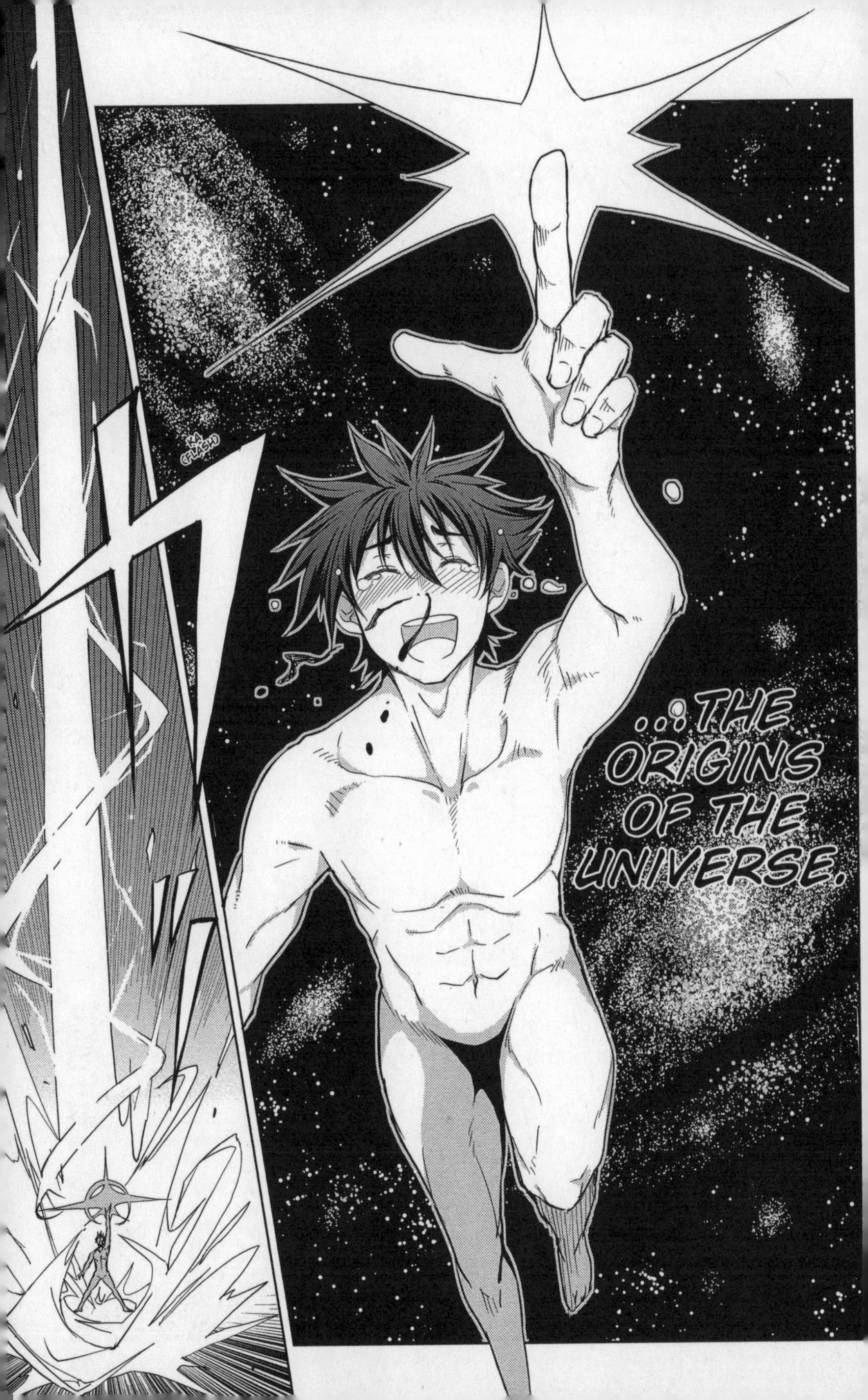
...THE ORIGINS OF THE UNIVERSE.
KA (FLASH)

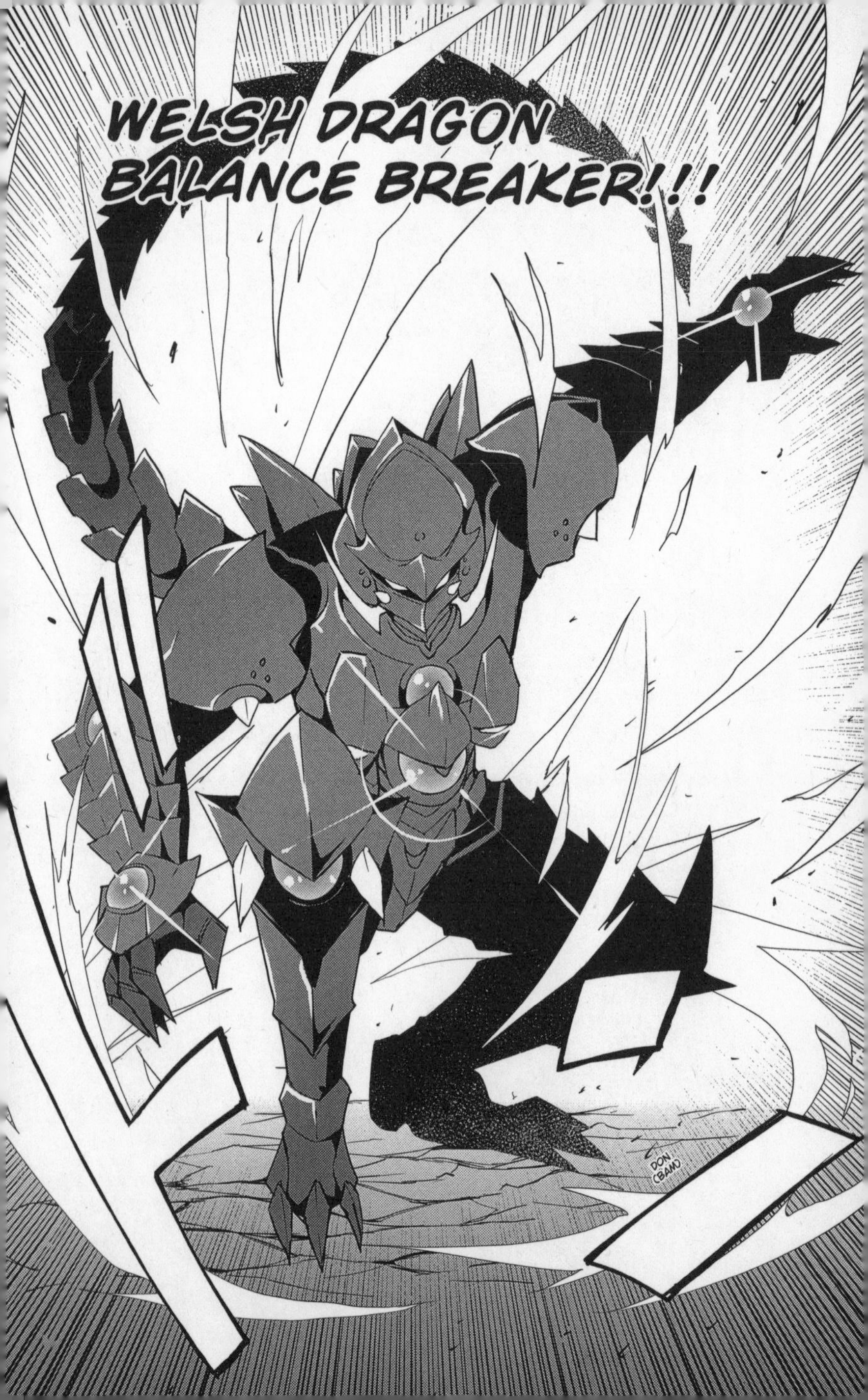
WELSH DRAGON BALANCE BREAKER!!!
DON (BAM)

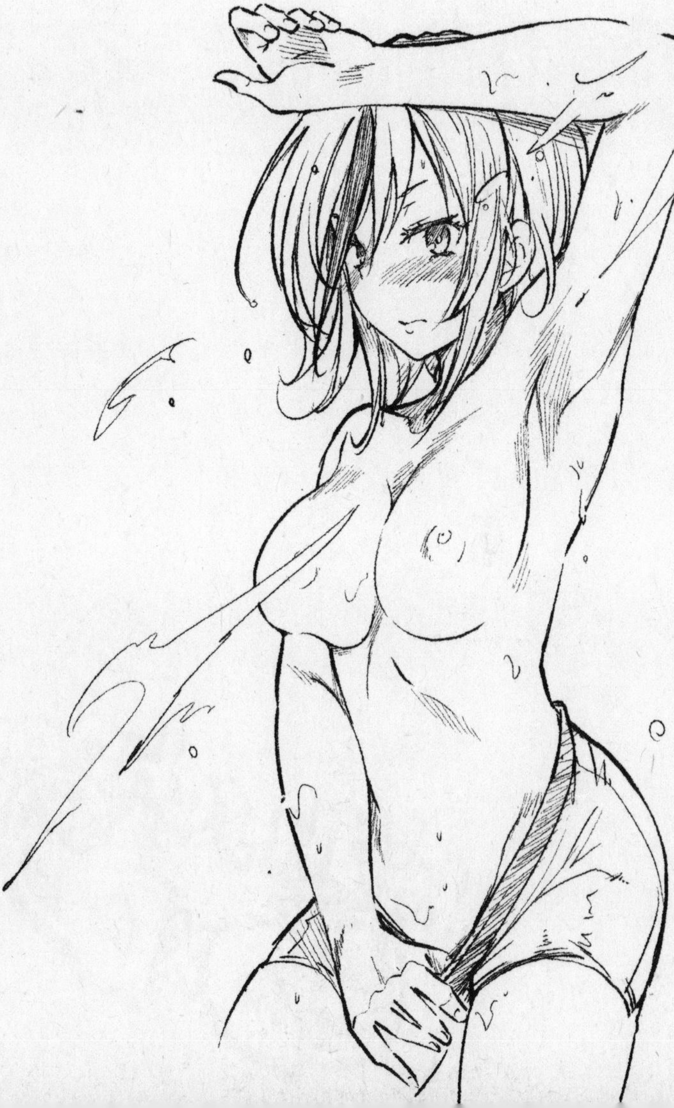

HIGH SCHOOL DxD

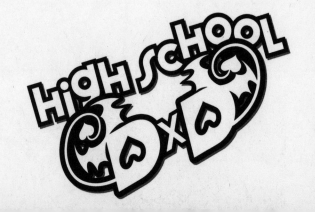

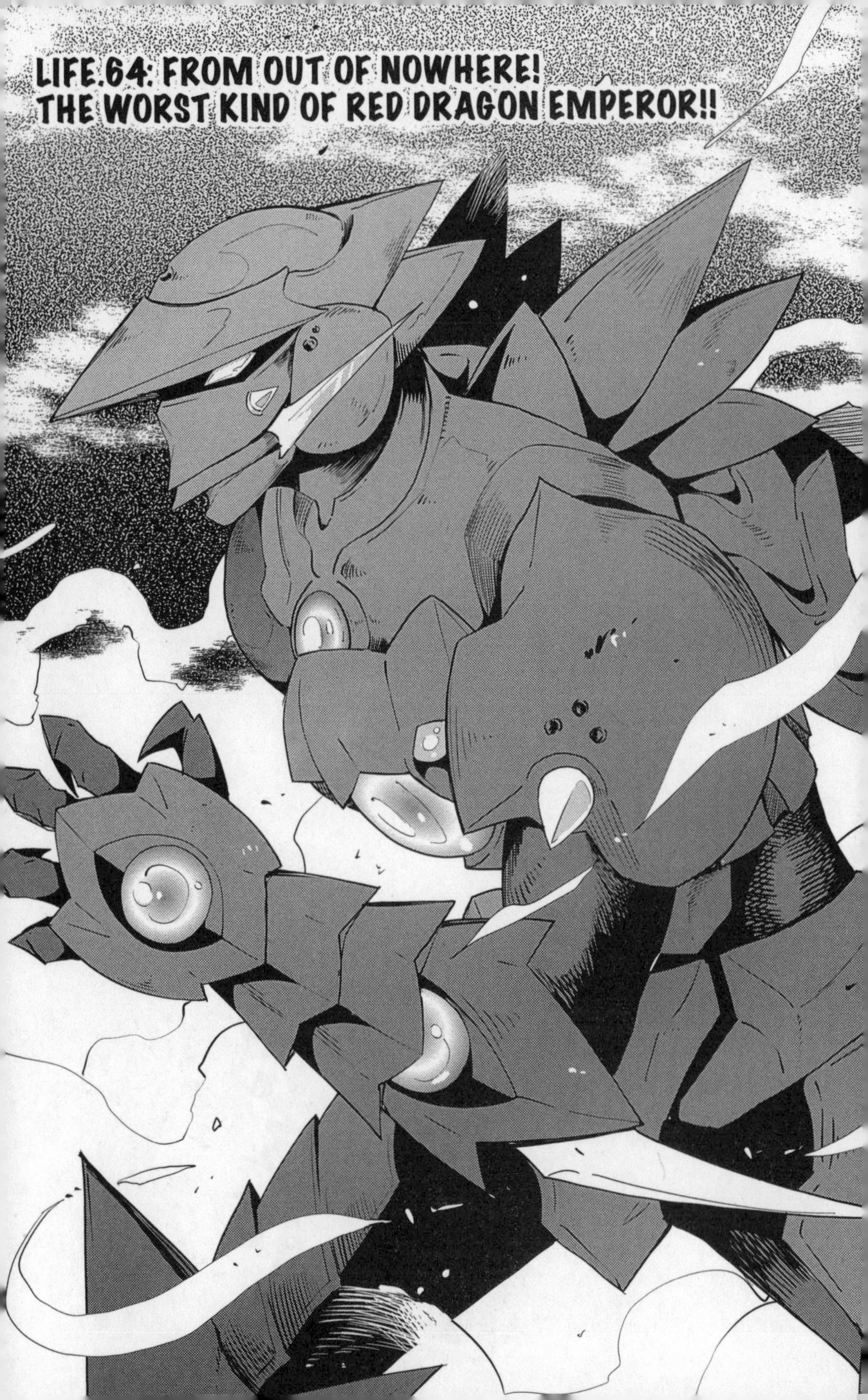
LIFE.64: FROM OUT OF NOWHERE!
THE WORST KIND OF RED DRAGON EMPEROR!!

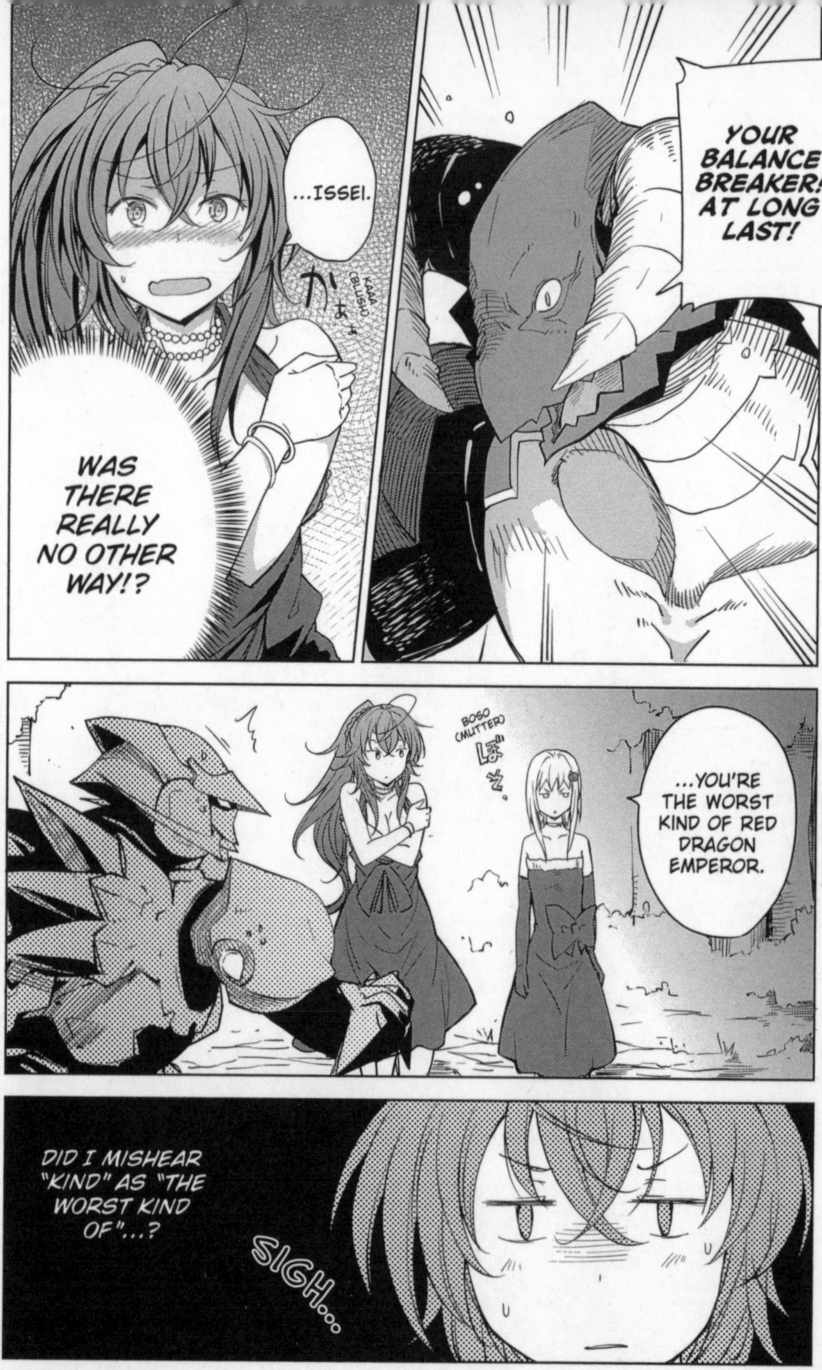
YOUR BALANCE BREAKER! AT LONG LAST!
...ISSEI.
かぁ
KAAA (BLUSH)
WAS THERE REALLY NO OTHER WAY!?
ぼそ
BOSO (MUTTER)
...YOU'RE THE WORST KIND OF RED DRAGON EMPEROR.
DID I MISHEAR "KIND" AS "THE WORST KIND OF"...?
SIGH...

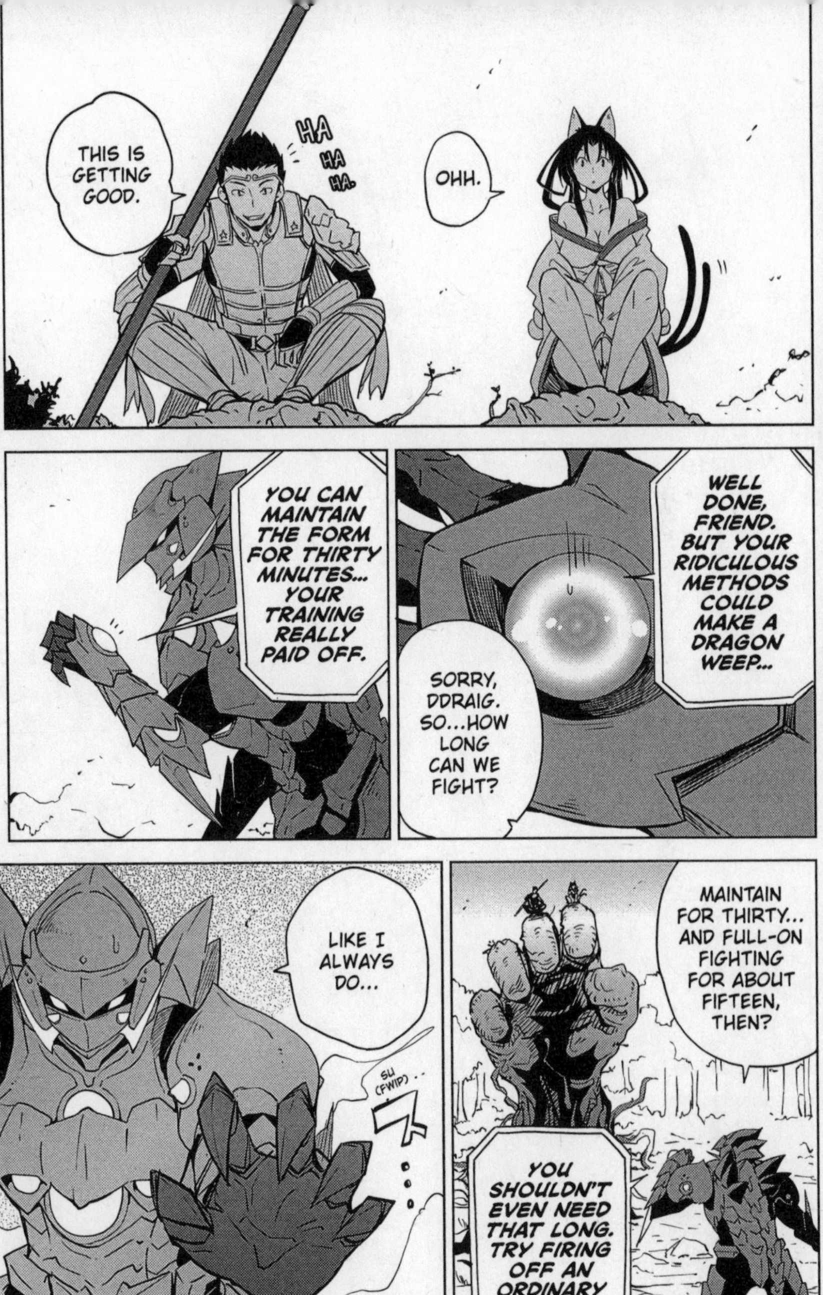
OHH.
HA HA HA.
THIS IS GETTING GOOD.
WELL DONE, FRIEND. BUT YOUR RIDICULOUS METHODS COULD MAKE A DRAGON WEEP...
SORRY, DDRAIG. SO...HOW LONG CAN WE FIGHT?
YOU CAN MAINTAIN THE FORM FOR THIRTY MINUTES... YOUR TRAINING REALLY PAID OFF.
MAINTAIN FOR THIRTY... AND FULL-ON FIGHTING FOR ABOUT FIFTEEN, THEN?
YOU SHOULDN'T EVEN NEED THAT LONG. TRY FIRING OFF AN ORDINARY MAGIC ORB.
LIKE I ALWAYS DO...
SU (FWIP)

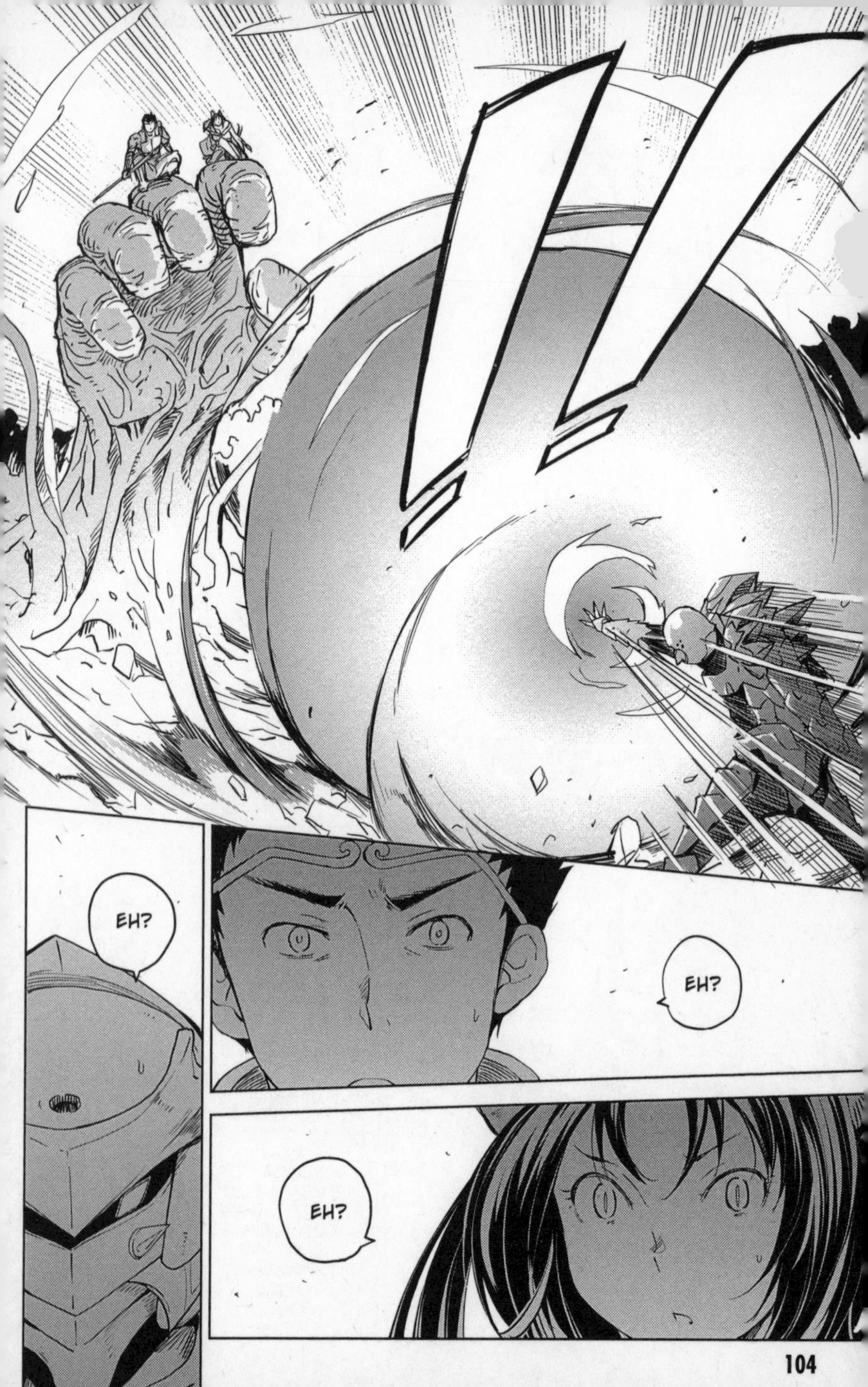
EH?
EH?
EH?

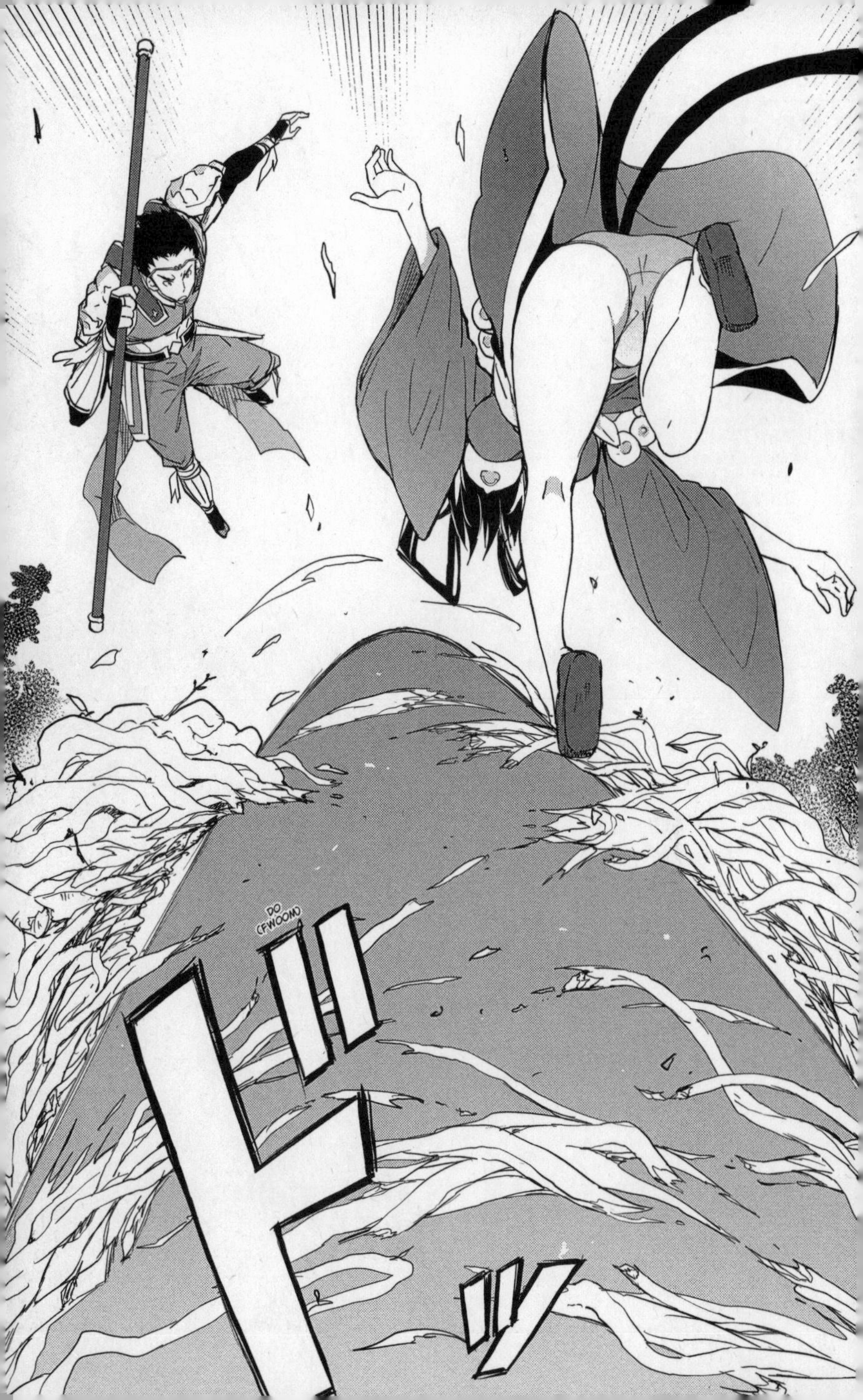
DO
(FWOOM)

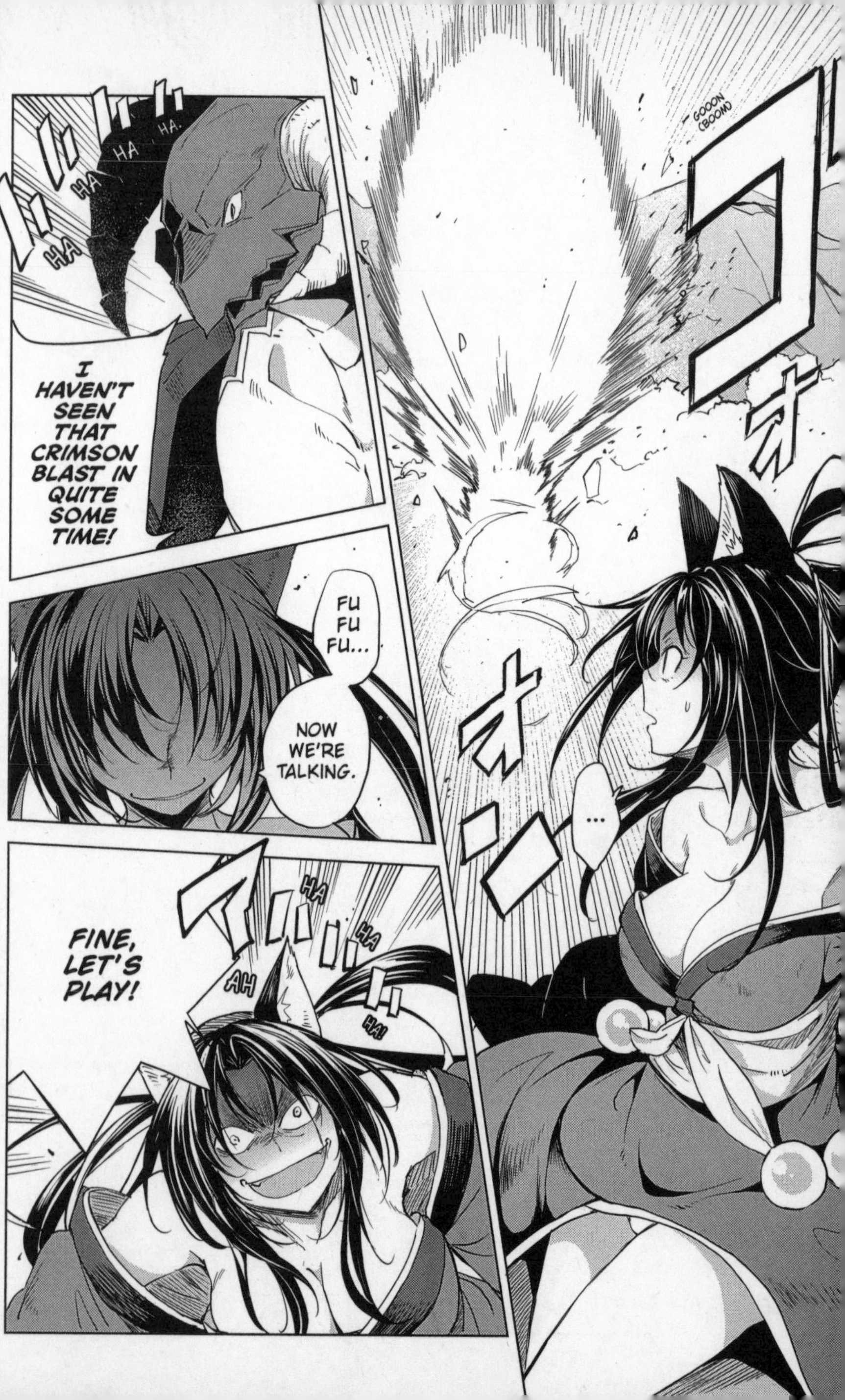
GOOON (BOOM)
...
HA HA HA HA
I HAVEN'T SEEN THAT CRIMSON BLAST IN QUITE SOME TIME!
FU FU FU...
NOW WE'RE TALKING.
HA HA AH HA!
FINE, LET'S PLAY!

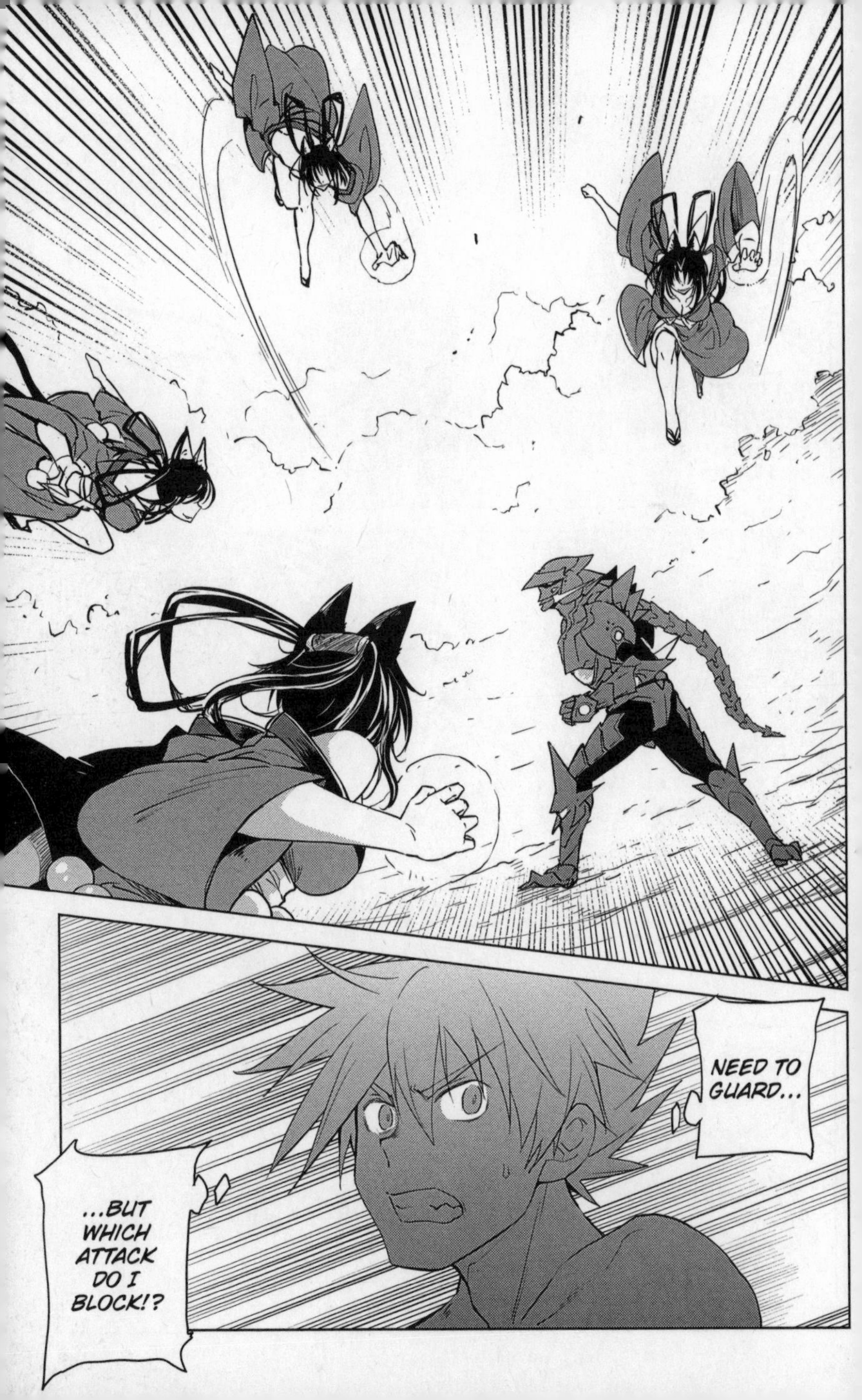
NEED TO GUARD...
...BUT WHICH ATTACK DO I BLOCK!?

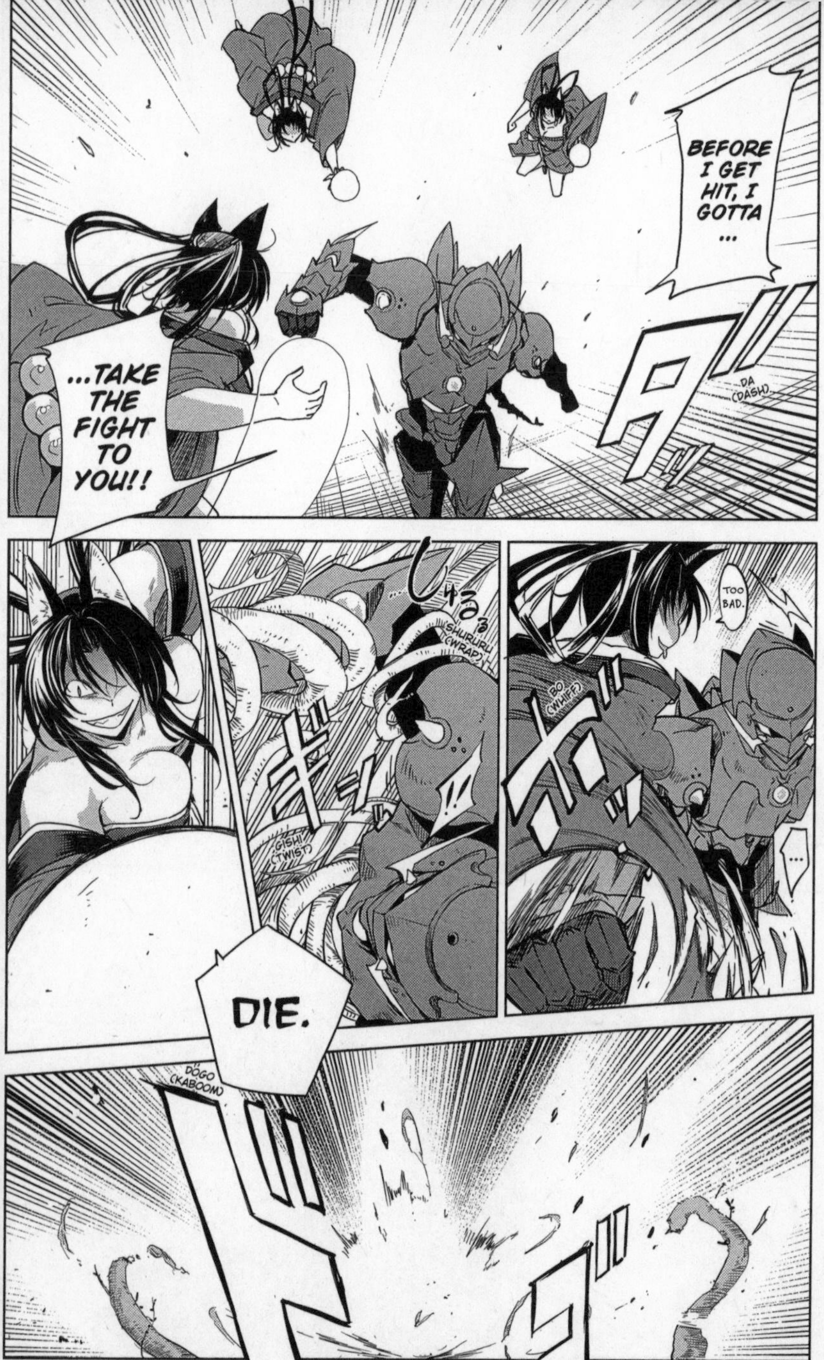
BEFORE I GET HIT, I GOTTA ...
DA (DASH)
...TAKE THE FIGHT TO YOU!!
TOO BAD.
BO (WHIFF)
...
SHURURU (WRAP)
GISHI (TWIST)
!!
DIE.
DOGO (KABOOM)

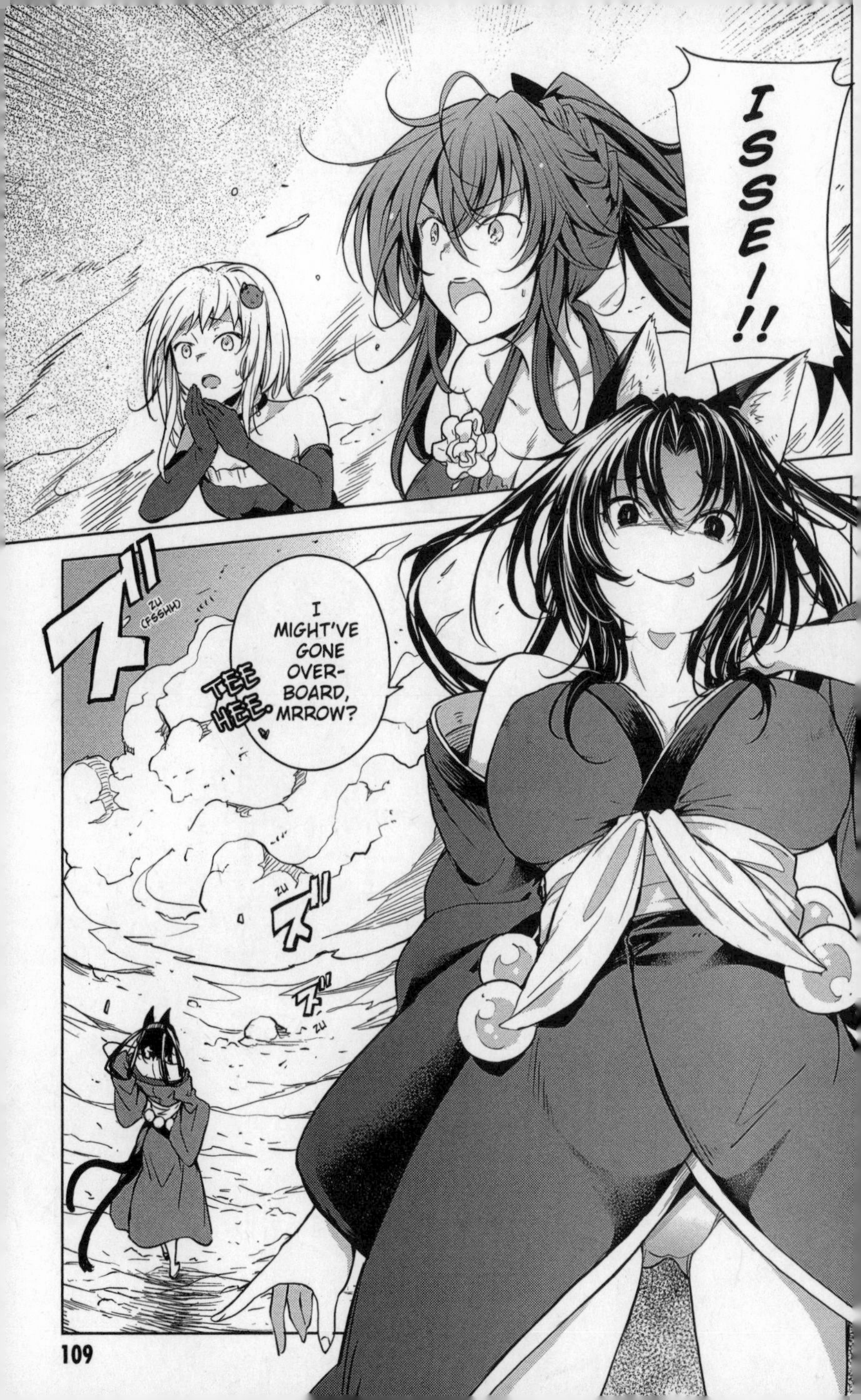
ISSE!!!
I MIGHT'VE GONE OVER-BOARD, MRROW?
TEE HEE.
ZU (FSSHH)
ZU
ZU

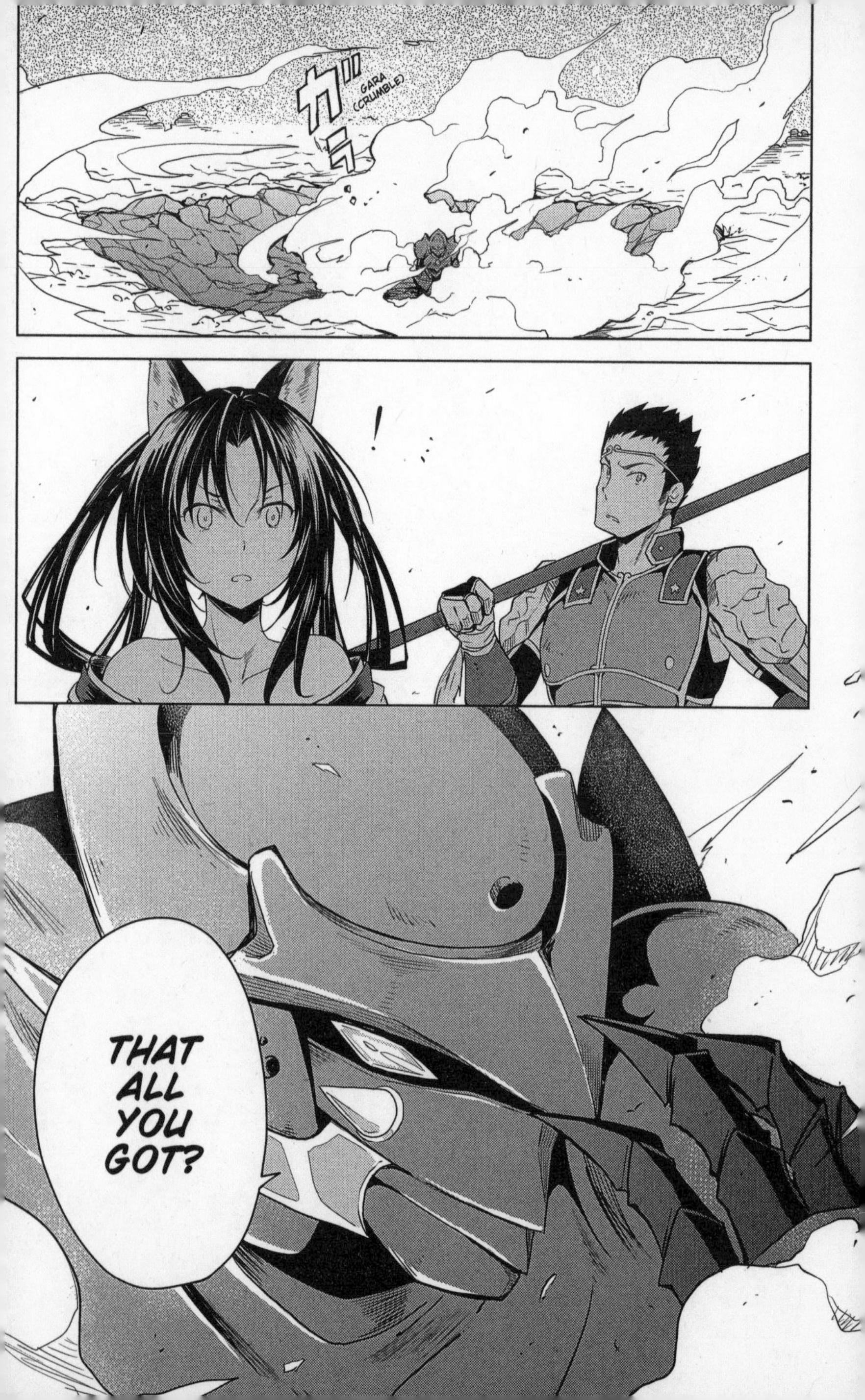
ガラ
GARA (CRUMBLE)
!
THAT ALL YOU GOT?

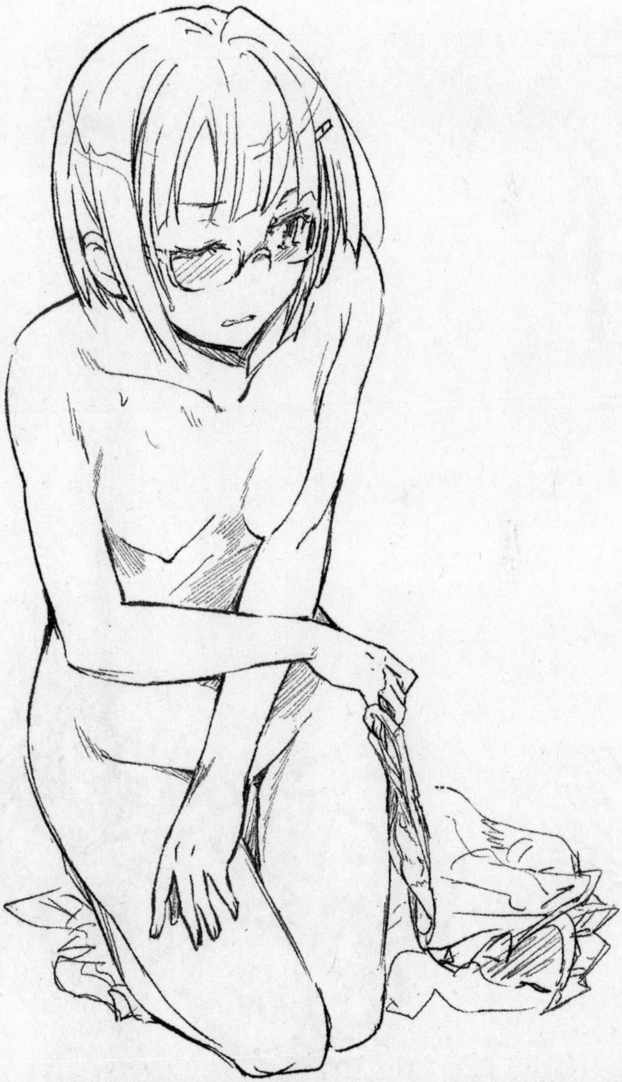

HIGH SCHOOL DxD

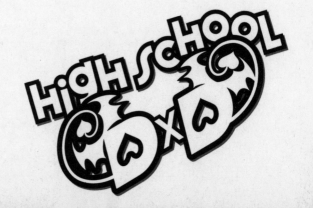

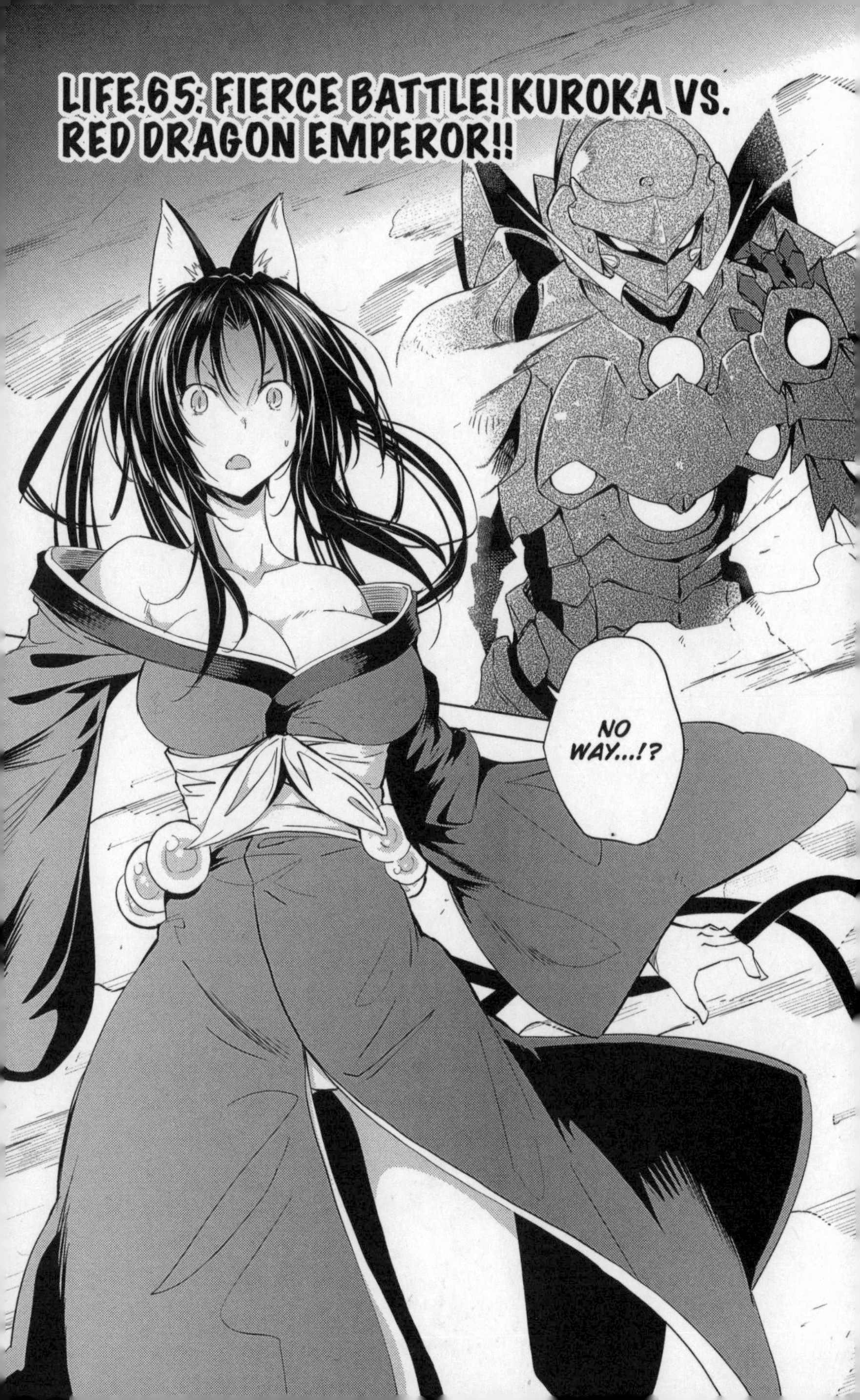
LIFE.65: FIERCE BATTLE! KUROKA VS. RED DRAGON EMPEROR!!
NO WAY...!?

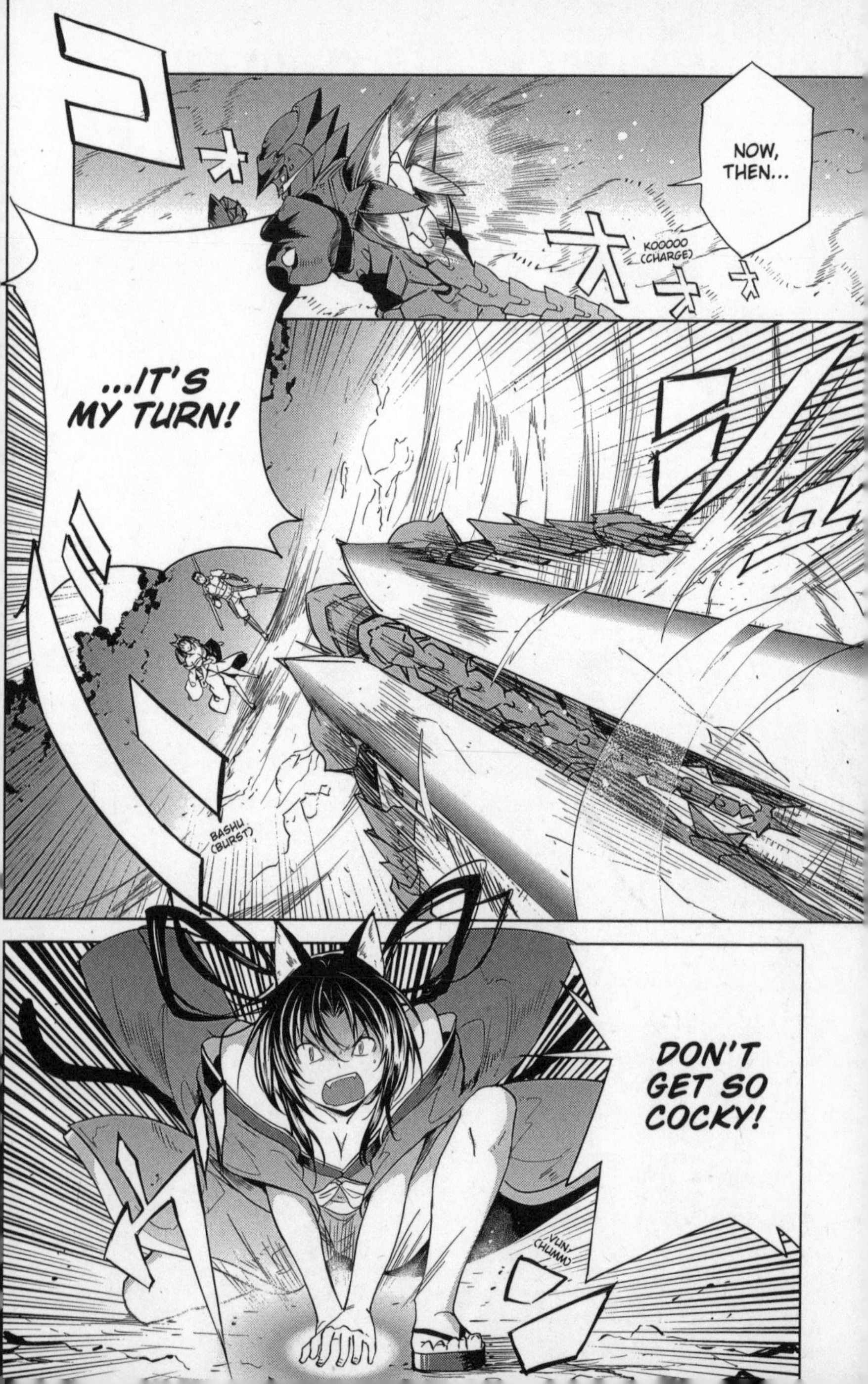
NOW, THEN...
KOOOOO (CHARGE)
...IT'S MY TURN!
BASHU (BURST)
DON'T GET SO COCKY!
VUN-CHUMM

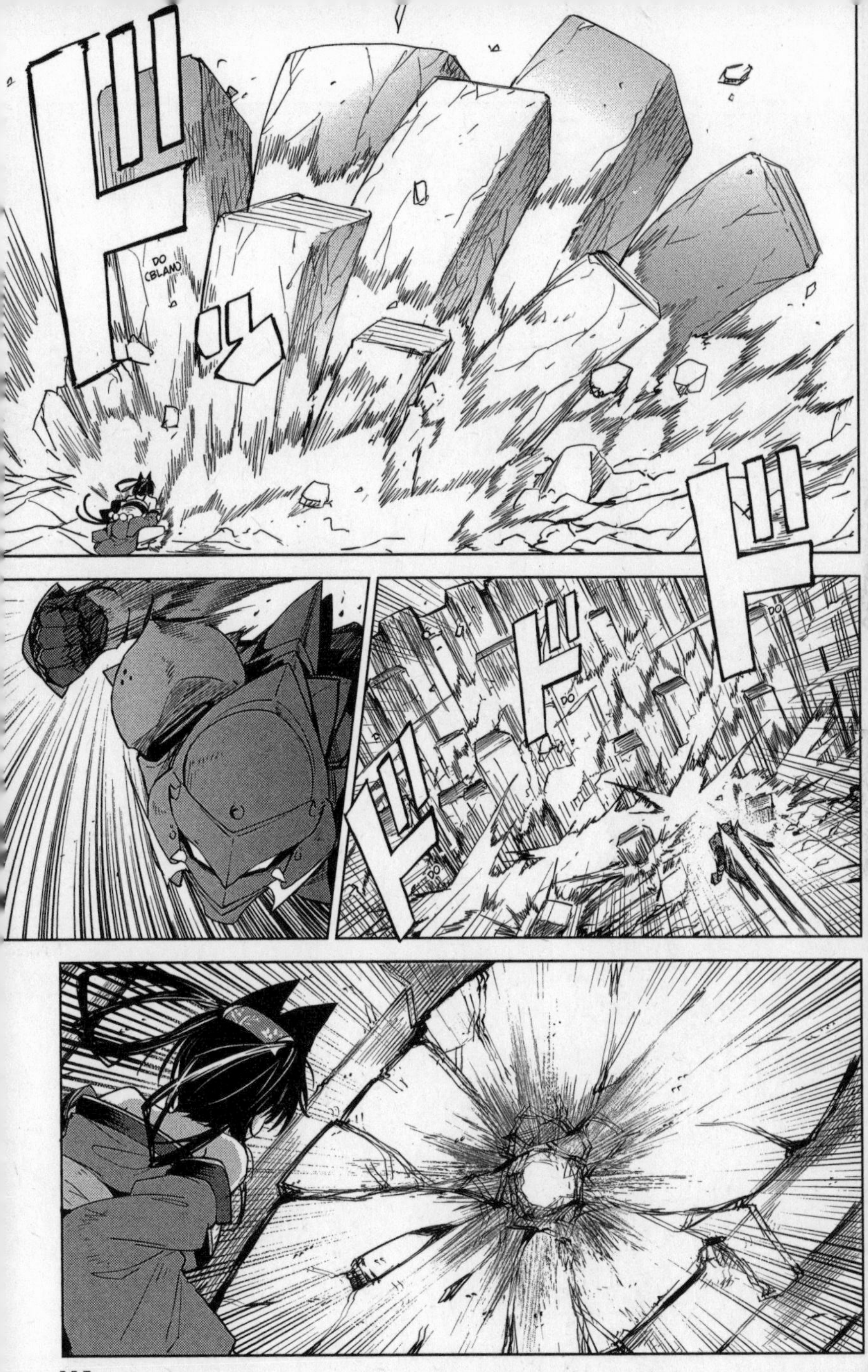
DO
(BLAM)
DO
DO
DO

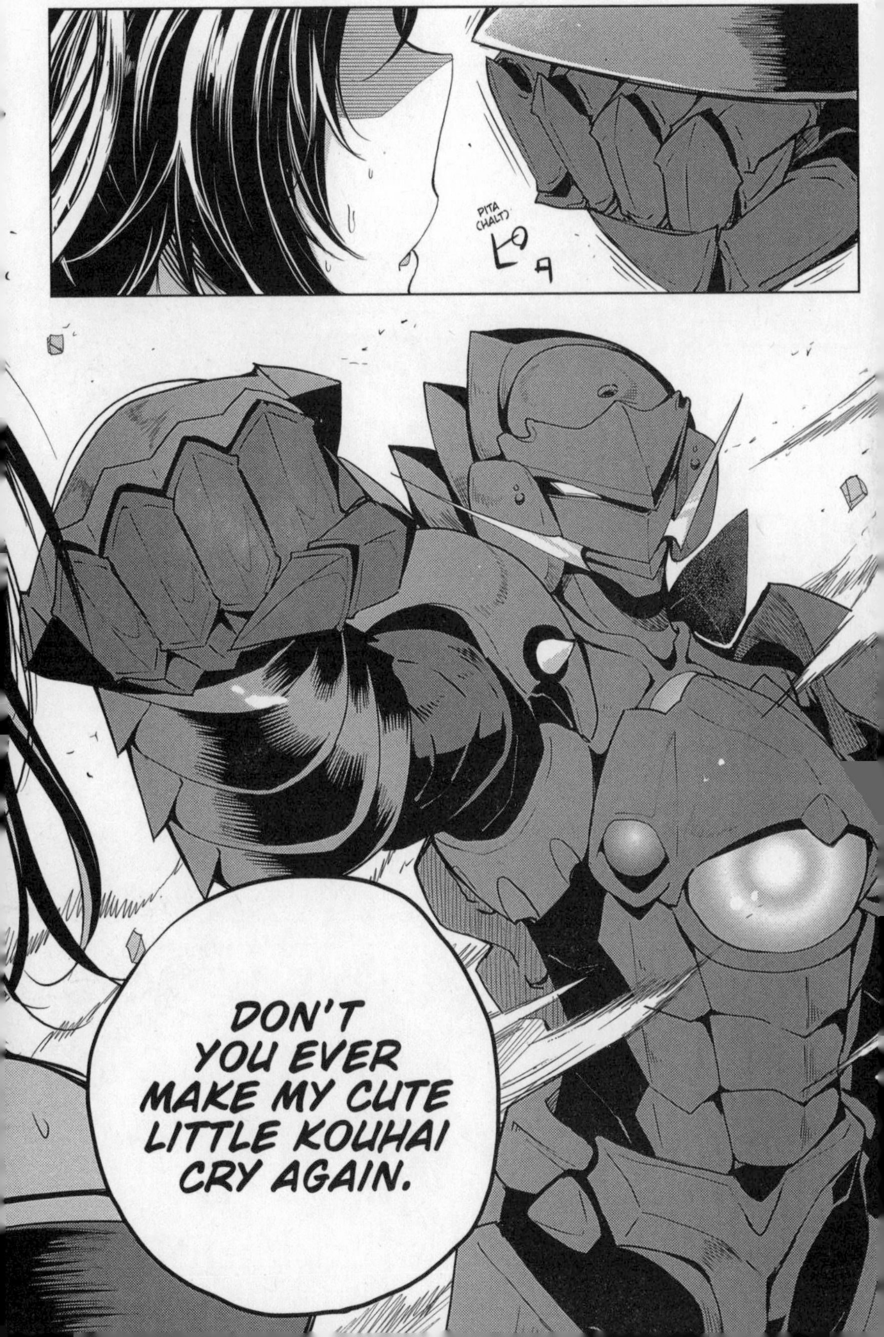
PITA (HALT)
ピタ
DON'T YOU EVER MAKE MY CUTE LITTLE KOUHAI CRY AGAIN.

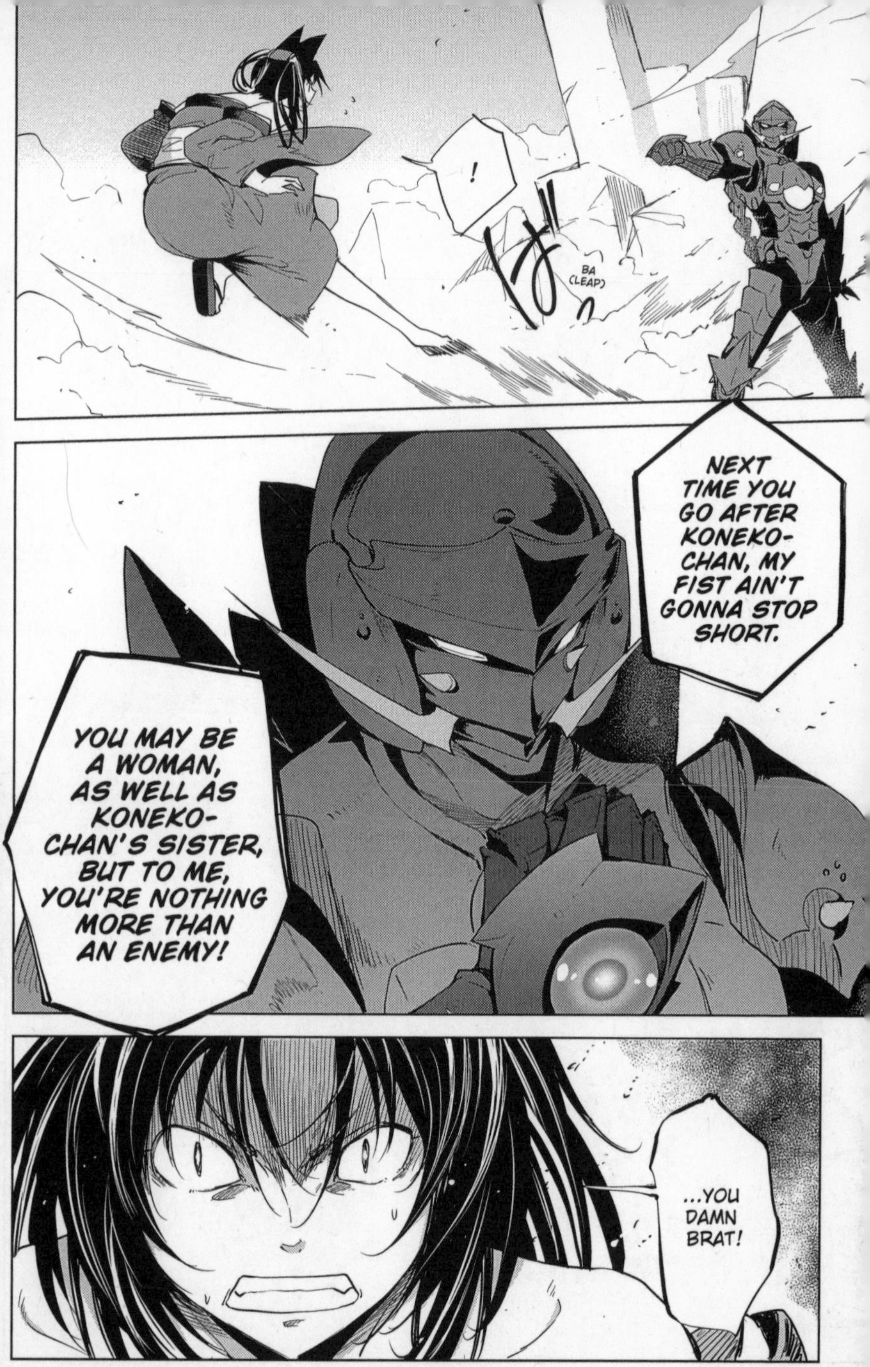
!
BA (LEAP)
NEXT TIME YOU GO AFTER KONEKO-CHAN, MY FIST AIN'T GONNA STOP SHORT.
YOU MAY BE A WOMAN, AS WELL AS KONEKO-CHAN'S SISTER, BUT TO ME, YOU'RE NOTHING MORE THAN AN ENEMY!
...YOU DAMN BRAT!

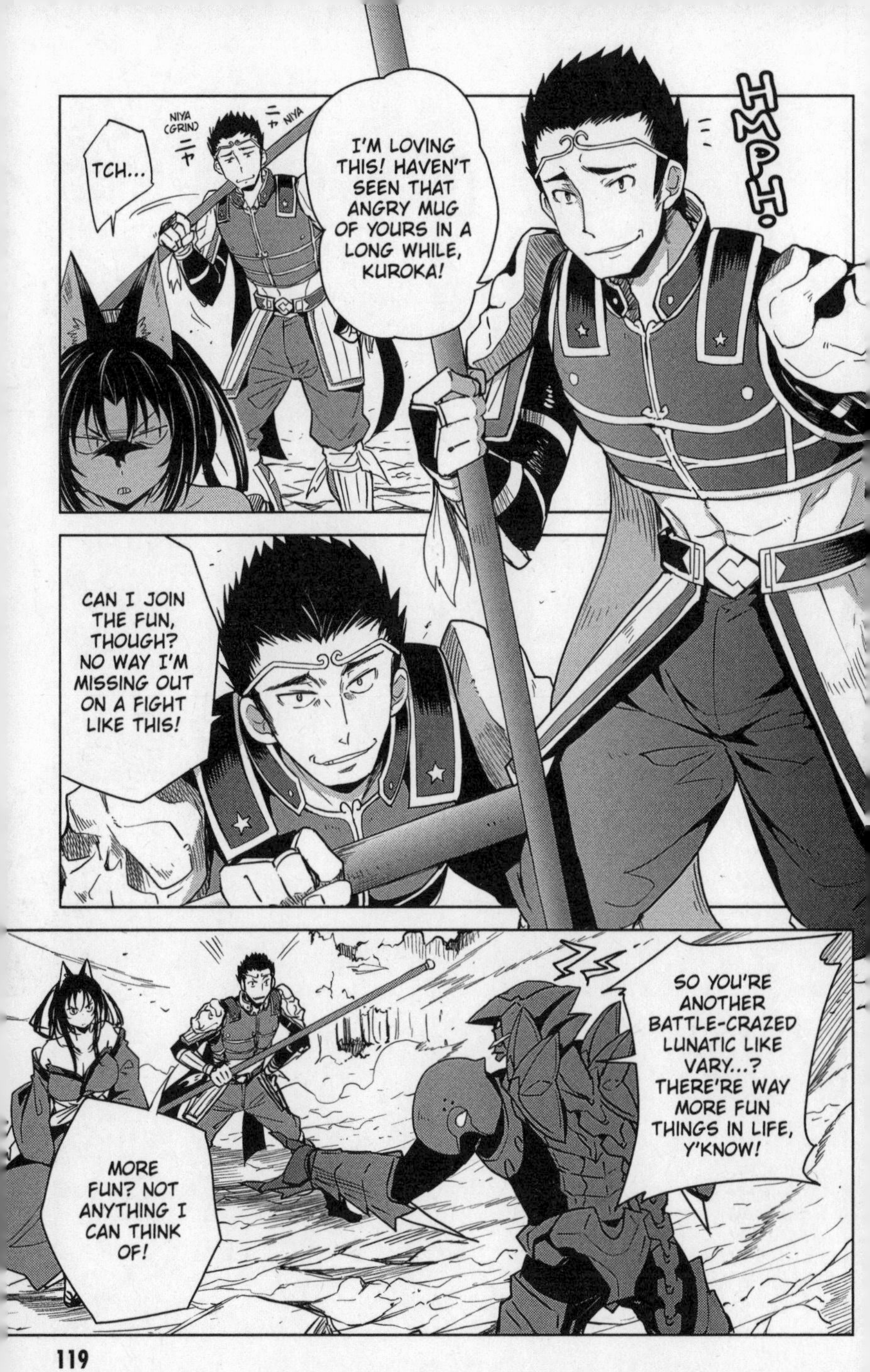
HMPH.
I'M LOVING THIS! HAVEN'T SEEN THAT ANGRY MUG OF YOURS IN A LONG WHILE, KUROKA!
NIYA
NIYA (GRIN)
TCH...
CAN I JOIN THE FUN, THOUGH? NO WAY I'M MISSING OUT ON A FIGHT LIKE THIS!
SO YOU'RE ANOTHER BATTLE-CRAZED LUNATIC LIKE VARY...? THERE'RE WAY MORE FUN THINGS IN LIFE, Y'KNOW!
MORE FUN? NOT ANYTHING I CAN THINK OF!

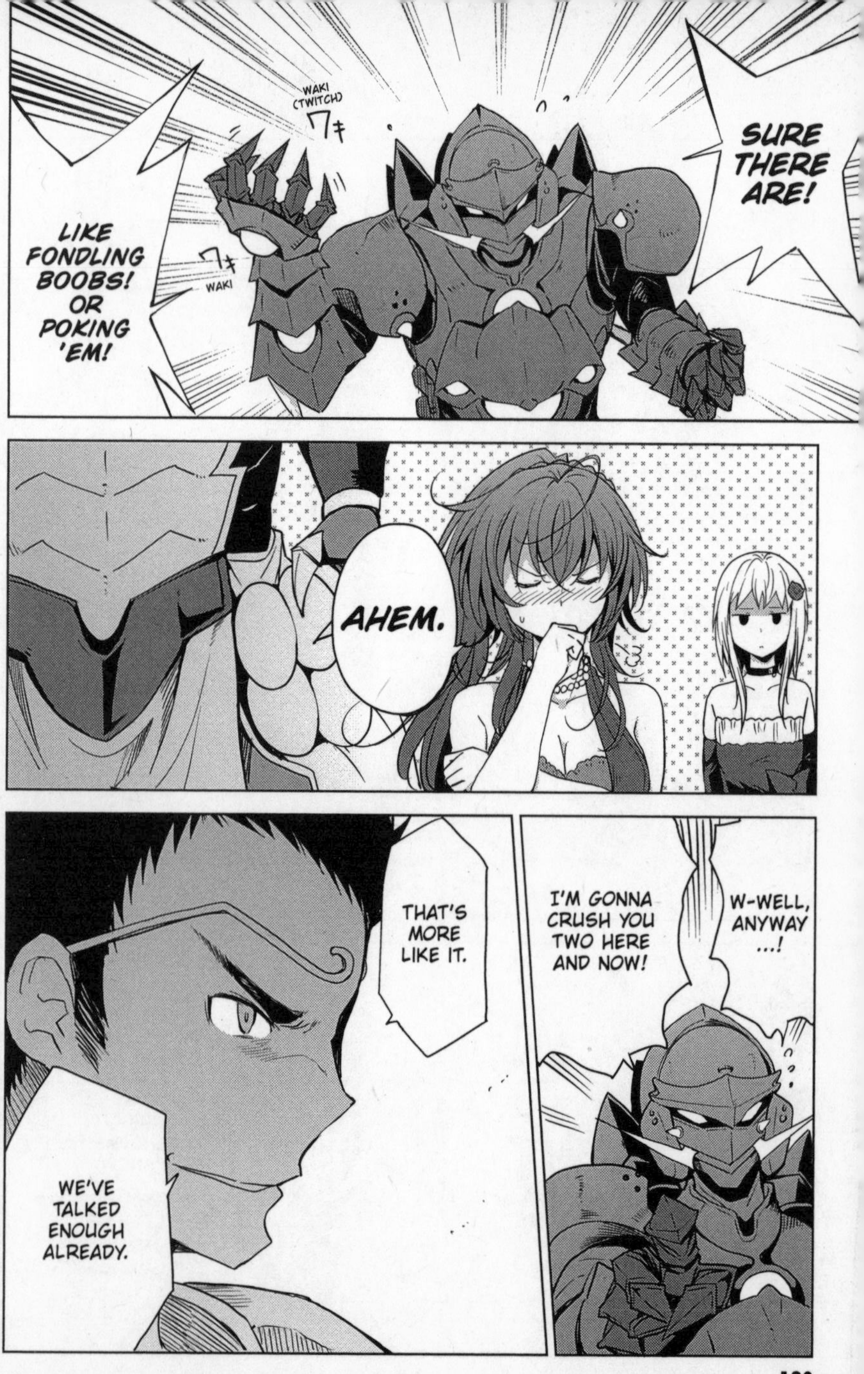
SURE THERE ARE!
WAKI (TWITCH)
ワキ
LIKE FONDLING BOOBS! OR POKING 'EM!
ワキ
WAKI
AHEM.
W-WELL, ANYWAY ...!
I'M GONNA CRUSH YOU TWO HERE AND NOW!
THAT'S MORE LIKE IT.
WE'VE TALKED ENOUGH ALREADY.

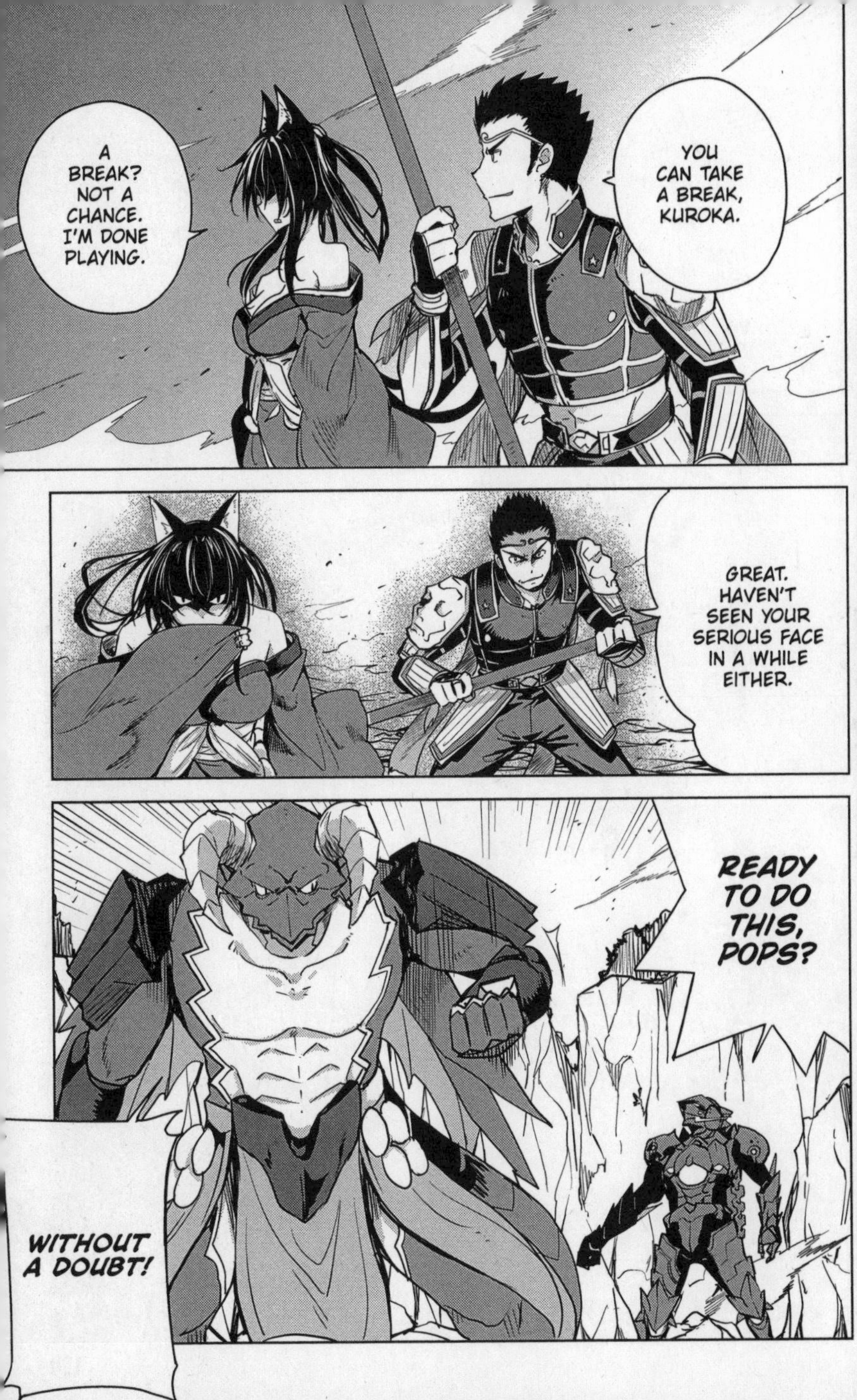
YOU CAN TAKE A BREAK, KUROKA.
A BREAK? NOT A CHANCE. I'M DONE PLAYING.
GREAT. HAVEN'T SEEN YOUR SERIOUS FACE IN A WHILE EITHER.
READY TO DO THIS, POPS?
WITHOUT A DOUBT!

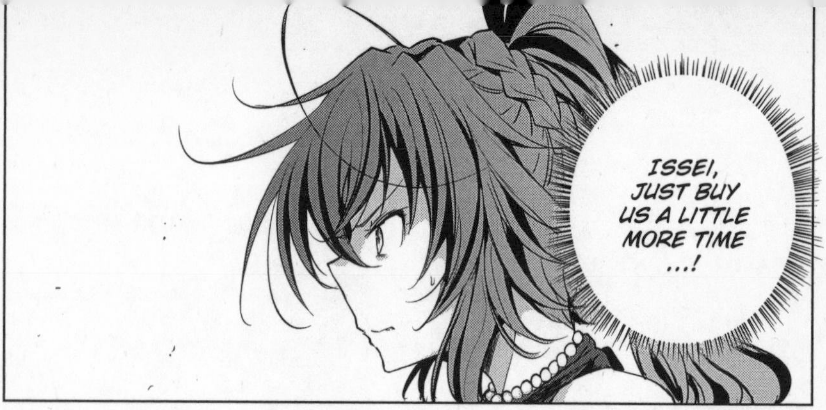
ISSEI, JUST BUY US A LITTLE MORE TIME ...!

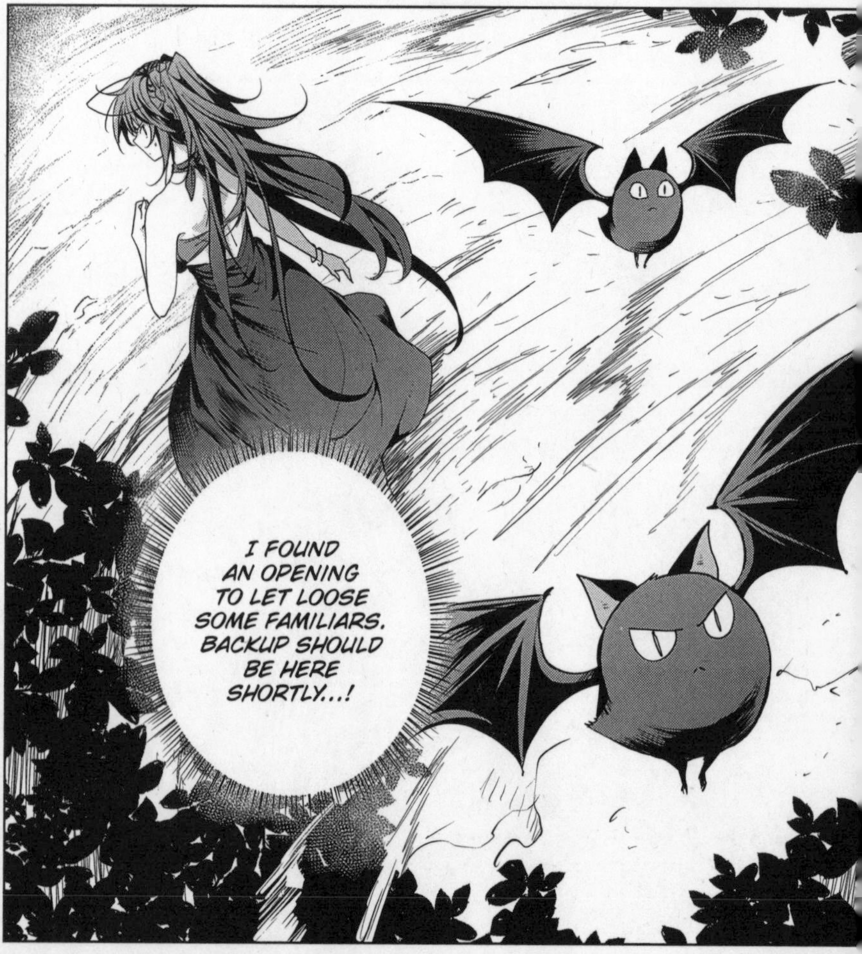
I FOUND AN OPENING TO LET LOOSE SOME FAMILIARS. BACKUP SHOULD BE HERE SHORTLY...!

HIGH SCHOOL DxD

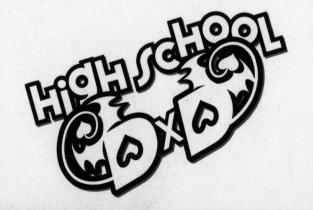

LIFE.66: ATTACK! ULTIMATE HOLY BLADE!!

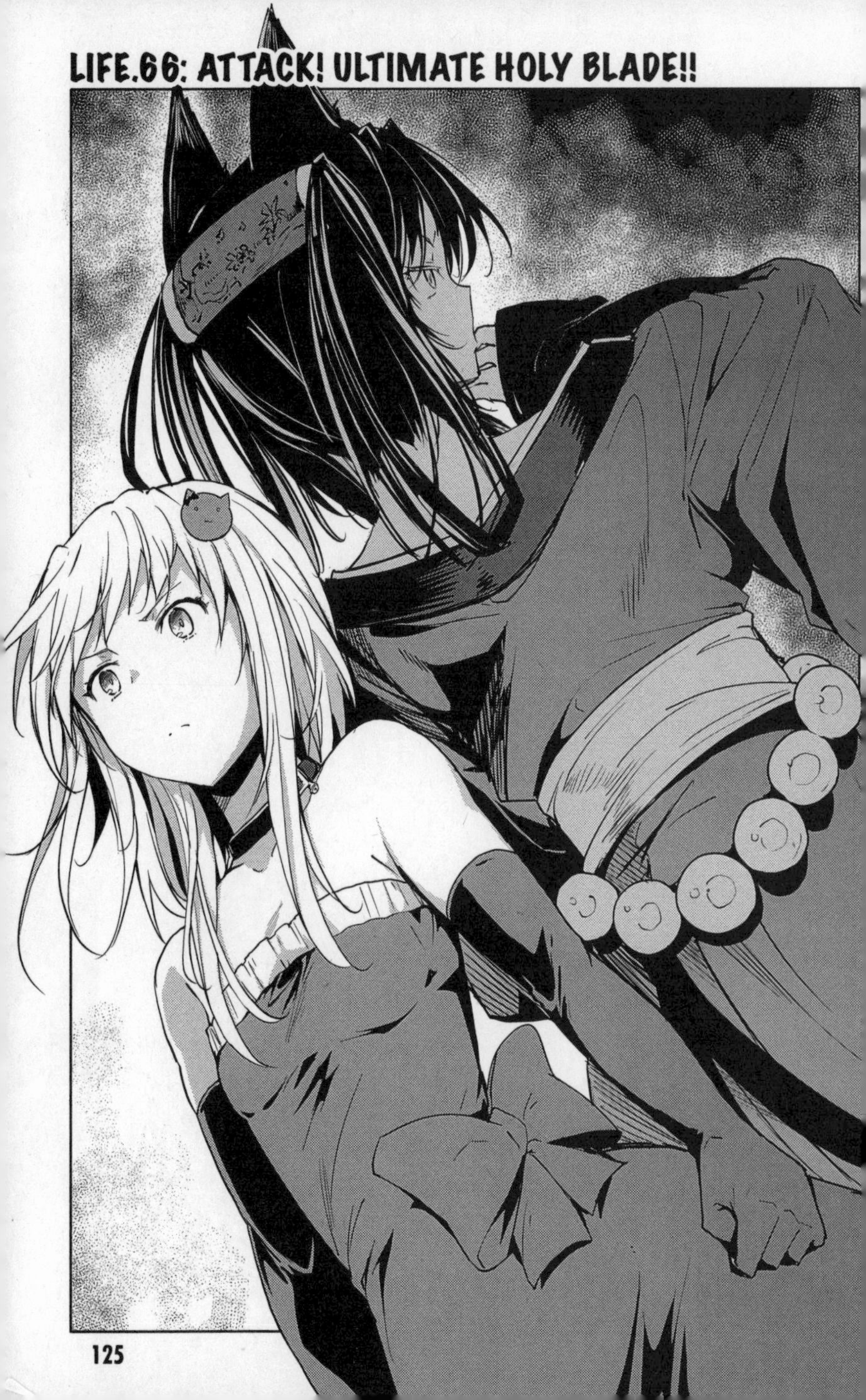

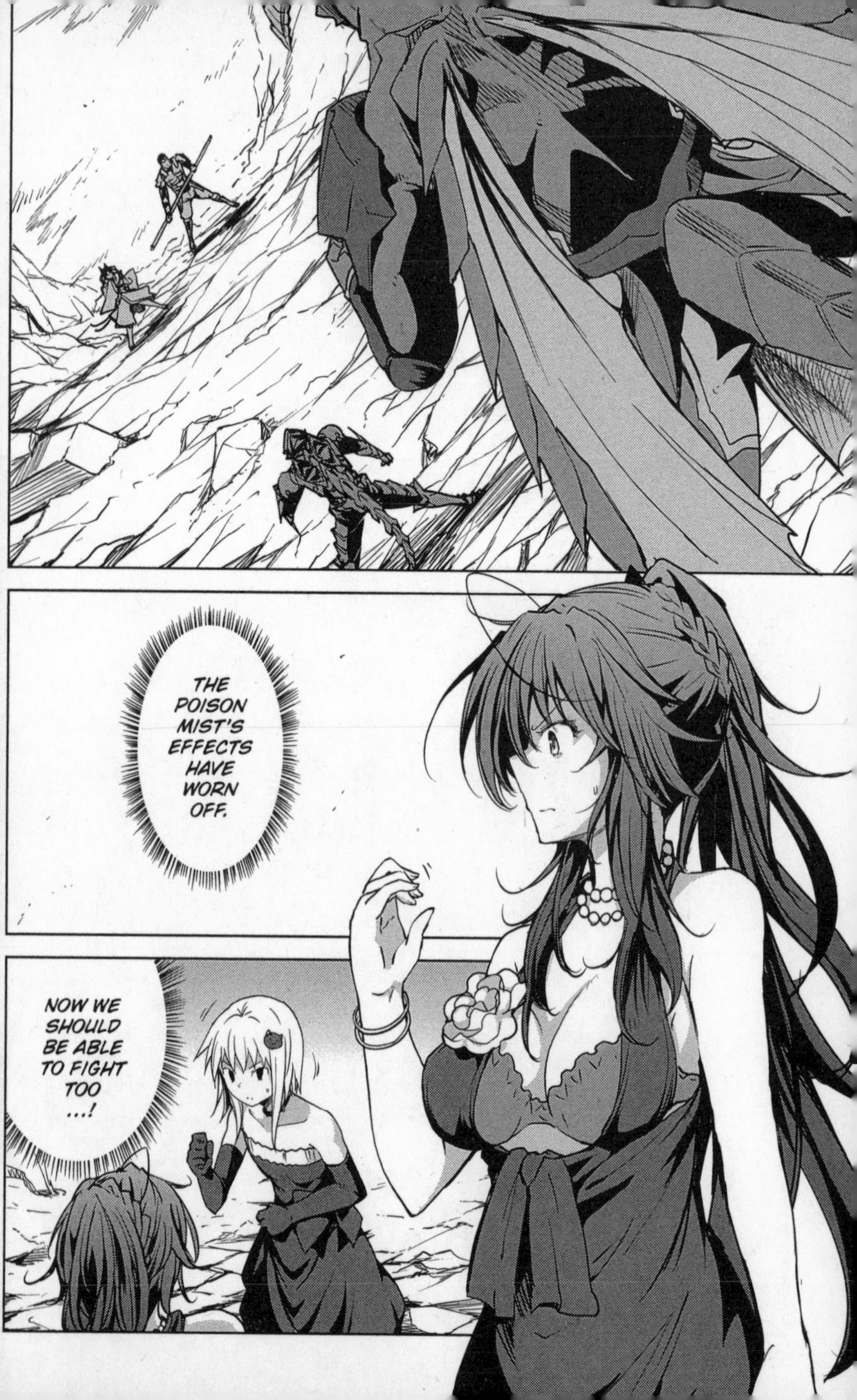
THE POISON MIST'S EFFECTS HAVE WORN OFF.
NOW WE SHOULD BE ABLE TO FIGHT TOO ...!

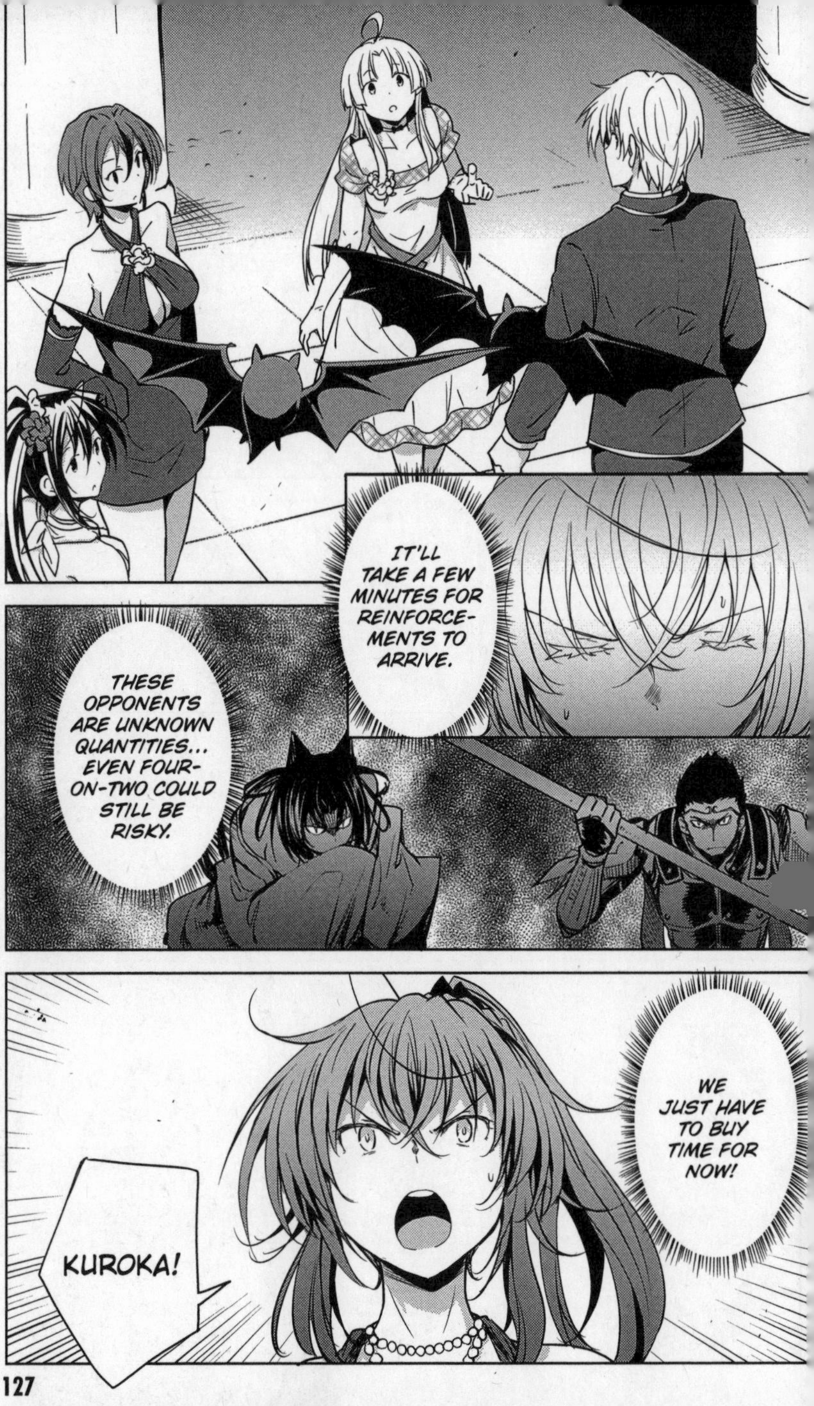
IT'LL TAKE A FEW MINUTES FOR REINFORCE-MENTS TO ARRIVE.
THESE OPPONENTS ARE UNKNOWN QUANTITIES... EVEN FOUR-ON-TWO COULD STILL BE RISKY.
WE JUST HAVE TO BUY TIME FOR NOW!
KUROKA!

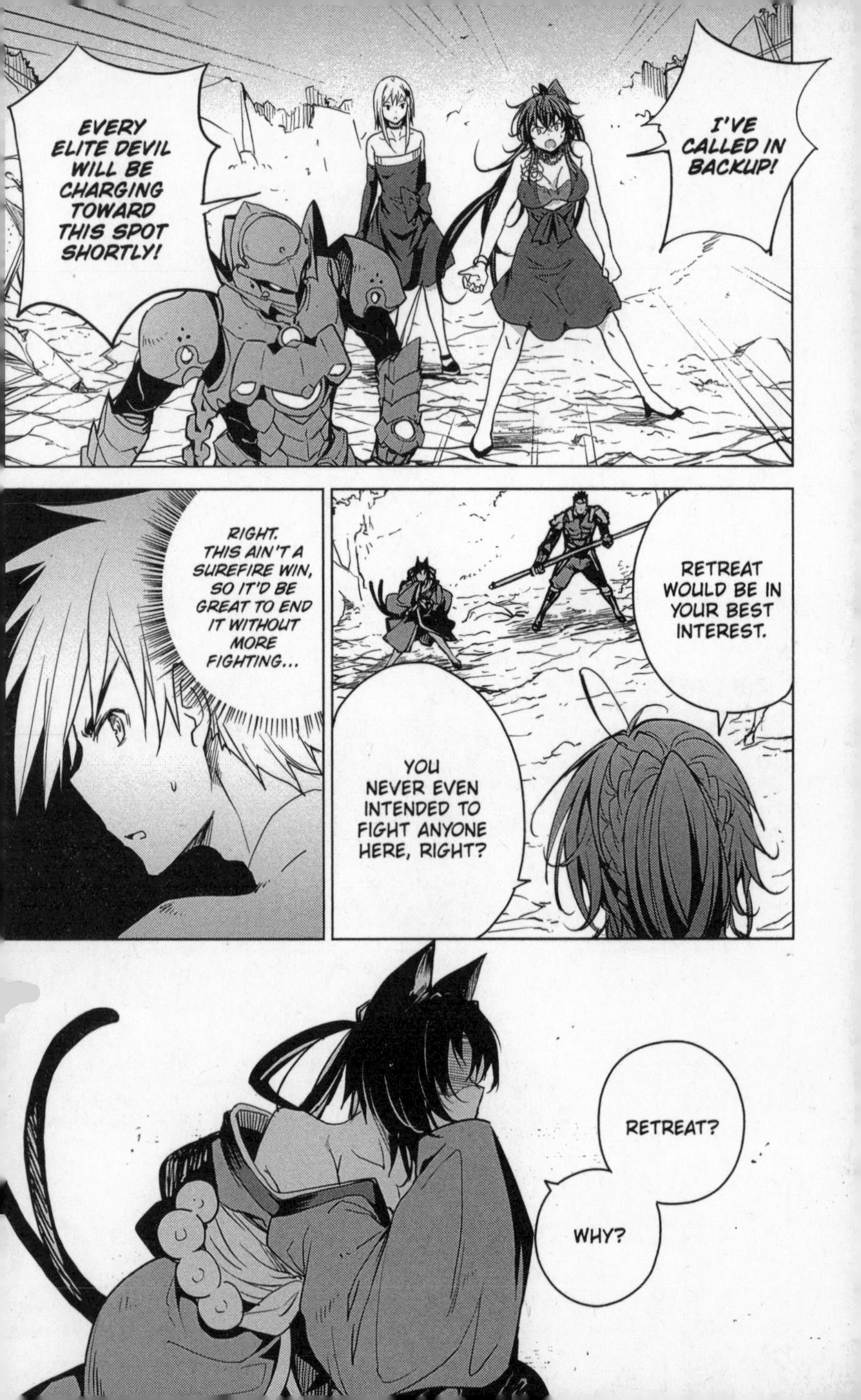
I'VE CALLED IN BACKUP!
EVERY ELITE DEVIL WILL BE CHARGING TOWARD THIS SPOT SHORTLY!
RETREAT WOULD BE IN YOUR BEST INTEREST.
YOU NEVER EVEN INTENDED TO FIGHT ANYONE HERE, RIGHT?
RIGHT. THIS AIN'T A SUREFIRE WIN, SO IT'D BE GREAT TO END IT WITHOUT MORE FIGHTING...
RETREAT?
WHY?

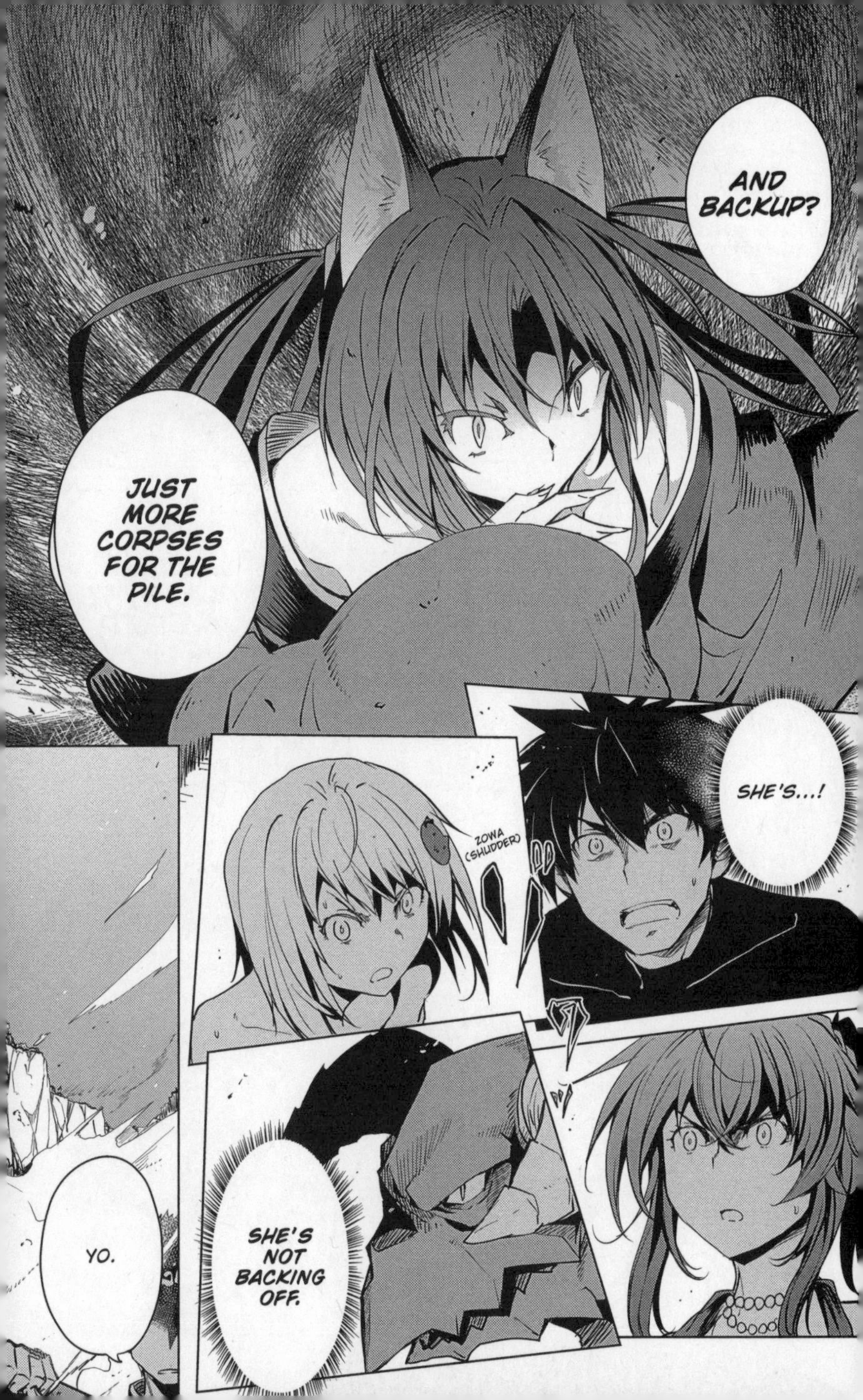
AND BACKUP?
JUST MORE CORPSES FOR THE PILE.
SHE'S...!
ZOWA (SHUDDER)
SHE'S NOT BACKING OFF.
YO.

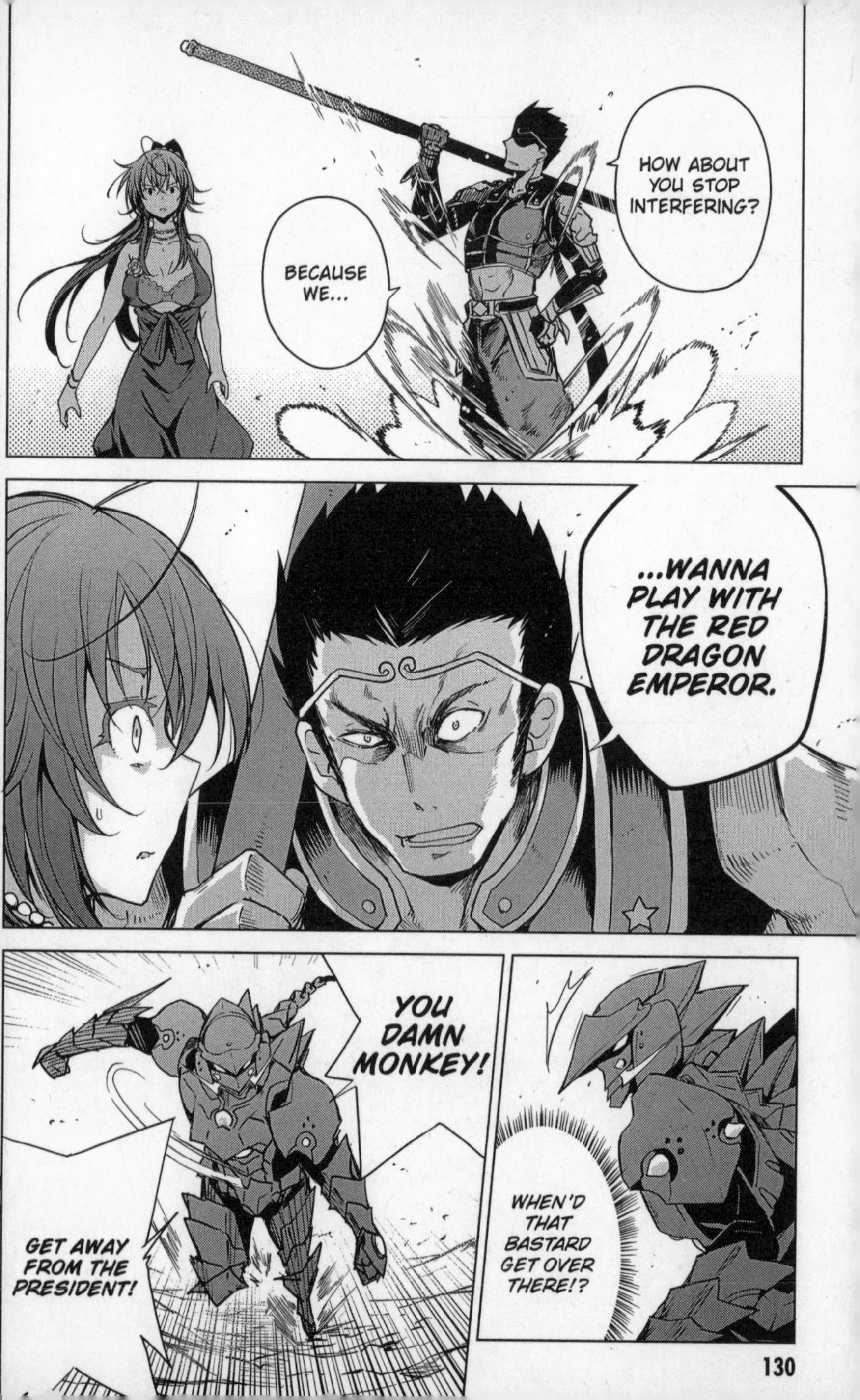
HOW ABOUT YOU STOP INTERFERING?
BECAUSE WE...
...WANNA PLAY WITH THE RED DRAGON EMPEROR.
WHEN'D THAT BASTARD GET OVER THERE!?
YOU DAMN MONKEY!
GET AWAY FROM THE PRESIDENT!

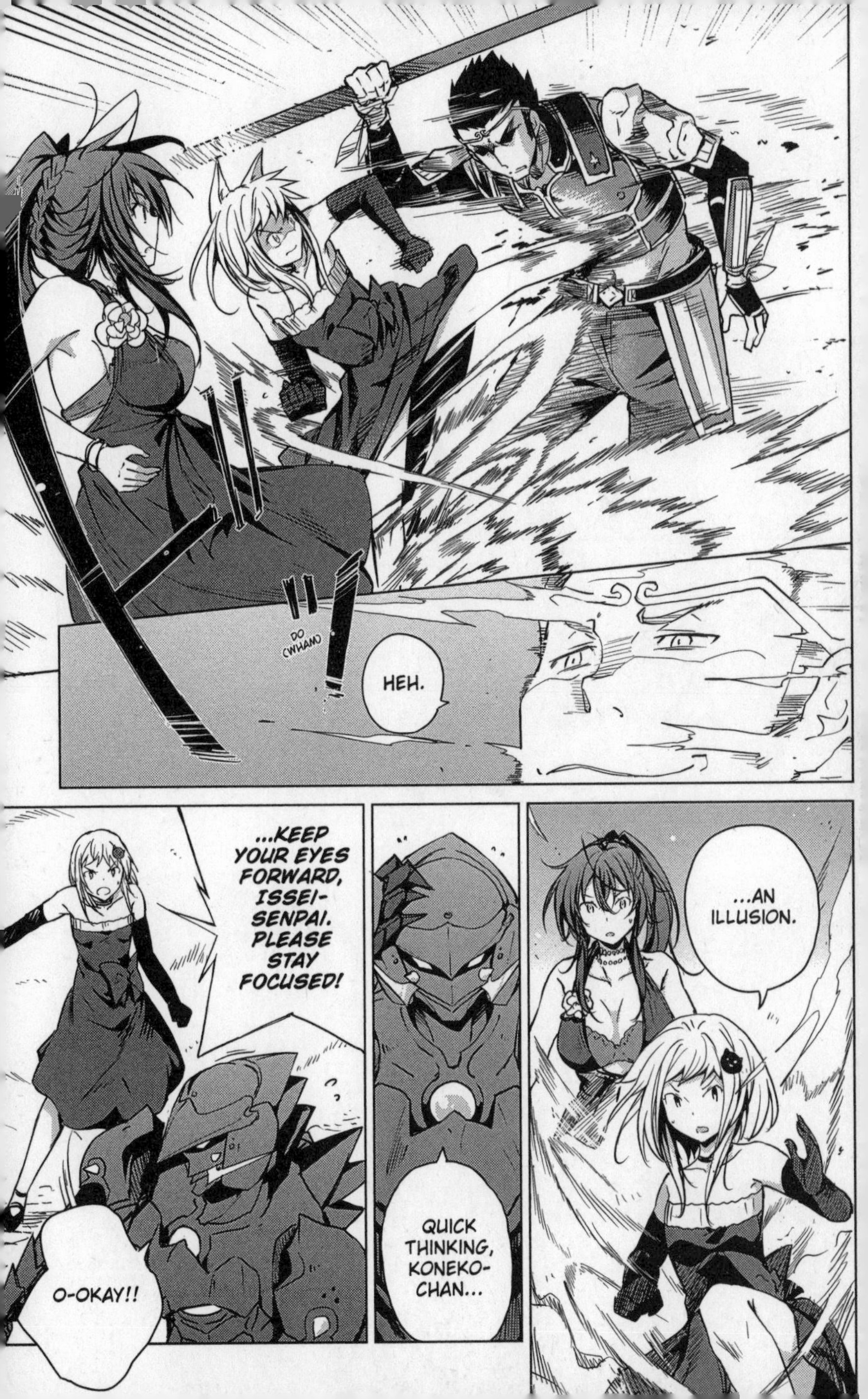
DO (WHAM)
HEH.
...AN ILLUSION.
QUICK THINKING, KONEKO-CHAN...
...KEEP YOUR EYES FORWARD, ISSEI-SENPAI. PLEASE STAY FOCUSED!
O-OKAY!!

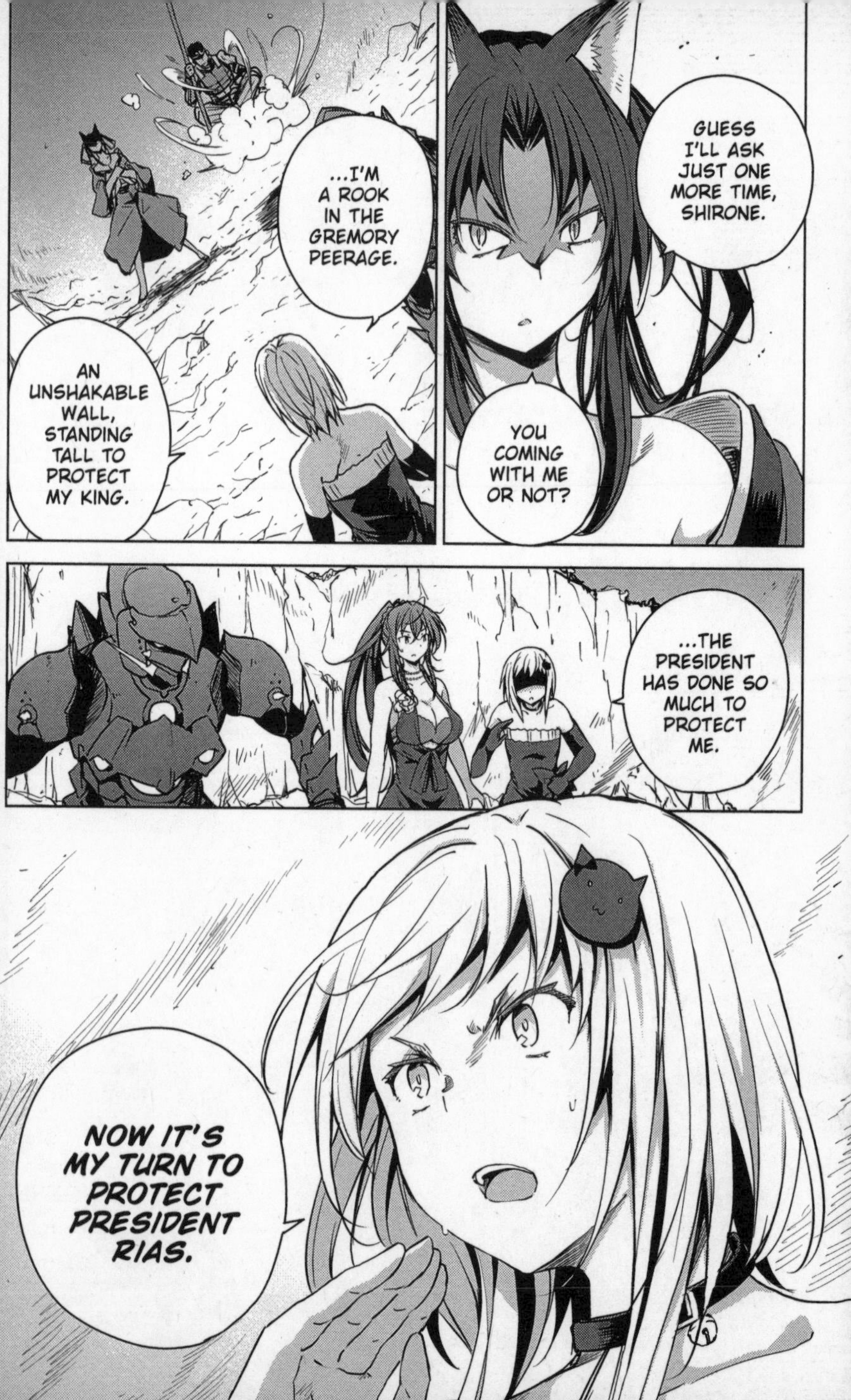
GUESS I'LL ASK JUST ONE MORE TIME, SHIRONE.
YOU COMING WITH ME OR NOT?
...I'M A ROOK IN THE GREMORY PEERAGE.
AN UNSHAKABLE WALL, STANDING TALL TO PROTECT MY KING.
...THE PRESIDENT HAS DONE SO MUCH TO PROTECT ME.
NOW IT'S MY TURN TO PROTECT PRESIDENT RIAS.

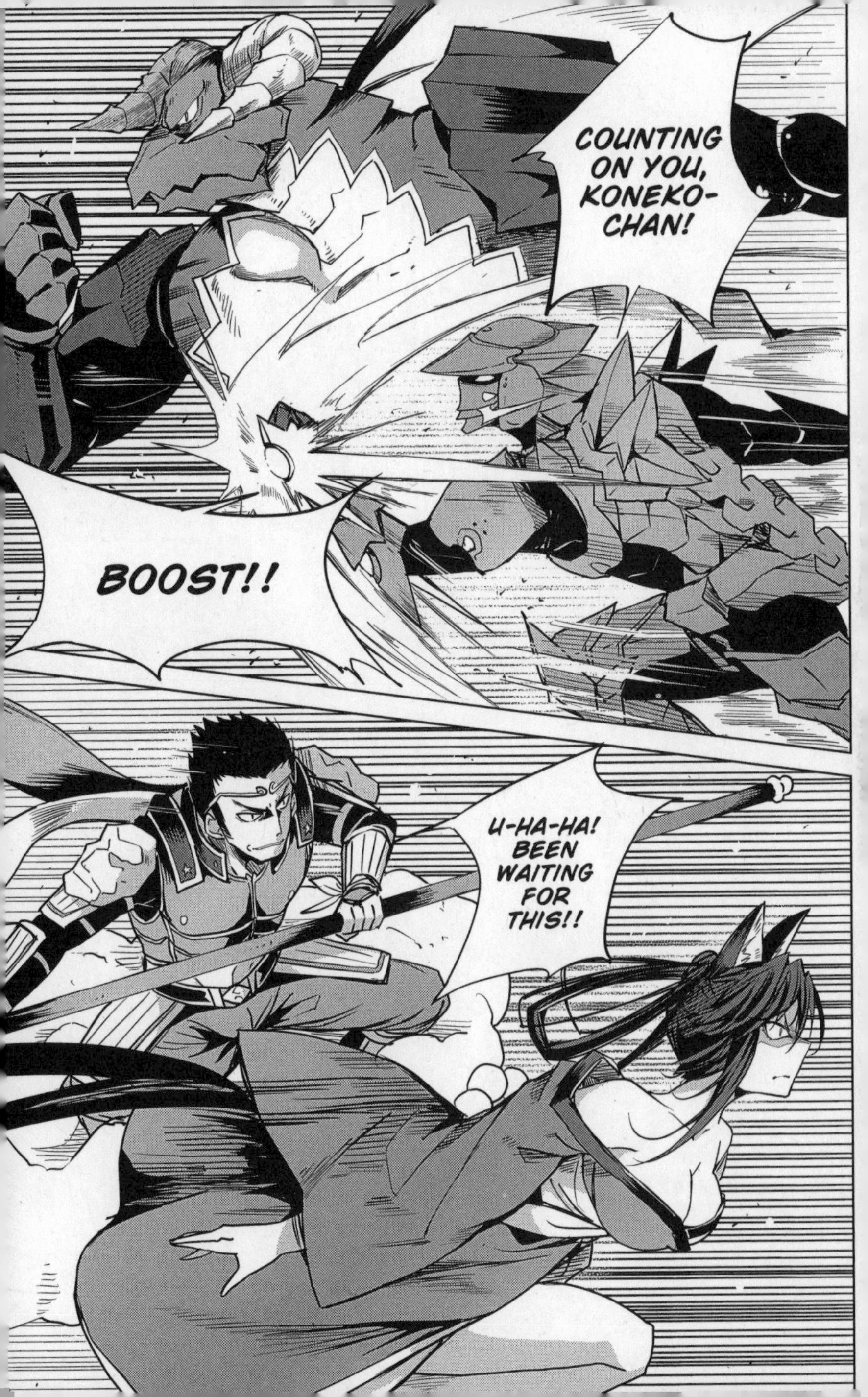
COUNTING ON YOU, KONEKO-CHAN!
BOOST!!
U-HA-HA! BEEN WAITING FOR THIS!!

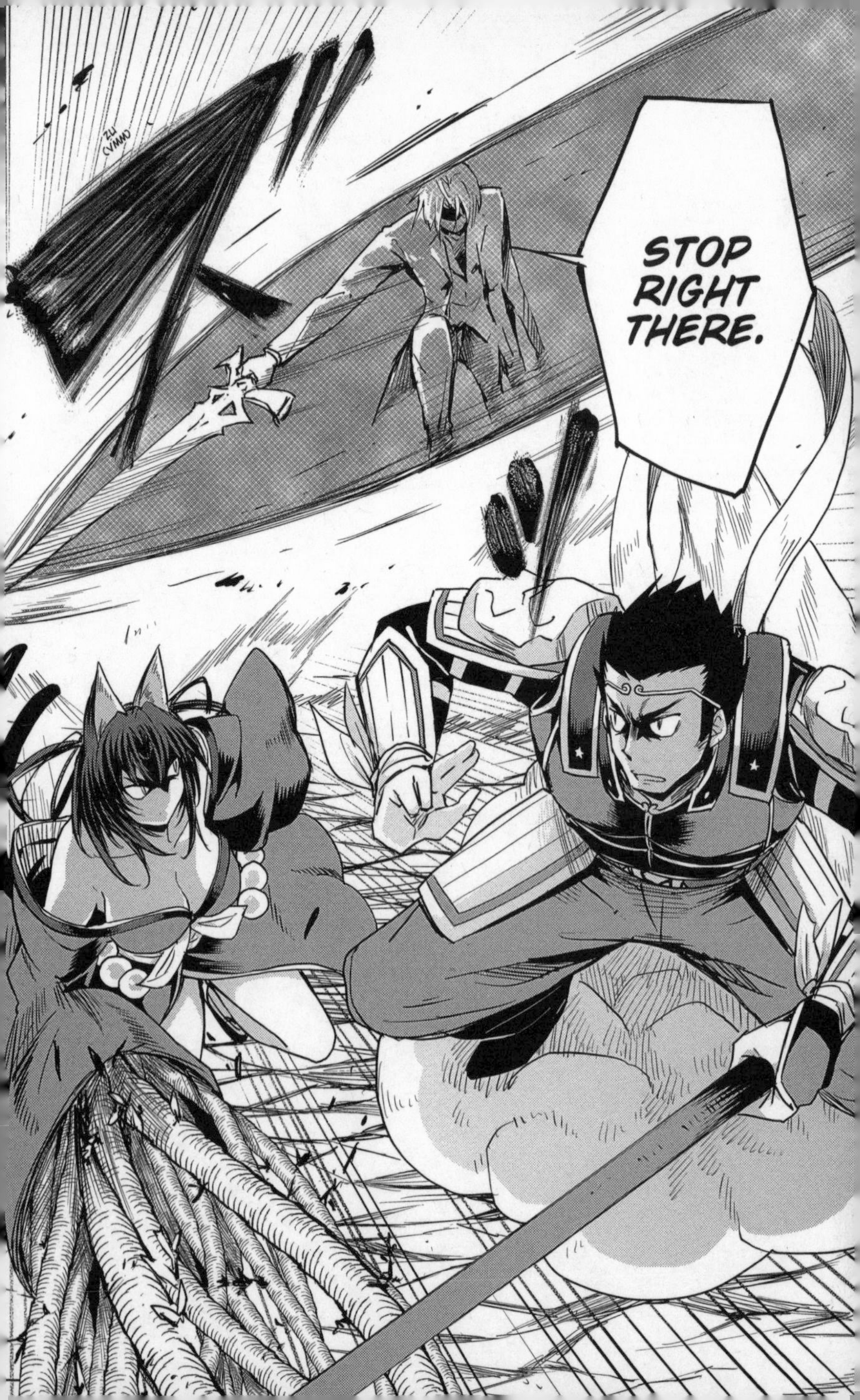
STOP RIGHT THERE.

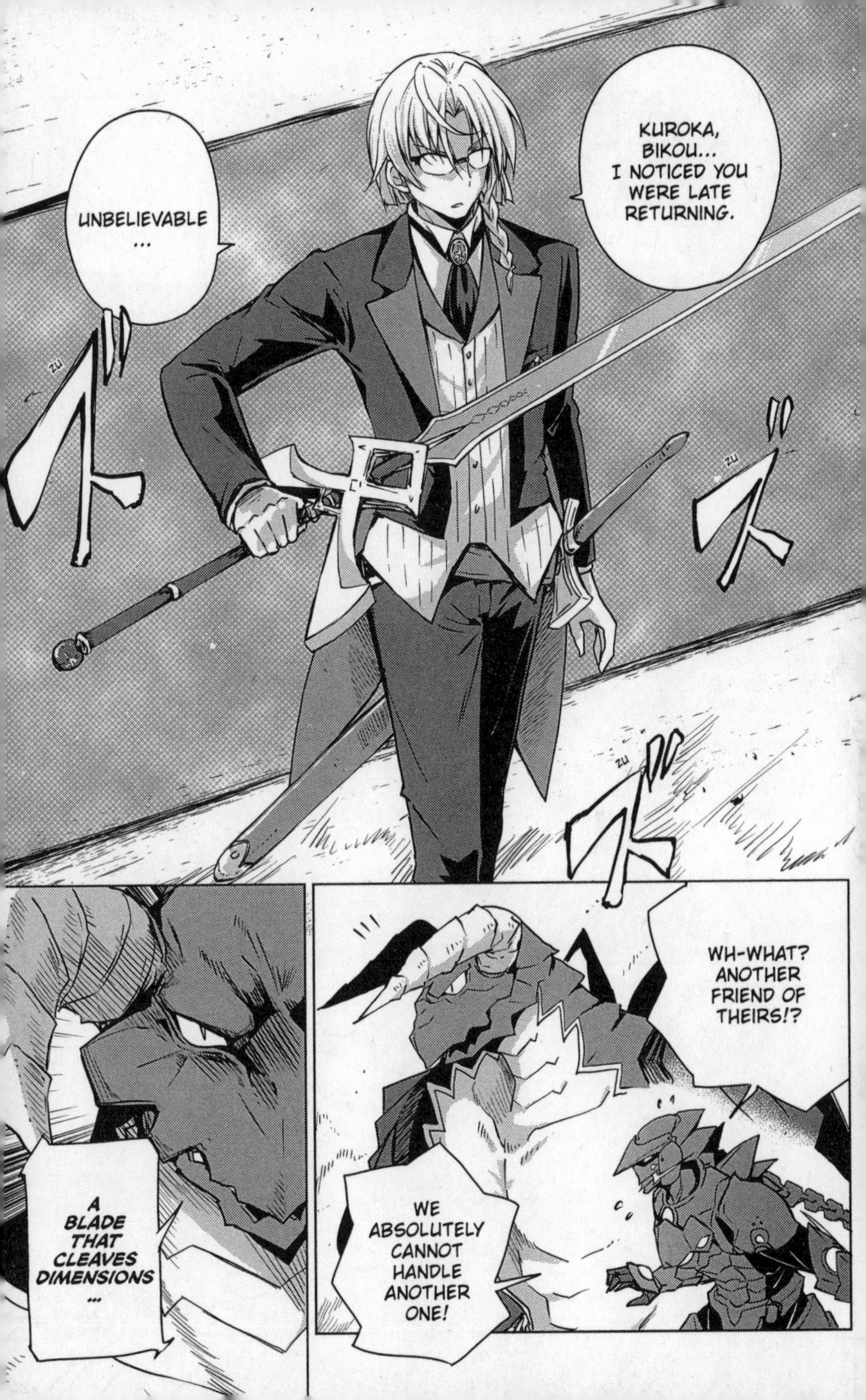
KUROKA, BIKOU... I NOTICED YOU WERE LATE RETURNING.
ZU
ZU
UNBELIEVABLE...
ZU
WH-WHAT? ANOTHER FRIEND OF THEIRS!?
WE ABSOLUTELY CANNOT HANDLE ANOTHER ONE!
A BLADE THAT CLEAVES DIMENSIONS...

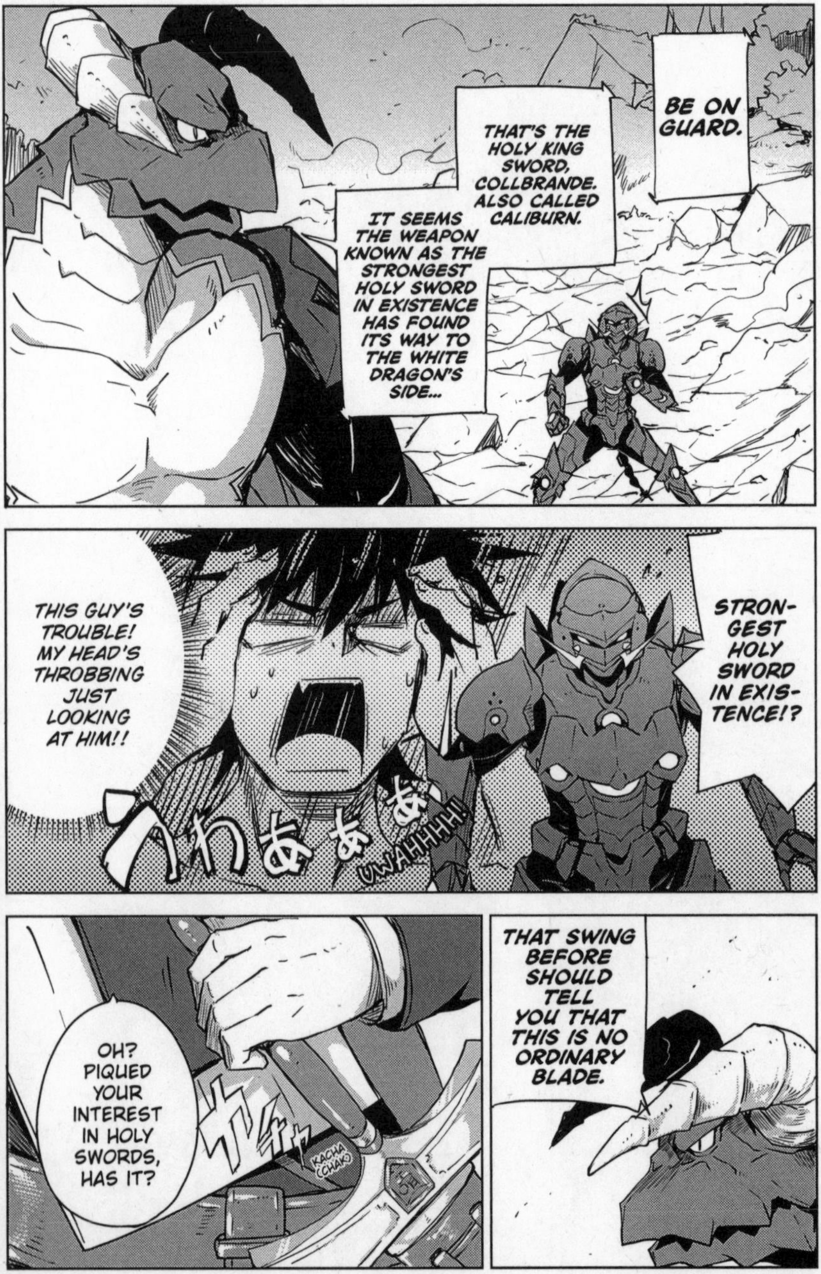

BE ON GUARD.
THAT'S THE HOLY KING SWORD, COLLBRANDE. ALSO CALLED CALIBURN.
IT SEEMS THE WEAPON KNOWN AS THE STRONGEST HOLY SWORD IN EXISTENCE HAS FOUND ITS WAY TO THE WHITE DRAGON'S SIDE...
STRON-GEST HOLY SWORD IN EXIS-TENCE!?
THIS GUY'S TROUBLE! MY HEAD'S THROBBING JUST LOOKING AT HIM!!
UWAHHHH!
THAT SWING BEFORE SHOULD TELL YOU THAT THIS IS NO ORDINARY BLADE.
OH? PIQUED YOUR INTEREST IN HOLY SWORDS, HAS IT?
KACHA (CHAK)

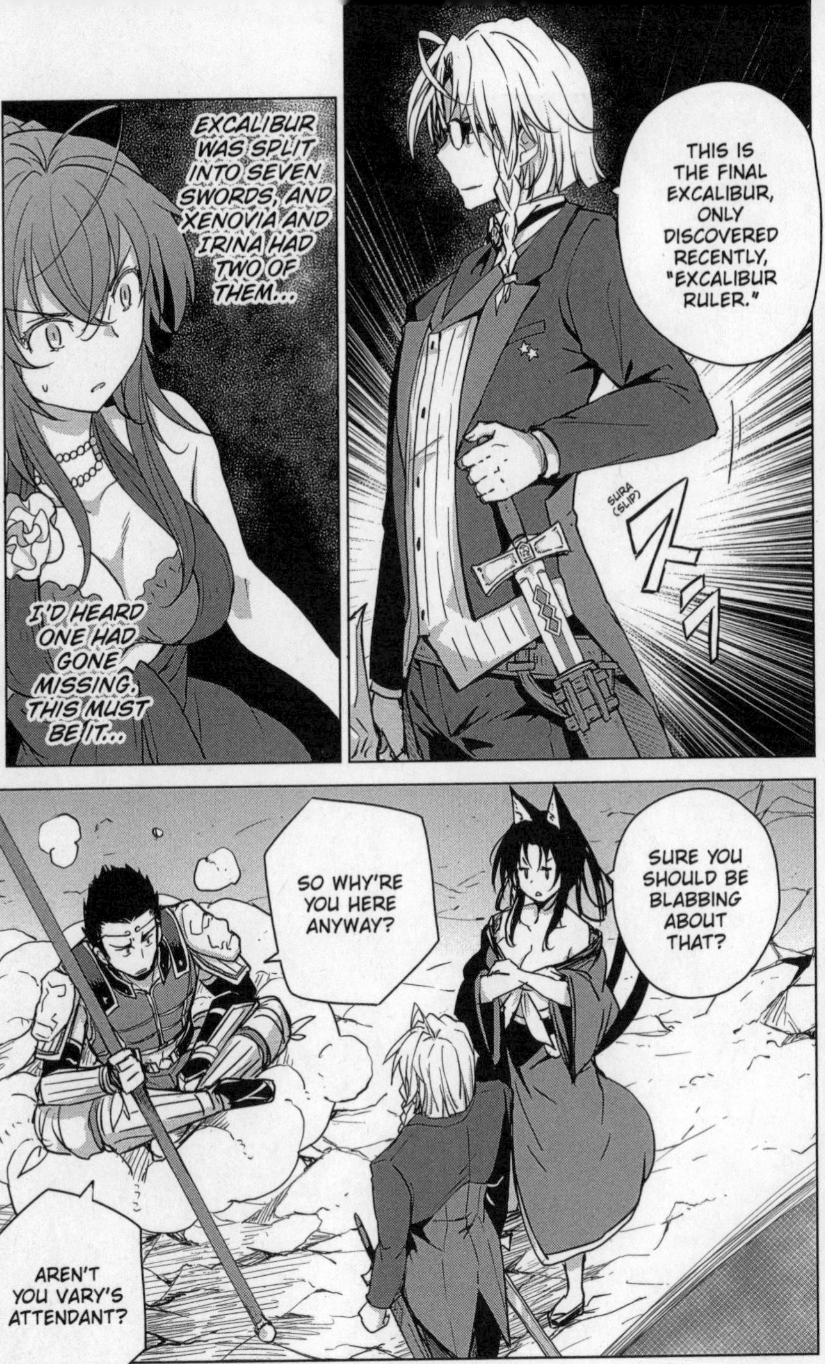
THIS IS THE FINAL EXCALIBUR, ONLY DISCOVERED RECENTLY, "EXCALIBUR RULER."
SURA (SLIP)
EXCALIBUR WAS SPLIT INTO SEVEN SWORDS, AND XENOVIA AND IRINA HAD TWO OF THEM...
I'D HEARD ONE HAD GONE MISSING. THIS MUST BE IT...
SURE YOU SHOULD BE BLABBING ABOUT THAT?
SO WHY'RE YOU HERE ANYWAY?
AREN'T YOU VARY'S ATTENDANT?

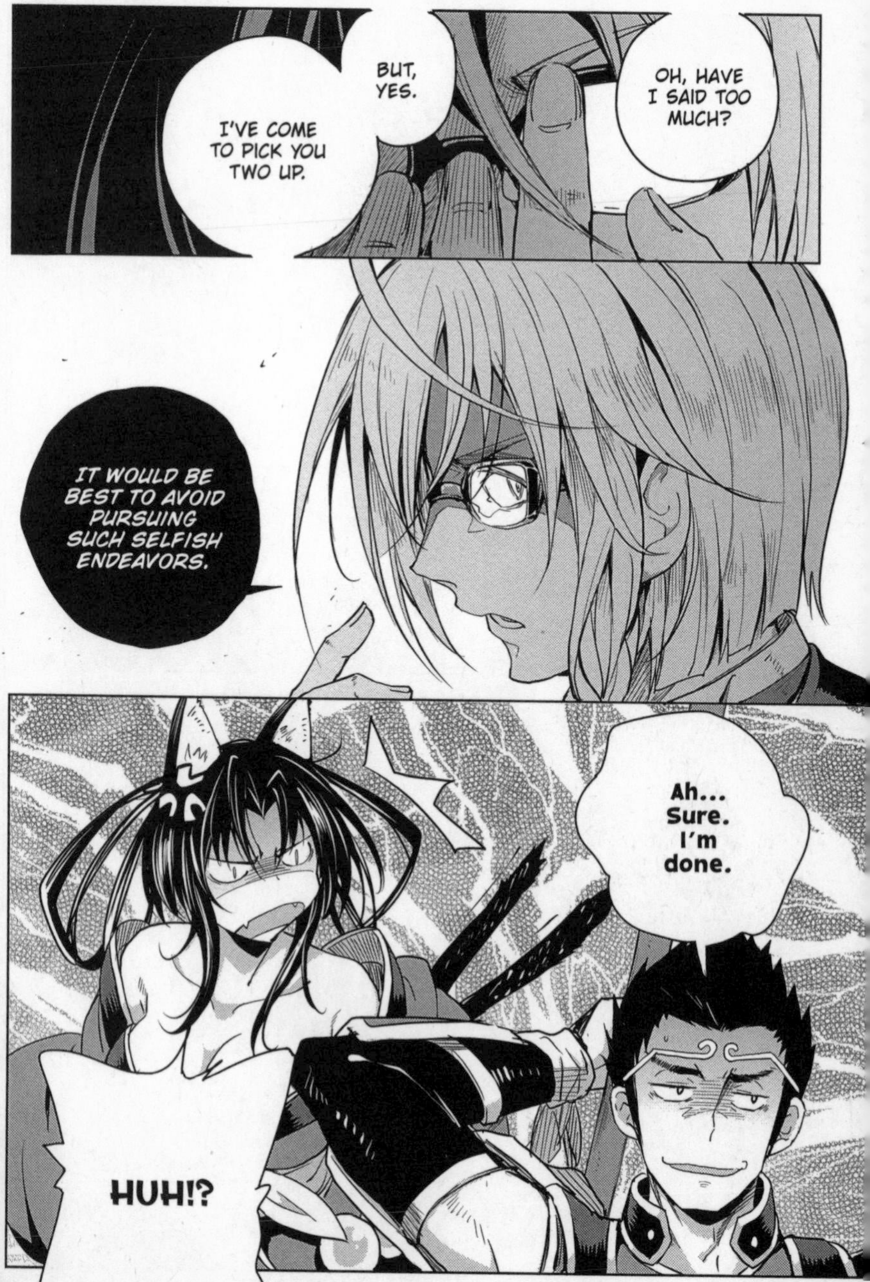
OH, HAVE I SAID TOO MUCH?
BUT, YES.
I'VE COME TO PICK YOU TWO UP.
IT WOULD BE BEST TO AVOID PURSUING SUCH SELFISH ENDEAVORS.
Ah... Sure. I'm done.
HUH!?

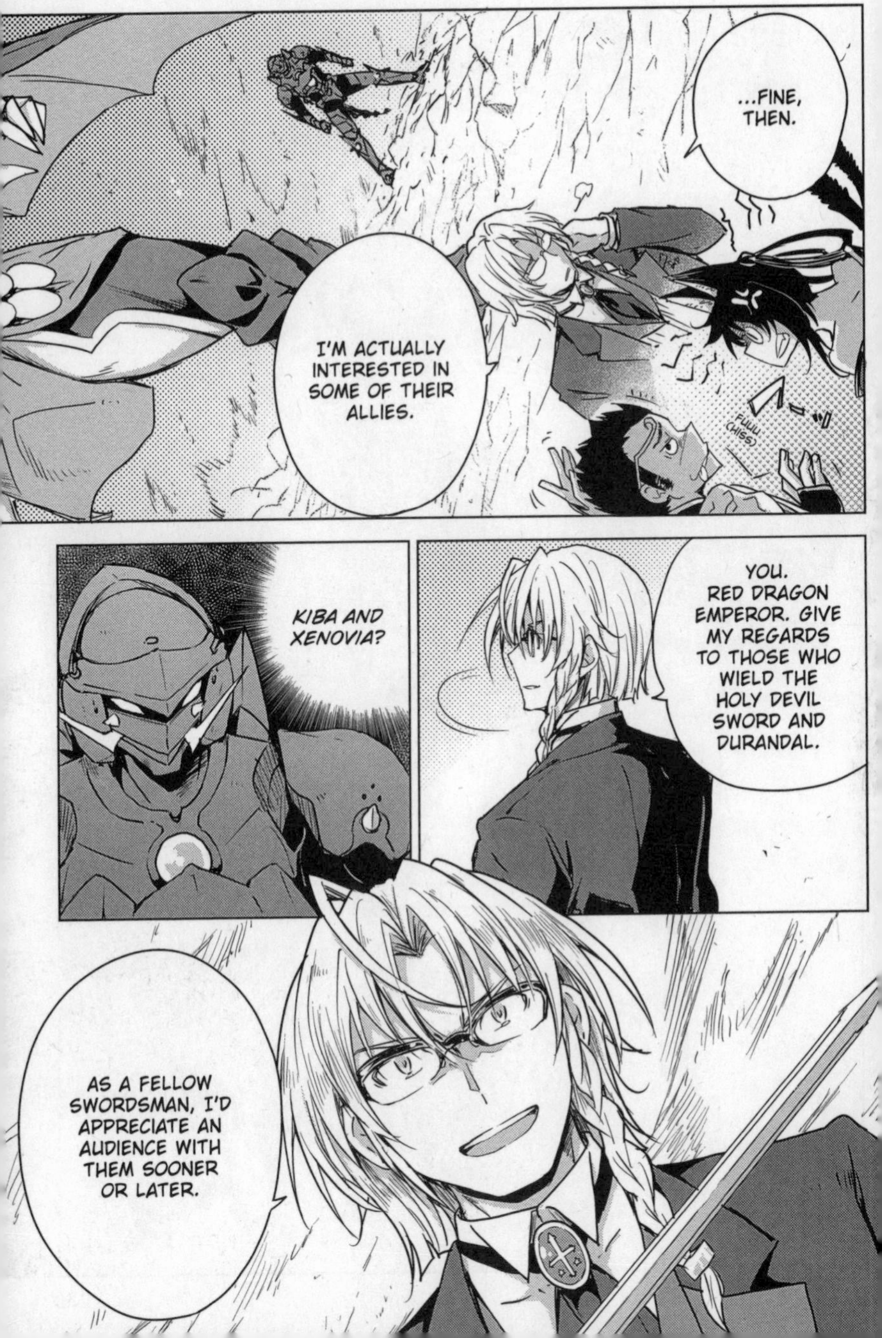
...FINE, THEN.
FUUU (HISS)
I'M ACTUALLY INTERESTED IN SOME OF THEIR ALLIES.
YOU. RED DRAGON EMPEROR. GIVE MY REGARDS TO THOSE WHO WIELD THE HOLY DEVIL SWORD AND DURANDAL.
KIBA AND XENOVIA?
AS A FELLOW SWORDSMAN, I'D APPRECIATE AN AUDIENCE WITH THEM SOONER OR LATER.

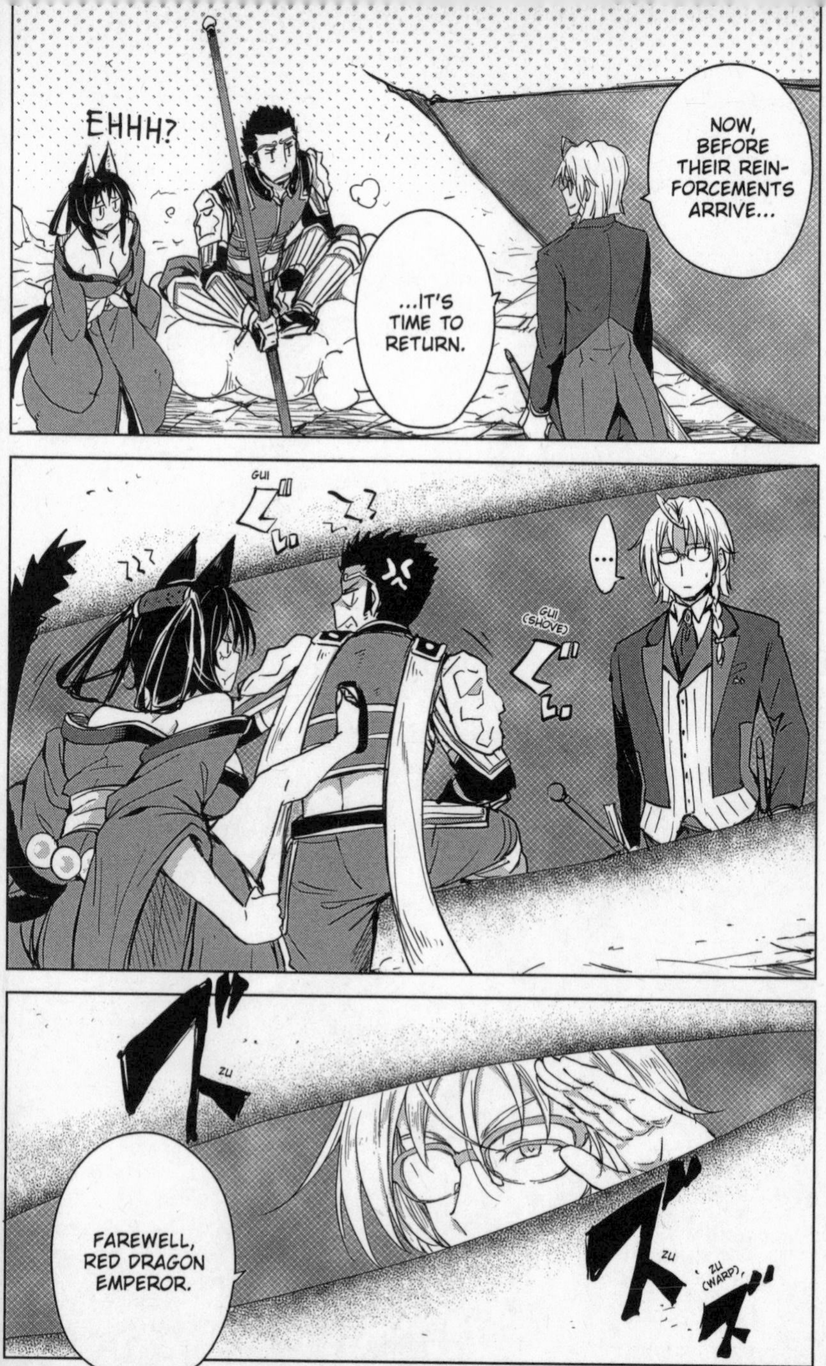
NOW, BEFORE THEIR REIN-FORCEMENTS ARRIVE...
...IT'S TIME TO RETURN.
EHHH?
...
GUI (SHOVE)
GUI
ZU
ZU
ZU (WARP)
FAREWELL, RED DRAGON EMPEROR.

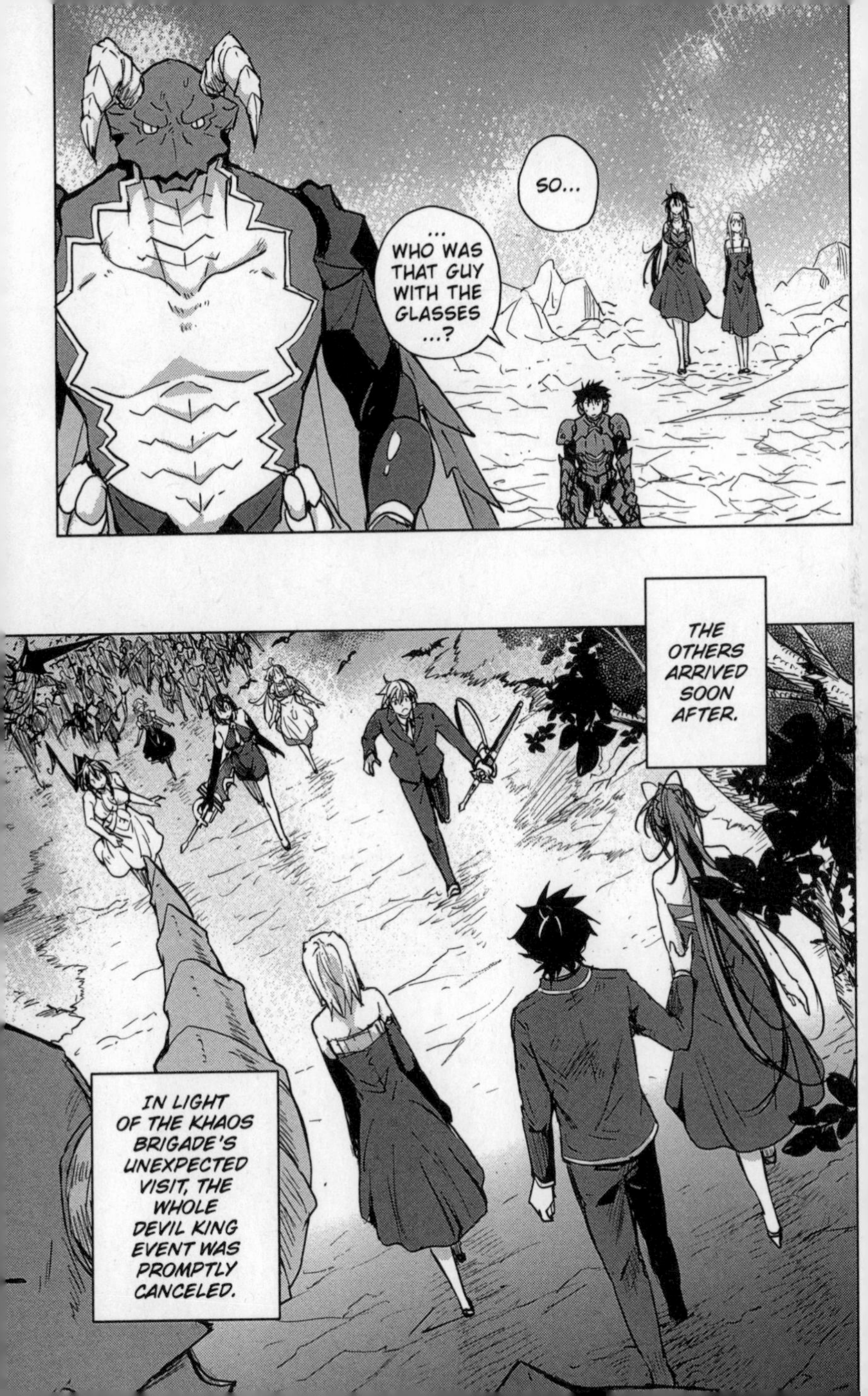
SO...
... WHO WAS THAT GUY WITH THE GLASSES ...?
THE OTHERS ARRIVED SOON AFTER.
IN LIGHT OF THE KHAOS BRIGADE'S UNEXPECTED VISIT, THE WHOLE DEVIL KING EVENT WAS PROMPTLY CANCELED.

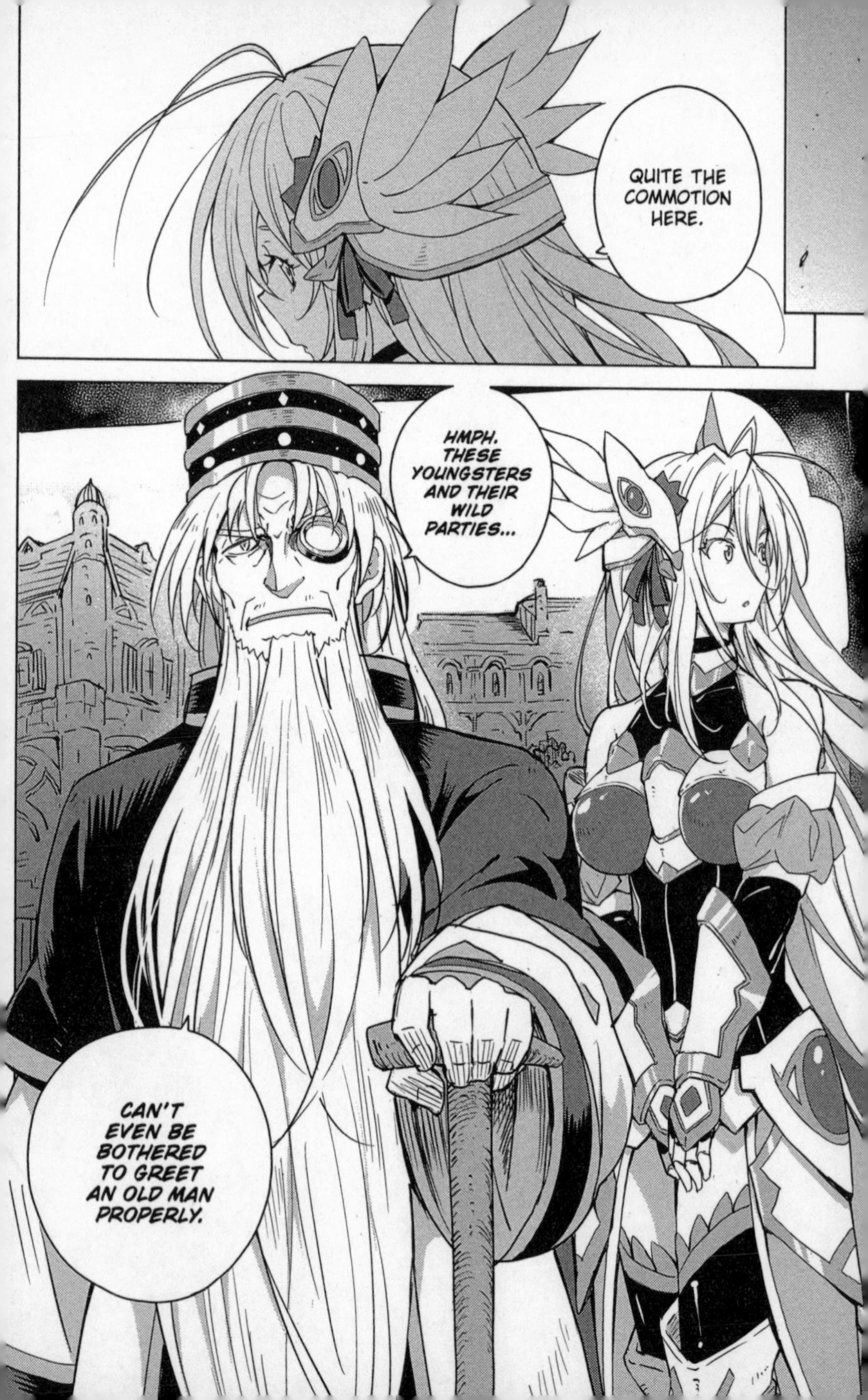
QUITE THE COMMOTION HERE.
HMPH. THESE YOUNGSTERS AND THEIR WILD PARTIES...
CAN'T EVEN BE BOTHERED TO GREET AN OLD MAN PROPERLY.

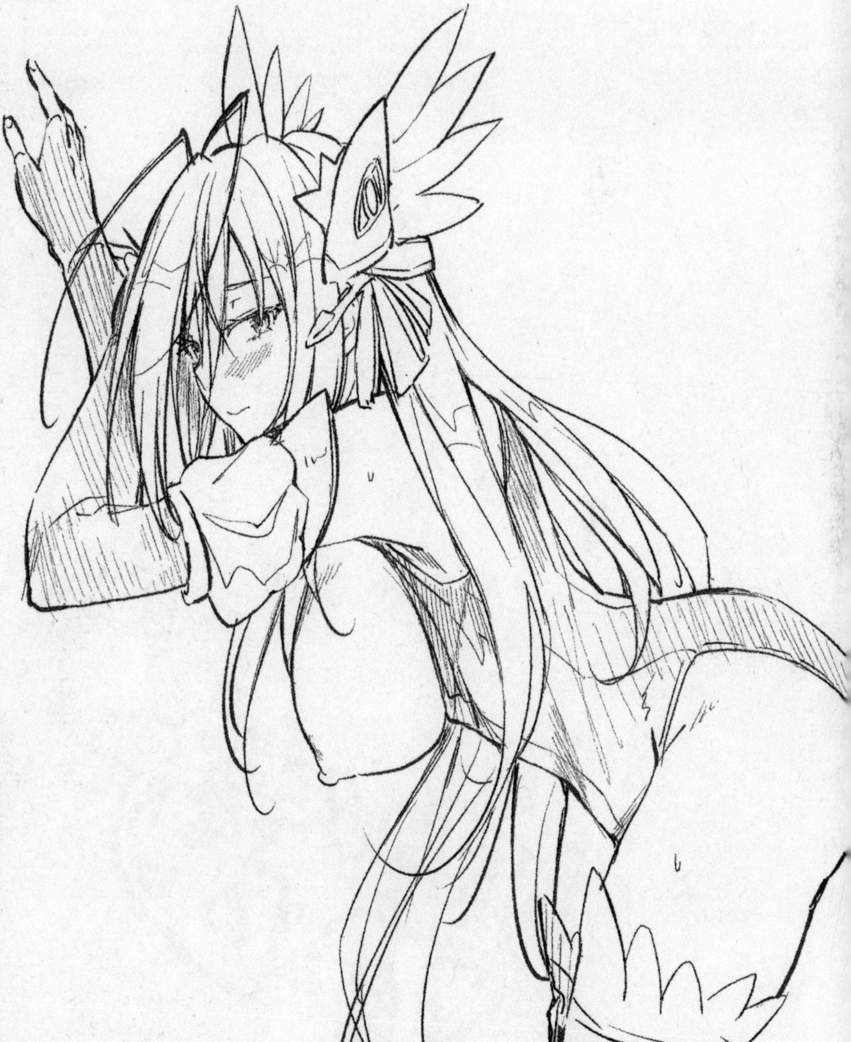

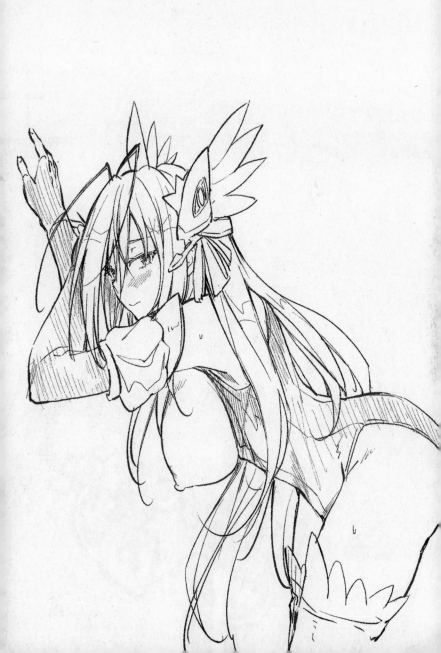

HIGH SCHOOL DxD

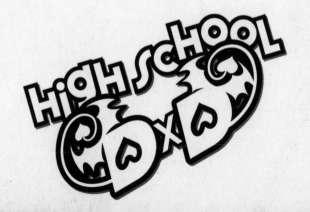

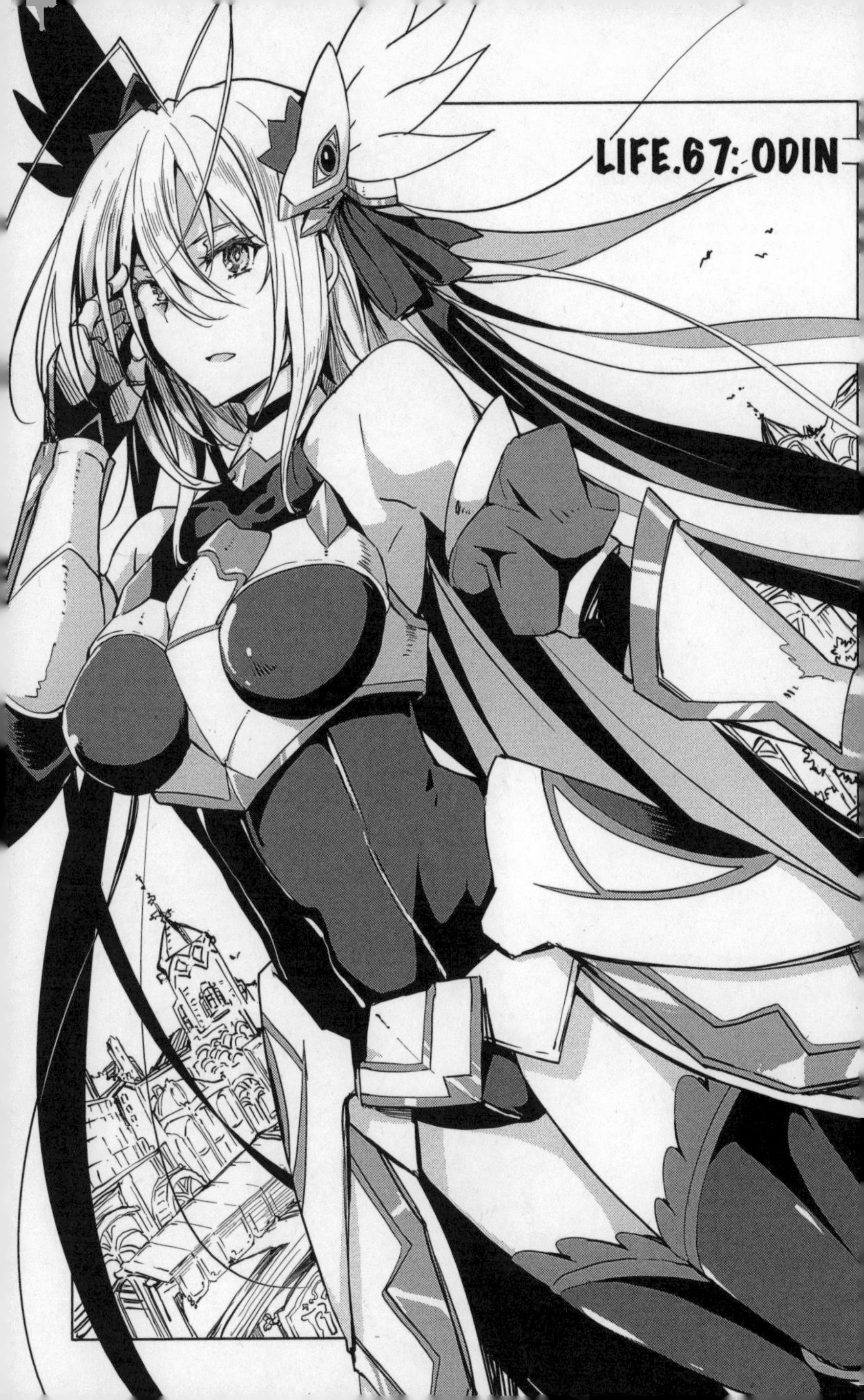
LIFE.67: ODIN

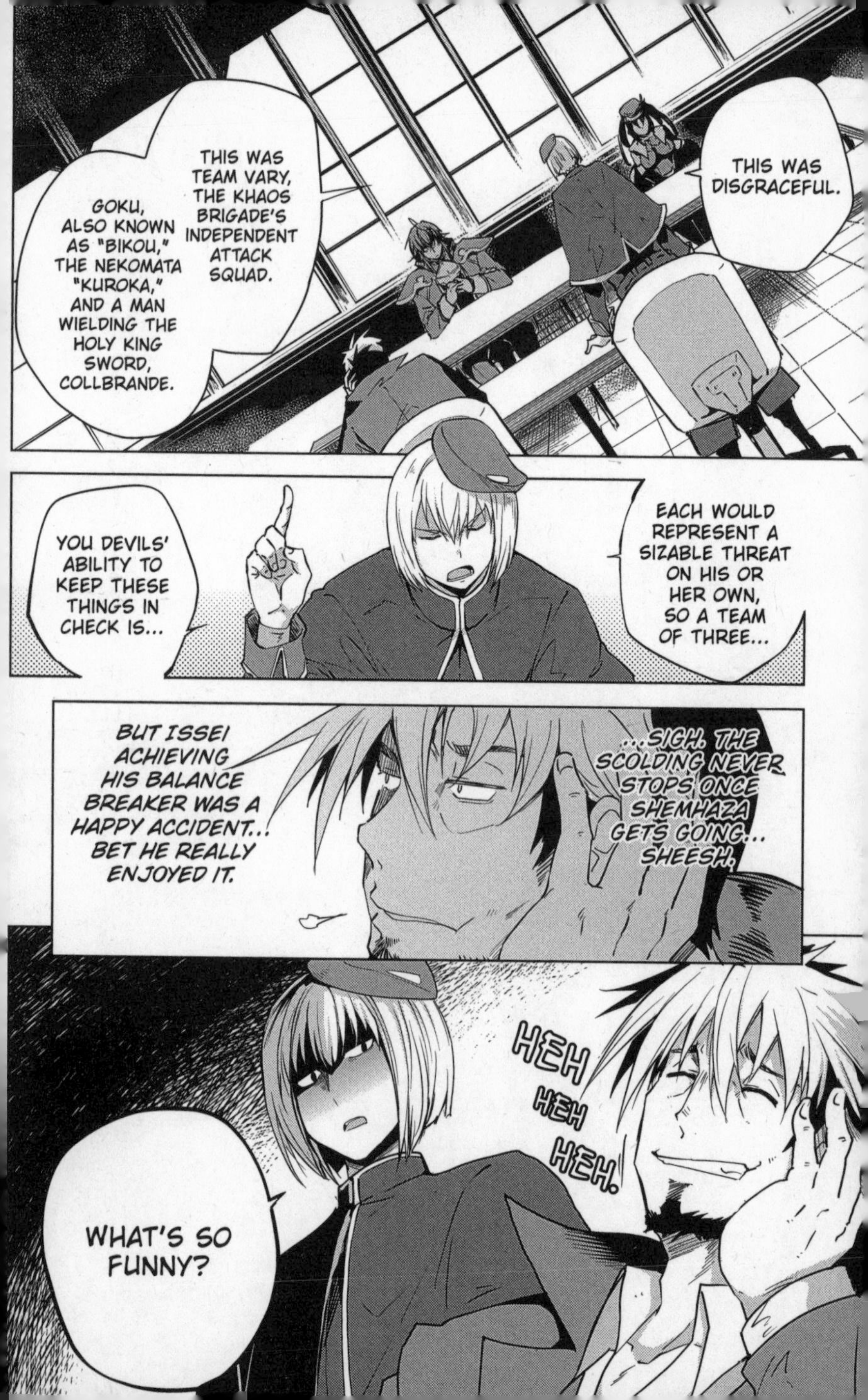
THIS WAS DISGRACEFUL.
THIS WAS TEAM VARY, THE KHAOS BRIGADE'S INDEPENDENT ATTACK SQUAD.
GOKU, ALSO KNOWN AS "BIKOU," THE NEKOMATA "KUROKA," AND A MAN WIELDING THE HOLY KING SWORD, COLLBRANDE.
EACH WOULD REPRESENT A SIZABLE THREAT ON HIS OR HER OWN, SO A TEAM OF THREE...
YOU DEVILS' ABILITY TO KEEP THESE THINGS IN CHECK IS...
...SIGH. THE SCOLDING NEVER STOPS ONCE SHEMHAZA GETS GOING... SHEESH.
BUT ISSEI ACHIEVING HIS BALANCE BREAKER WAS A HAPPY ACCIDENT... BET HE REALLY ENJOYED IT.
HEH HEH HEH.
WHAT'S SO FUNNY?

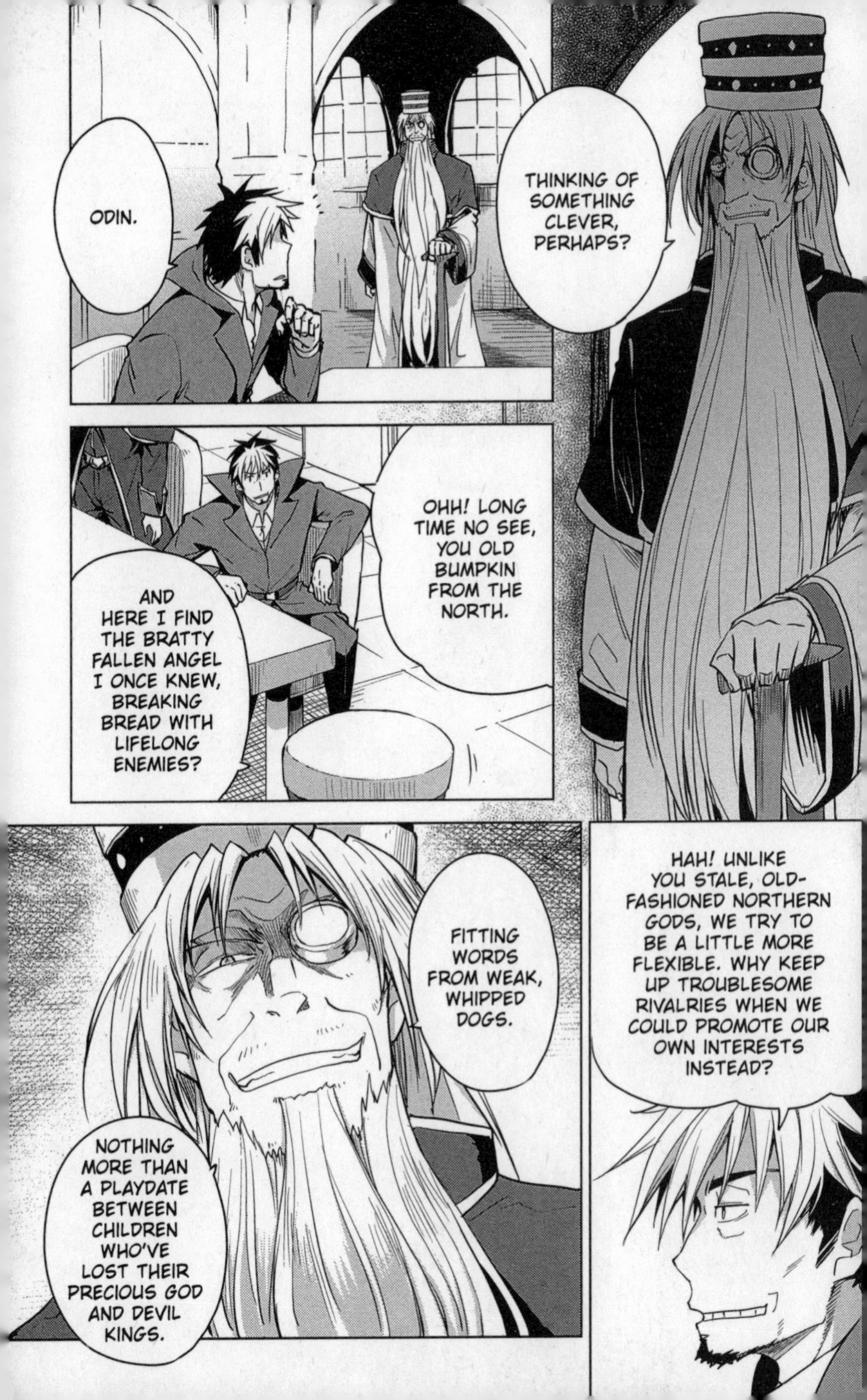
THINKING OF SOMETHING CLEVER, PERHAPS?
ODIN.
OHH! LONG TIME NO SEE, YOU OLD BUMPKIN FROM THE NORTH.
AND HERE I FIND THE BRATTY FALLEN ANGEL I ONCE KNEW, BREAKING BREAD WITH LIFELONG ENEMIES?
HAH! UNLIKE YOU STALE, OLD-FASHIONED NORTHERN GODS, WE TRY TO BE A LITTLE MORE FLEXIBLE. WHY KEEP UP TROUBLESOME RIVALRIES WHEN WE COULD PROMOTE OUR OWN INTERESTS INSTEAD?
FITTING WORDS FROM WEAK, WHIPPED DOGS.
NOTHING MORE THAN A PLAYDATE BETWEEN CHILDREN WHO'VE LOST THEIR PRECIOUS GOD AND DEVIL KINGS.

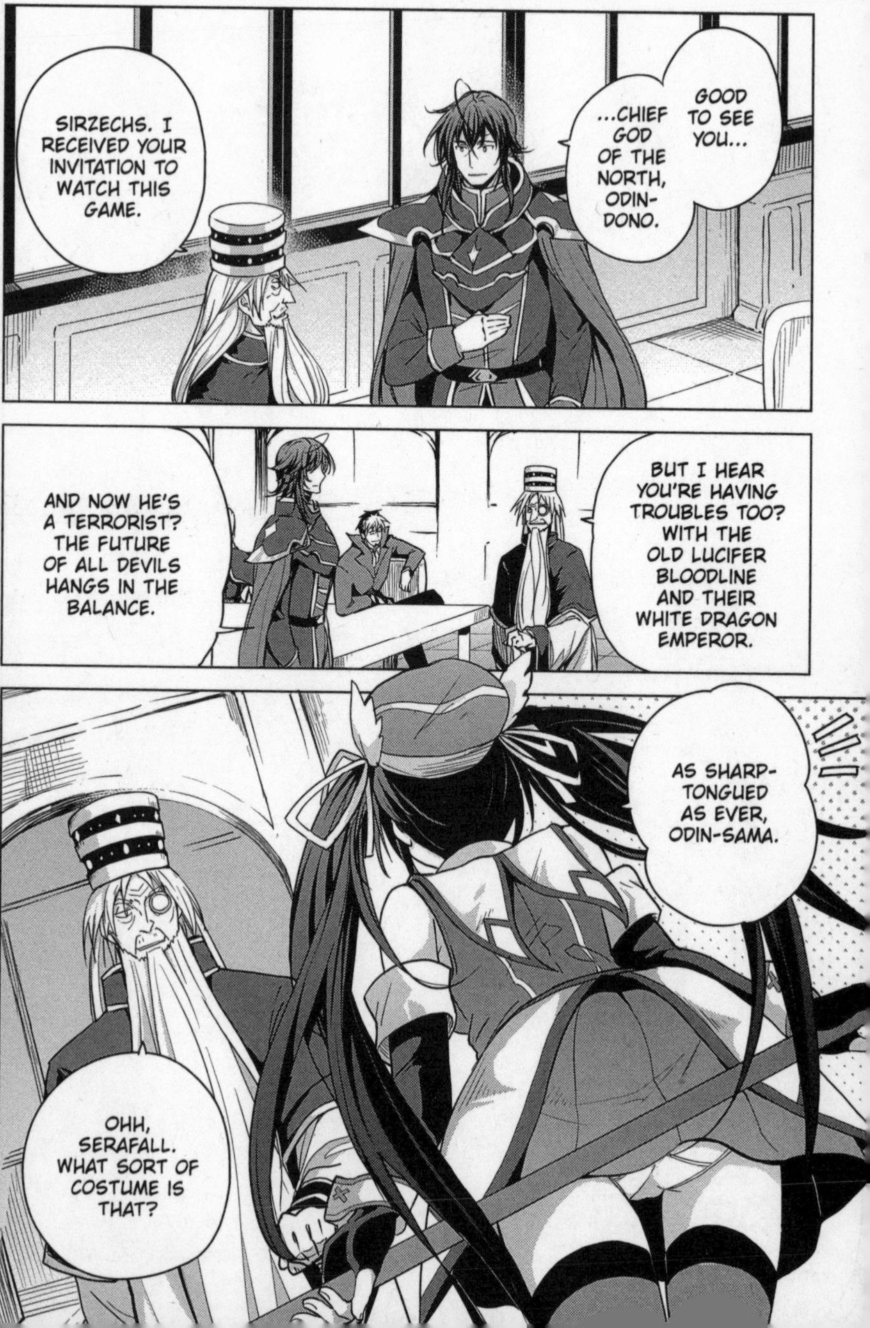
GOOD TO SEE YOU... ...CHIEF GOD OF THE NORTH, ODIN-DONO.
SIRZECHS. I RECEIVED YOUR INVITATION TO WATCH THIS GAME.
BUT I HEAR YOU'RE HAVING TROUBLES TOO? WITH THE OLD LUCIFER BLOODLINE AND THEIR WHITE DRAGON EMPEROR.
AND NOW HE'S A TERRORIST? THE FUTURE OF ALL DEVILS HANGS IN THE BALANCE.
AS SHARP-TONGUED AS EVER, ODIN-SAMA.
OHH, SERAFALL. WHAT SORT OF COSTUME IS THAT?

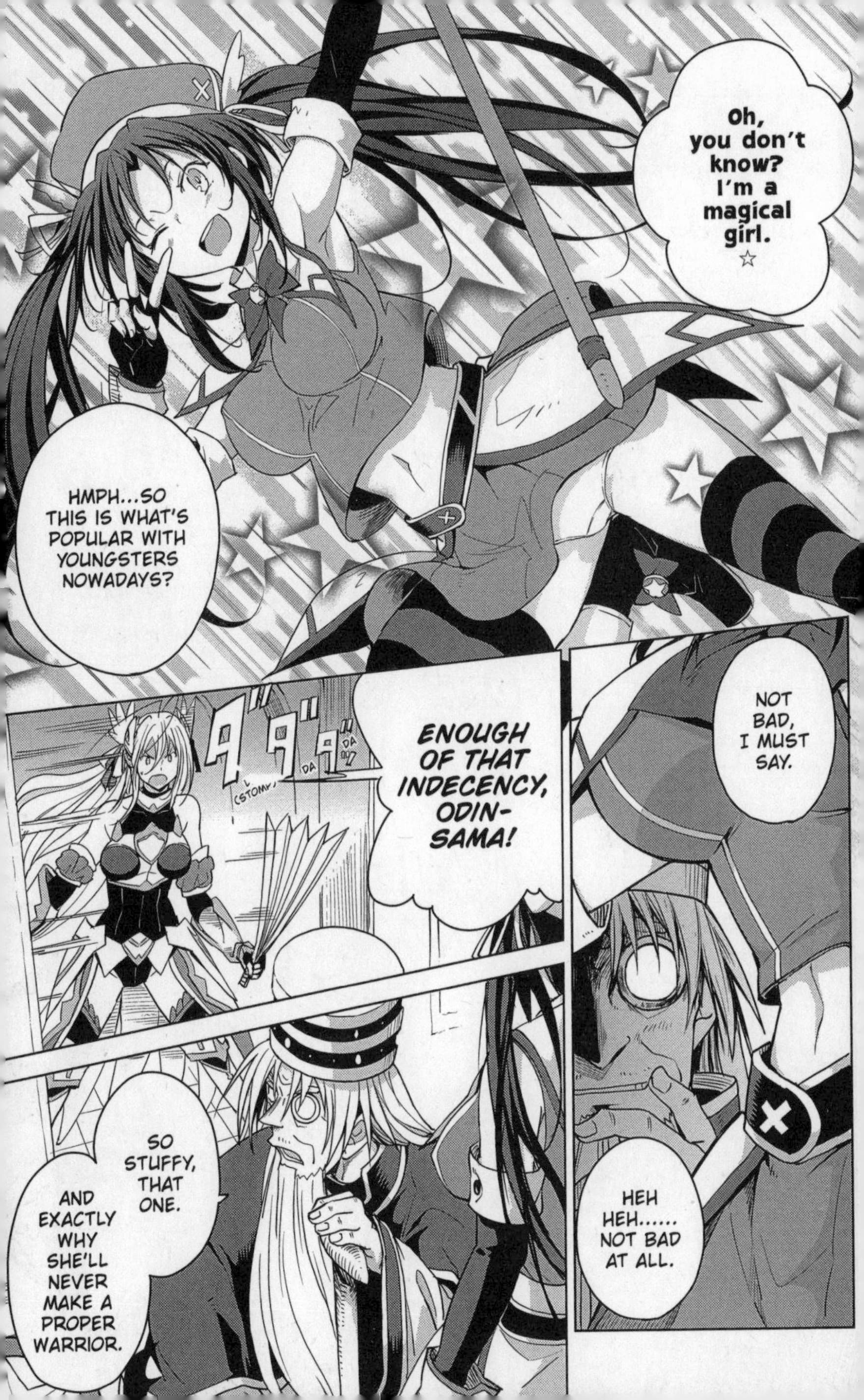
Oh, you don't know? I'm a magical girl. ☆
HMPH...SO THIS IS WHAT'S POPULAR WITH YOUNGSTERS NOWADAYS?
NOT BAD, I MUST SAY.
HEH HEH...... NOT BAD AT ALL.
DA
DA
(STOMP)
ENOUGH OF THAT INDECENCY, ODIN-SAMA!
SO STUFFY, THAT ONE.
AND EXACTLY WHY SHE'LL NEVER MAKE A PROPER WARRIOR.

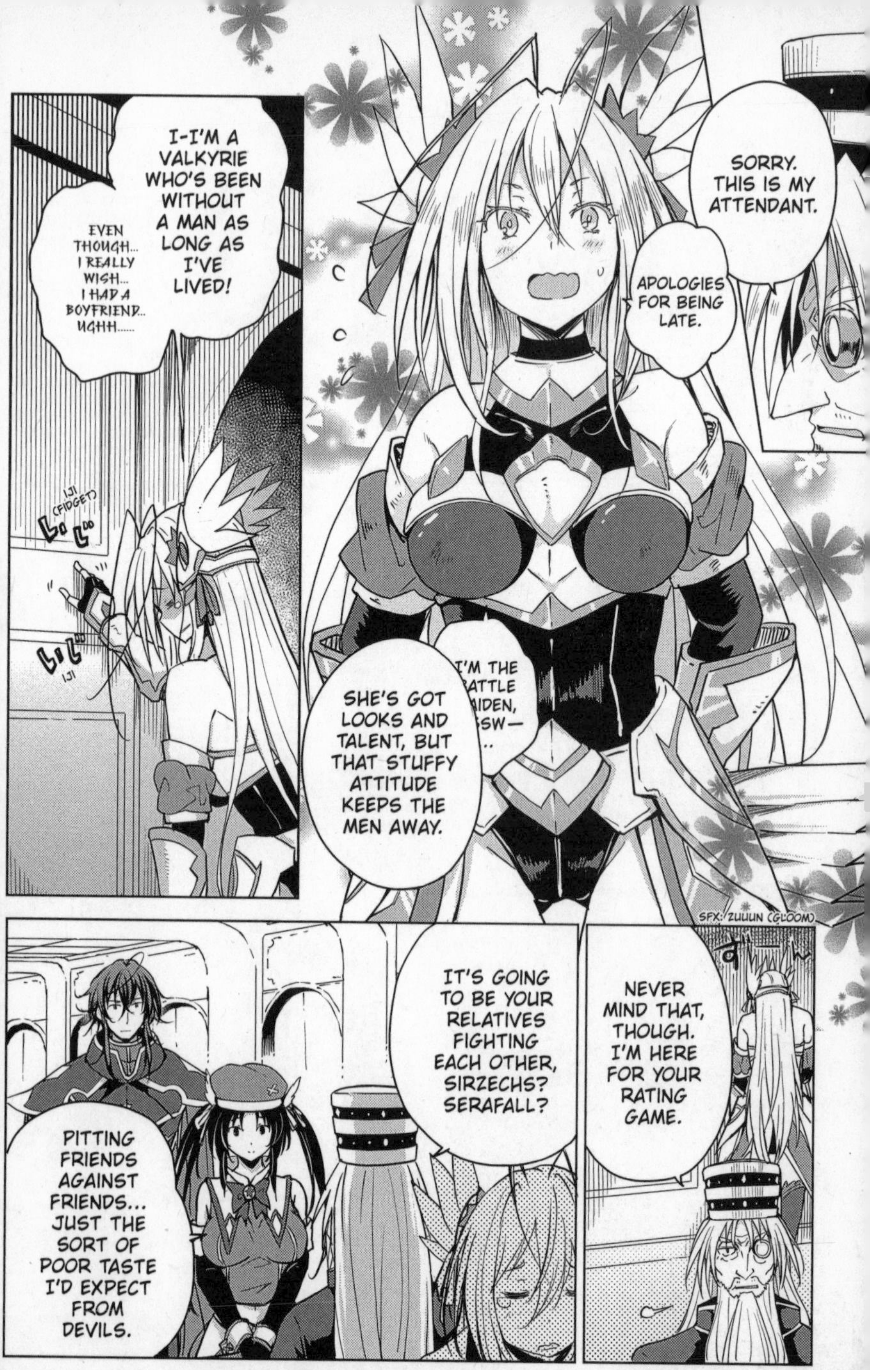
SORRY. THIS IS MY ATTENDANT.
APOLOGIES FOR BEING LATE.
I'M THE ATTLE AIDEN, SSW— ..
SHE'S GOT LOOKS AND TALENT, BUT THAT STUFFY ATTITUDE KEEPS THE MEN AWAY.
SFX: ZUUUN (GLOOM)
I-I'M A VALKYRIE WHO'S BEEN WITHOUT A MAN AS LONG AS I'VE LIVED!
EVEN THOUGH... I REALLY WISH... I HAD A BOYFRIEND... UGHH......
IJI (FIDGET)
IJI
NEVER MIND THAT, THOUGH. I'M HERE FOR YOUR RATING GAME.
IT'S GOING TO BE YOUR RELATIVES FIGHTING EACH OTHER, SIRZECHS? SERAFALL?
PITTING FRIENDS AGAINST FRIENDS... JUST THE SORT OF POOR TASTE I'D EXPECT FROM DEVILS.

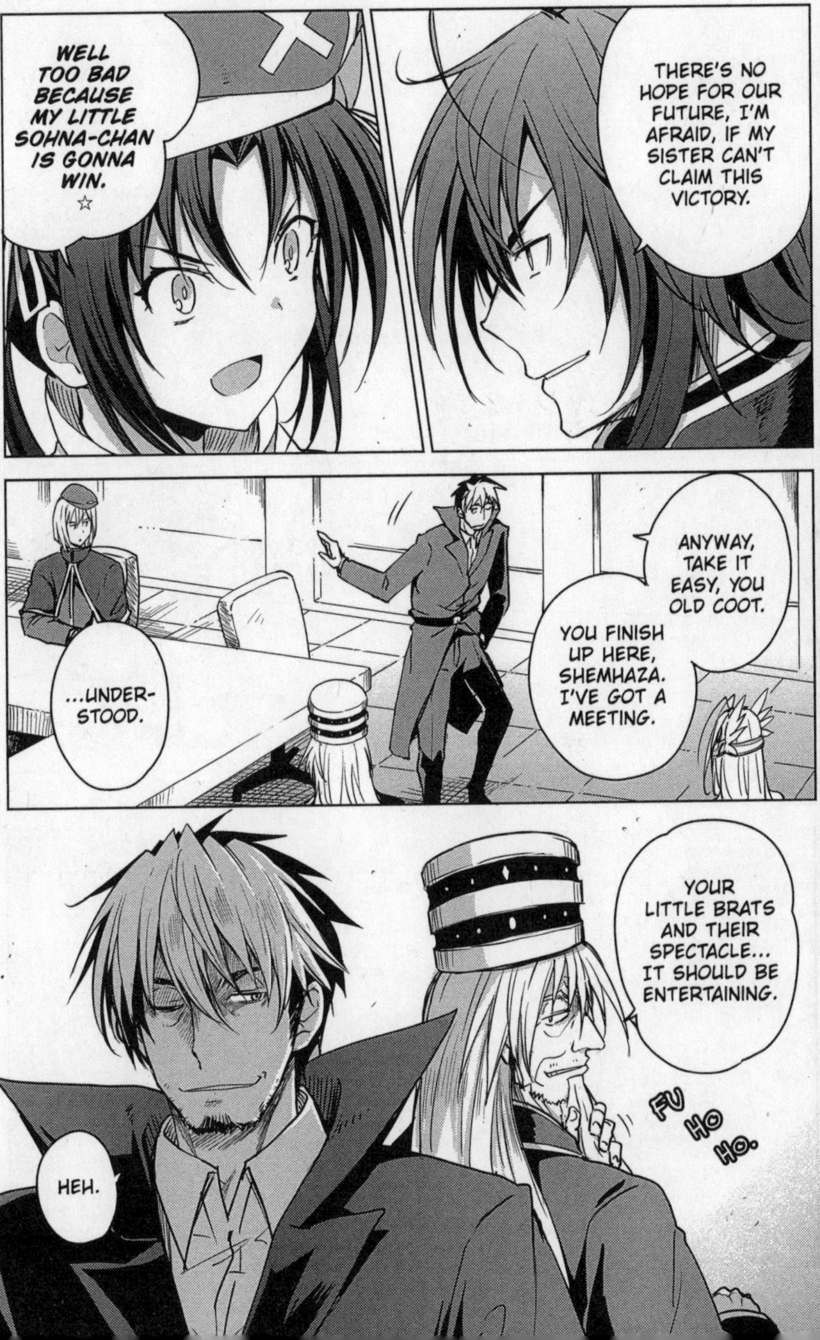
THERE'S NO HOPE FOR OUR FUTURE, I'M AFRAID, IF MY SISTER CAN'T CLAIM THIS VICTORY.
WELL TOO BAD BECAUSE MY LITTLE SOHNA-CHAN IS GONNA WIN. ☆
ANYWAY, TAKE IT EASY, YOU OLD COOT.
YOU FINISH UP HERE, SHEMHAZA. I'VE GOT A MEETING.
...UNDER-STOOD.
YOUR LITTLE BRATS AND THEIR SPECTACLE... IT SHOULD BE ENTERTAINING.
FU HO HO.
HEH.

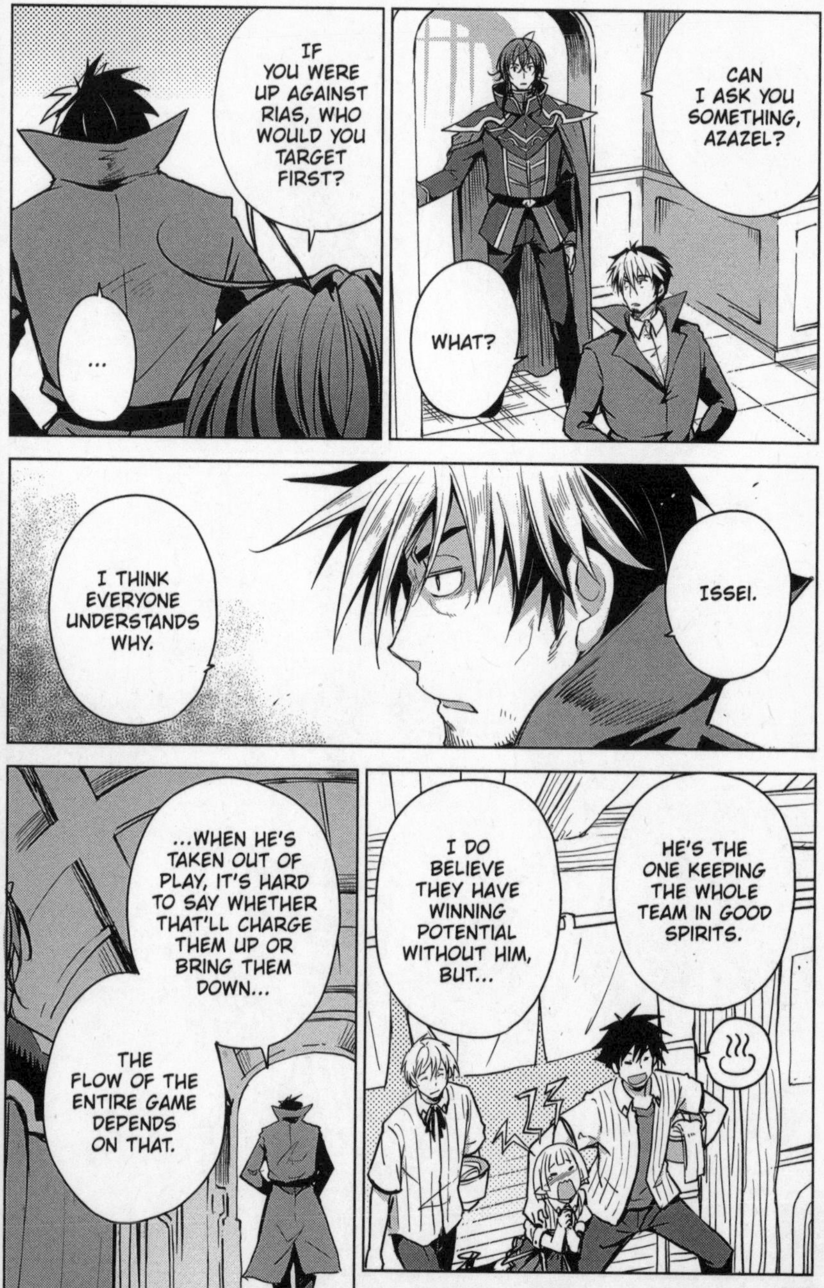
CAN I ASK YOU SOMETHING, AZAZEL?
WHAT?
IF YOU WERE UP AGAINST RIAS, WHO WOULD YOU TARGET FIRST?
...
ISSEI.
I THINK EVERYONE UNDERSTANDS WHY.
HE'S THE ONE KEEPING THE WHOLE TEAM IN GOOD SPIRITS.
I DO BELIEVE THEY HAVE WINNING POTENTIAL WITHOUT HIM, BUT...
...WHEN HE'S TAKEN OUT OF PLAY, IT'S HARD TO SAY WHETHER THAT'LL CHARGE THEM UP OR BRING THEM DOWN...
THE FLOW OF THE ENTIRE GAME DEPENDS ON THAT.

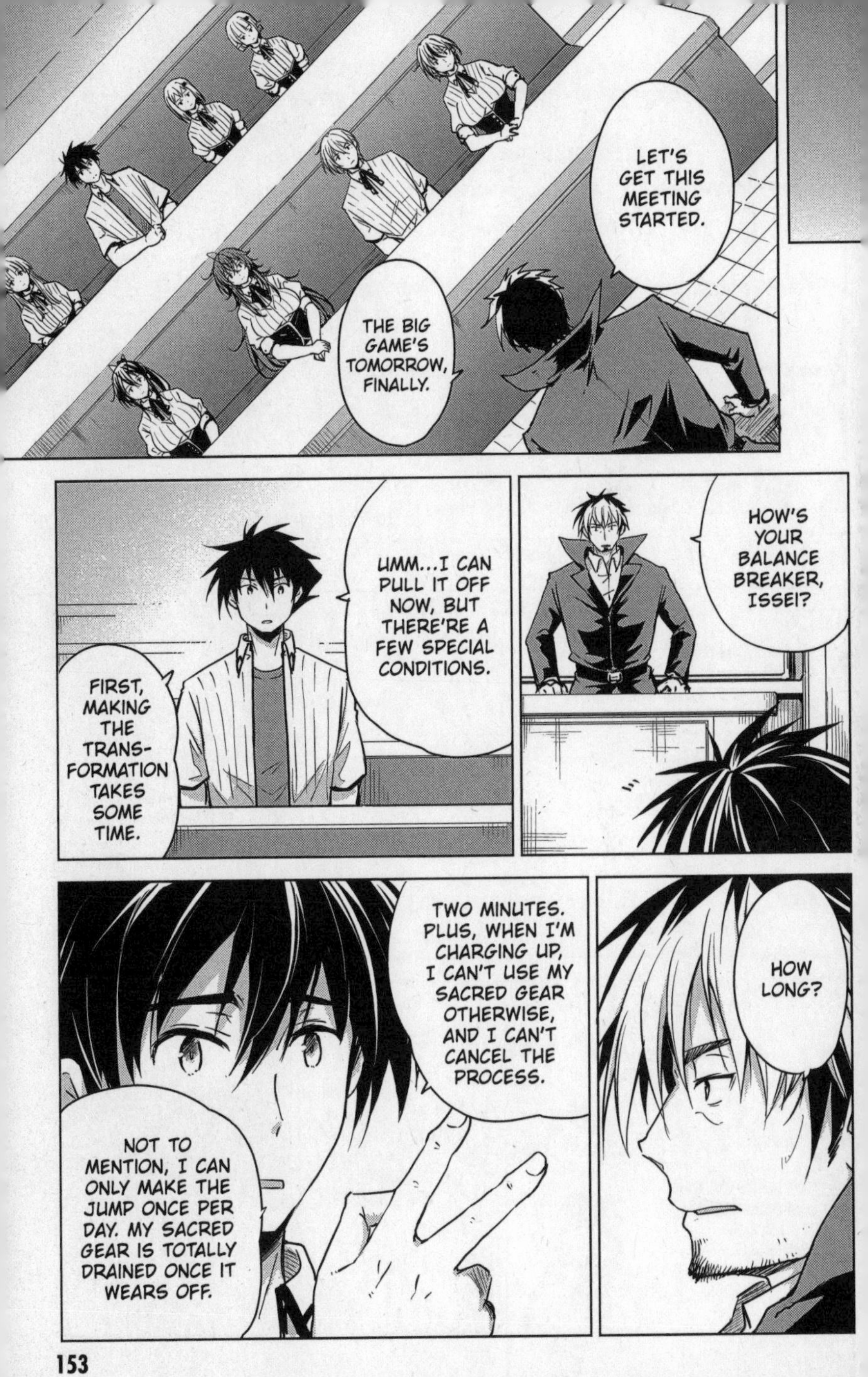
LET'S GET THIS MEETING STARTED.
THE BIG GAME'S TOMORROW, FINALLY.
HOW'S YOUR BALANCE BREAKER, ISSEI?
UMM...I CAN PULL IT OFF NOW, BUT THERE'RE A FEW SPECIAL CONDITIONS.
FIRST, MAKING THE TRANS-FORMATION TAKES SOME TIME.
HOW LONG?
TWO MINUTES. PLUS, WHEN I'M CHARGING UP, I CAN'T USE MY SACRED GEAR OTHERWISE, AND I CAN'T CANCEL THE PROCESS.
NOT TO MENTION, I CAN ONLY MAKE THE JUMP ONCE PER DAY. MY SACRED GEAR IS TOTALLY DRAINED ONCE IT WEARS OFF.

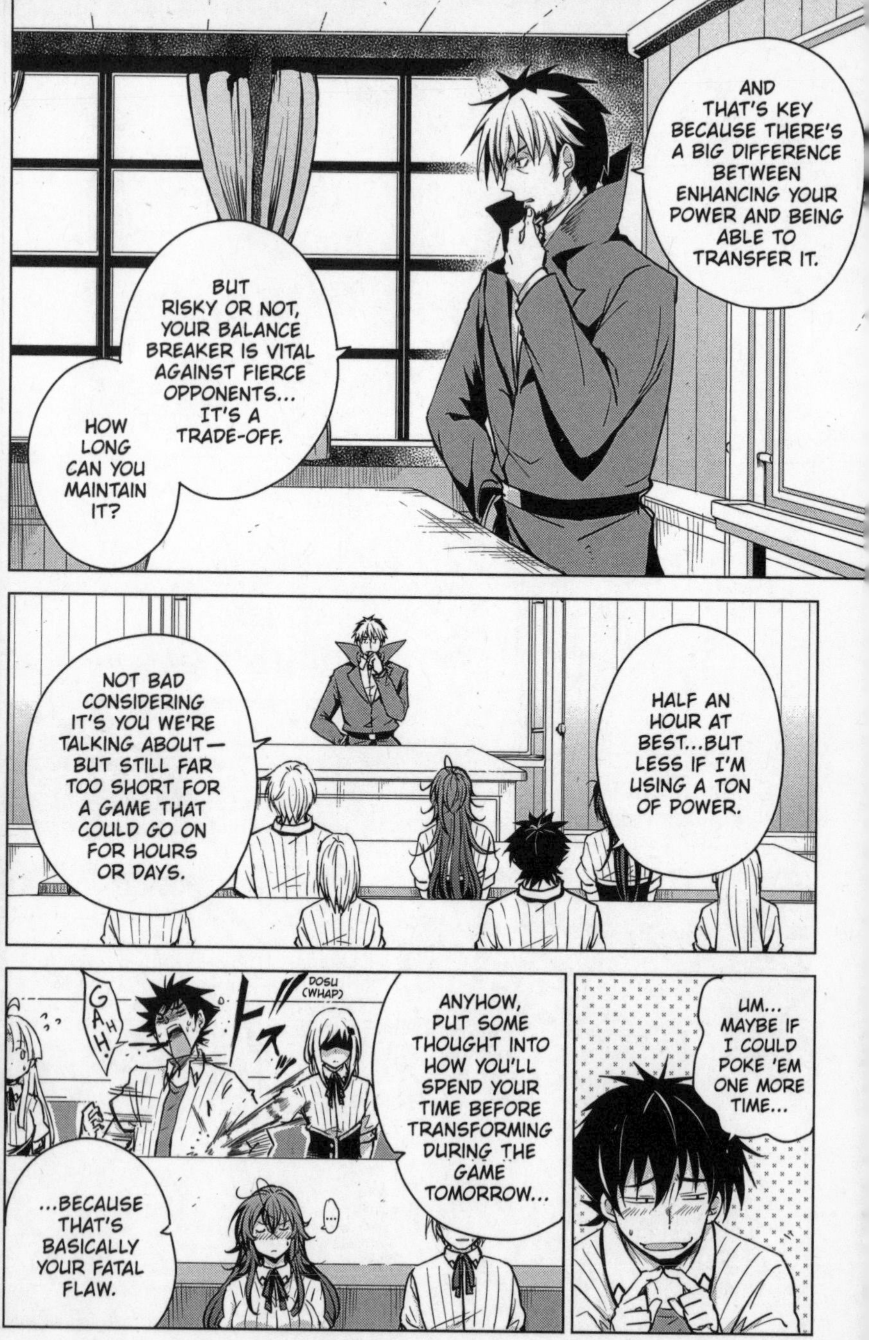
AND THAT'S KEY BECAUSE THERE'S A BIG DIFFERENCE BETWEEN ENHANCING YOUR POWER AND BEING ABLE TO TRANSFER IT.
BUT RISKY OR NOT, YOUR BALANCE BREAKER IS VITAL AGAINST FIERCE OPPONENTS... IT'S A TRADE-OFF.
HOW LONG CAN YOU MAINTAIN IT?
HALF AN HOUR AT BEST...BUT LESS IF I'M USING A TON OF POWER.
NOT BAD CONSIDERING IT'S YOU WE'RE TALKING ABOUT—BUT STILL FAR TOO SHORT FOR A GAME THAT COULD GO ON FOR HOURS OR DAYS.
UM... MAYBE IF I COULD POKE 'EM ONE MORE TIME...
ANYHOW, PUT SOME THOUGHT INTO HOW YOU'LL SPEND YOUR TIME BEFORE TRANSFORMING DURING THE GAME TOMORROW...
DOSU (WHAP)
GAH!
...
...BECAUSE THAT'S BASICALLY YOUR FATAL FLAW.

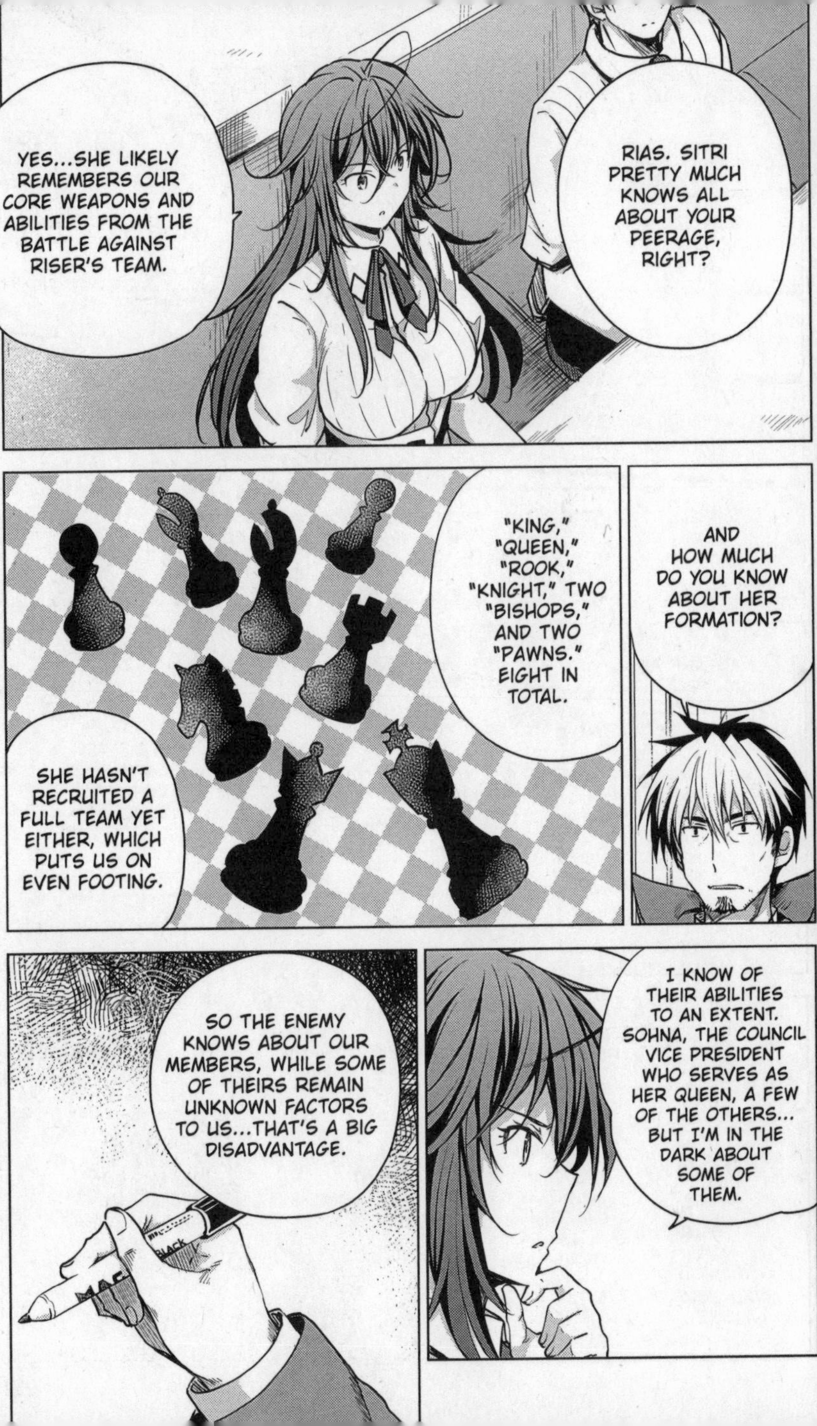
RIAS. SITRI PRETTY MUCH KNOWS ALL ABOUT YOUR PEERAGE, RIGHT?
YES...SHE LIKELY REMEMBERS OUR CORE WEAPONS AND ABILITIES FROM THE BATTLE AGAINST RISER'S TEAM.
AND HOW MUCH DO YOU KNOW ABOUT HER FORMATION?
"KING," "QUEEN," "ROOK," "KNIGHT," TWO "BISHOPS," AND TWO "PAWNS." EIGHT IN TOTAL.
SHE HASN'T RECRUITED A FULL TEAM YET EITHER, WHICH PUTS US ON EVEN FOOTING.
I KNOW OF THEIR ABILITIES TO AN EXTENT. SOHNA, THE COUNCIL VICE PRESIDENT WHO SERVES AS HER QUEEN, A FEW OF THE OTHERS... BUT I'M IN THE DARK ABOUT SOME OF THEM.
SO THE ENEMY KNOWS ABOUT OUR MEMBERS, WHILE SOME OF THEIRS REMAIN UNKNOWN FACTORS TO US...THAT'S A BIG DISADVANTAGE.

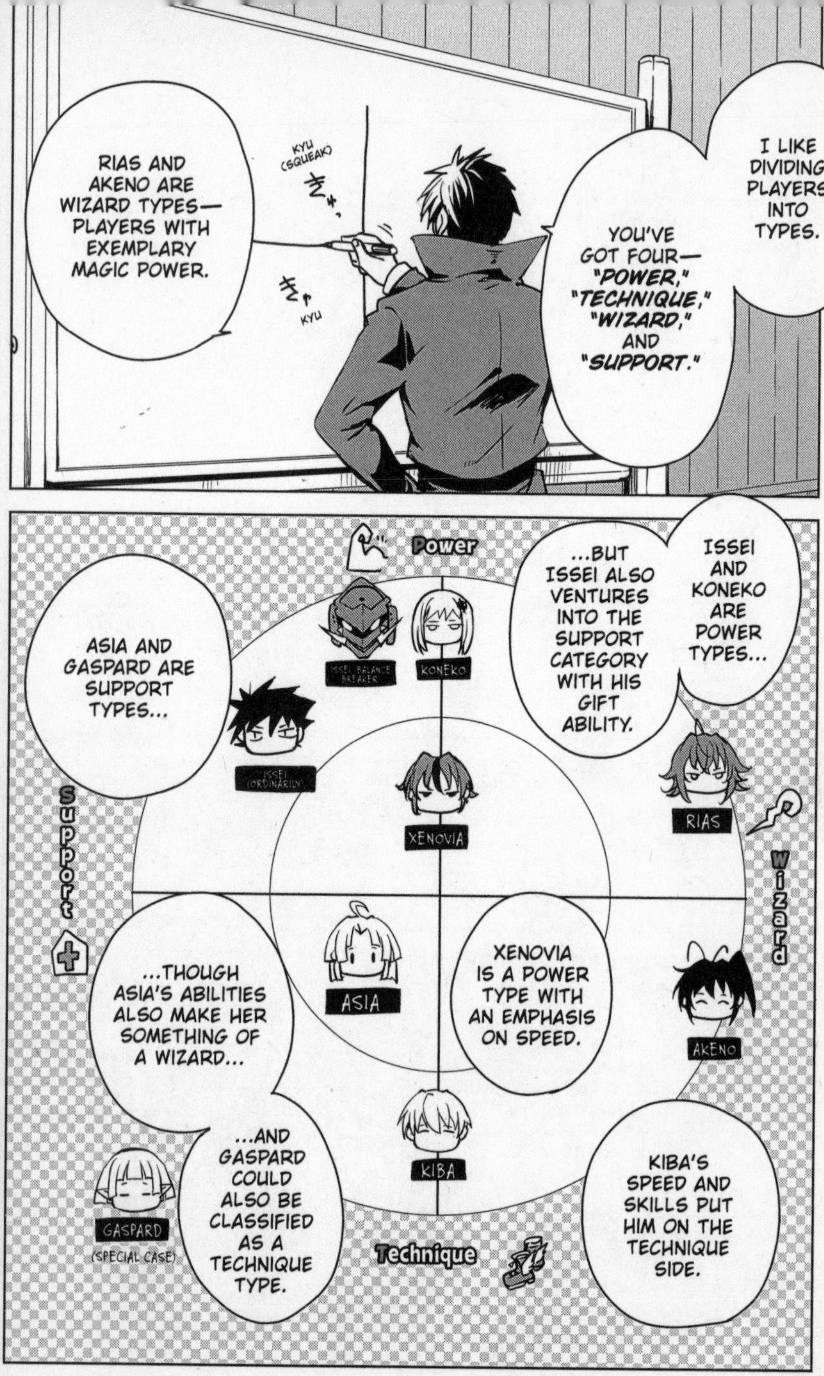
I LIKE DIVIDING PLAYERS INTO TYPES.
YOU'VE GOT FOUR—"*POWER*," "*TECHNIQUE*," "*WIZARD*," AND "*SUPPORT*."
KYU (SQUEAK)
KYU
RIAS AND AKENO ARE WIZARD TYPES—PLAYERS WITH EXEMPLARY MAGIC POWER.
ISSEI AND KONEKO ARE POWER TYPES...
...BUT ISSEI ALSO VENTURES INTO THE SUPPORT CATEGORY WITH HIS GIFT ABILITY.
Power
KONEKO
ISSEI BALANCE BREAKER
ASIA AND GASPARD ARE SUPPORT TYPES...
ISSEI (ORDINARILY)
RIAS
Wizard
XENOVIA
Support
XENOVIA IS A POWER TYPE WITH AN EMPHASIS ON SPEED.
AKENO
ASIA
...THOUGH ASIA'S ABILITIES ALSO MAKE HER SOMETHING OF A WIZARD...
KIBA
KIBA'S SPEED AND SKILLS PUT HIM ON THE TECHNIQUE SIDE.
...AND GASPARD COULD ALSO BE CLASSIFIED AS A TECHNIQUE TYPE.
Technique
GASPARD
(SPECIAL CASE)

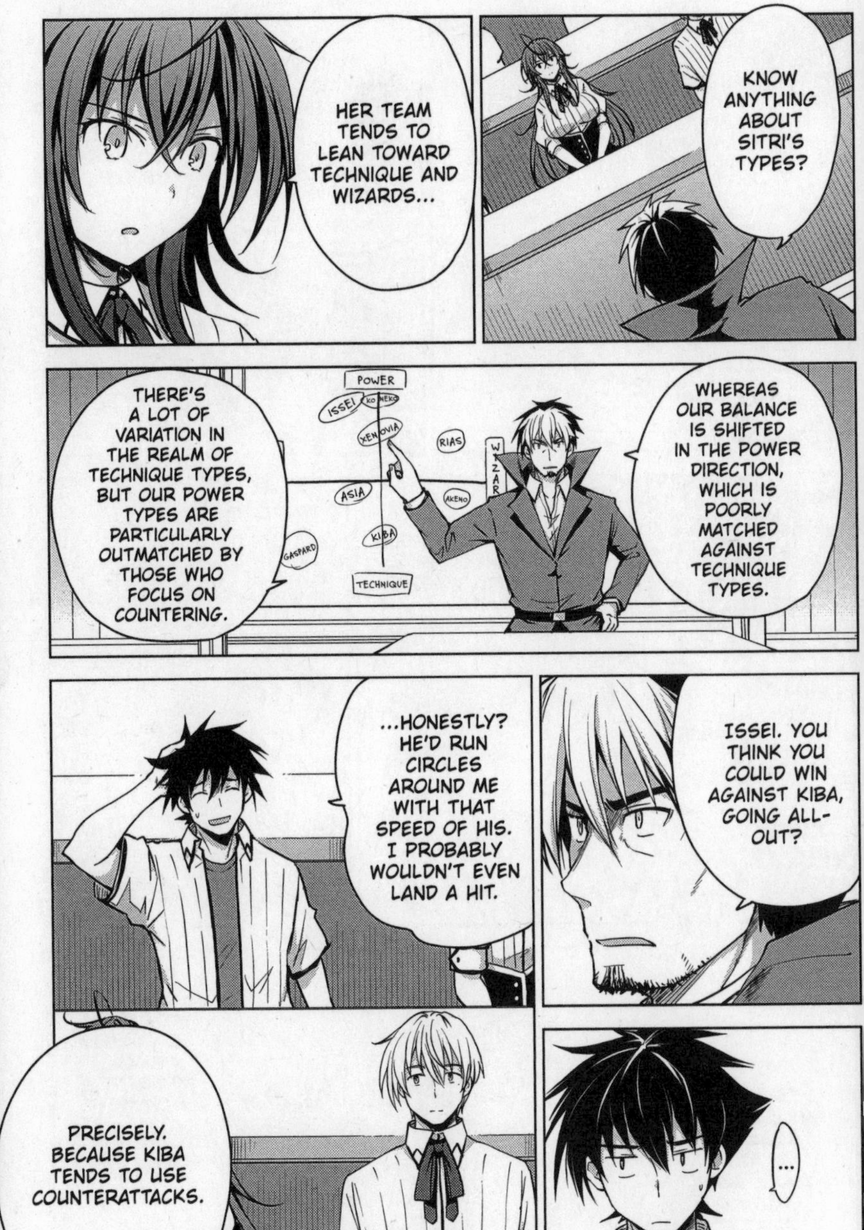
KNOW ANYTHING ABOUT SITRI'S TYPES?
HER TEAM TENDS TO LEAN TOWARD TECHNIQUE AND WIZARDS...
WHEREAS OUR BALANCE IS SHIFTED IN THE POWER DIRECTION, WHICH IS POORLY MATCHED AGAINST TECHNIQUE TYPES.
POWER
ISSEI
KONEKO
XENOVIA
RIAS
ASIA
AKENO
KIBA
GASPARD
TECHNIQUE
THERE'S A LOT OF VARIATION IN THE REALM OF TECHNIQUE TYPES, BUT OUR POWER TYPES ARE PARTICULARLY OUTMATCHED BY THOSE WHO FOCUS ON COUNTERING.
ISSEI. YOU THINK YOU COULD WIN AGAINST KIBA, GOING ALL-OUT?
...HONESTLY? HE'D RUN CIRCLES AROUND ME WITH THAT SPEED OF HIS. I PROBABLY WOULDN'T EVEN LAND A HIT.
...
PRECISELY. BECAUSE KIBA TENDS TO USE COUNTERATTACKS.

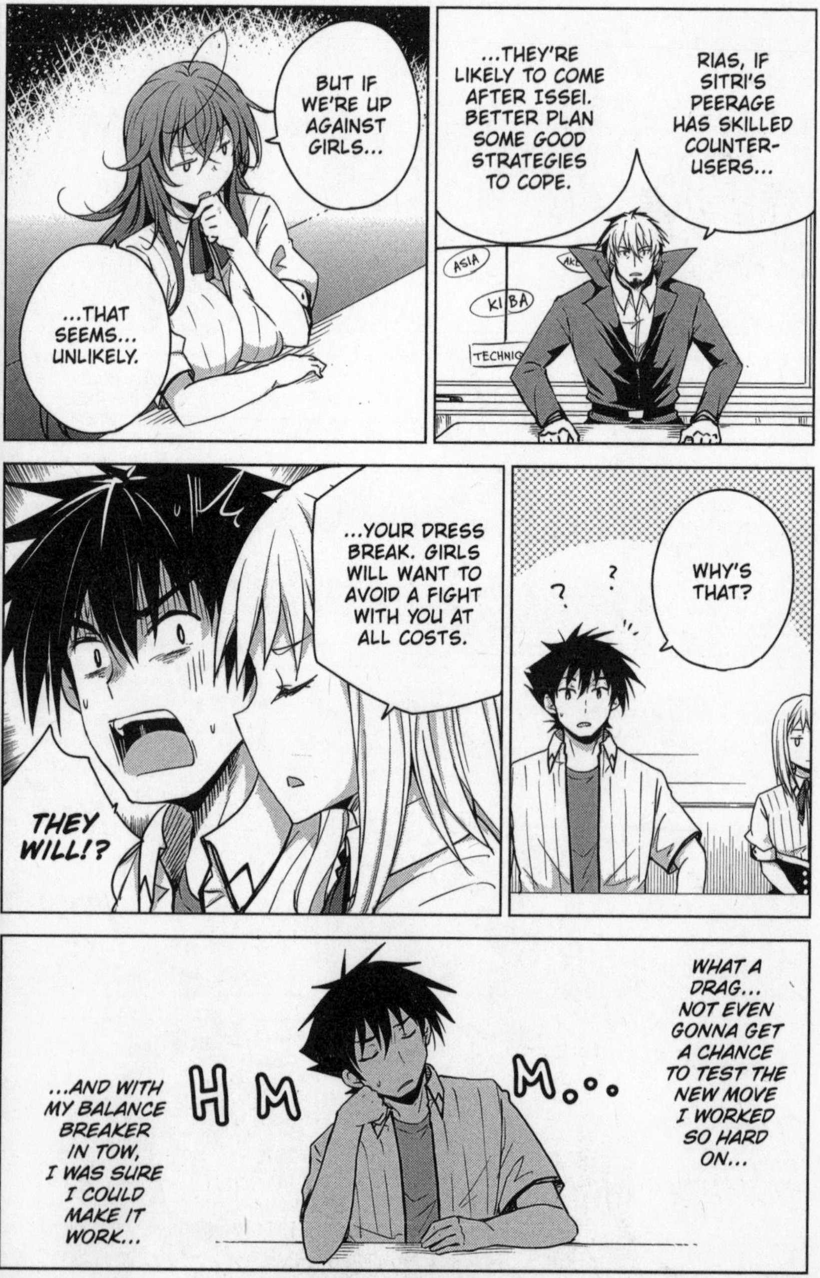
RIAS, IF SITRI'S PEERAGE HAS SKILLED COUNTER-USERS...
...THEY'RE LIKELY TO COME AFTER ISSEI. BETTER PLAN SOME GOOD STRATEGIES TO COPE.
ASIA
KIBA
BUT IF WE'RE UP AGAINST GIRLS...
...THAT SEEMS... UNLIKELY.
WHY'S THAT?
...YOUR DRESS BREAK. GIRLS WILL WANT TO AVOID A FIGHT WITH YOU AT ALL COSTS.
THEY WILL!?
WHAT A DRAG... NOT EVEN GONNA GET A CHANCE TO TEST THE NEW MOVE I WORKED SO HARD ON...
HMM...
...AND WITH MY BALANCE BREAKER IN TOW, I WAS SURE I COULD MAKE IT WORK...

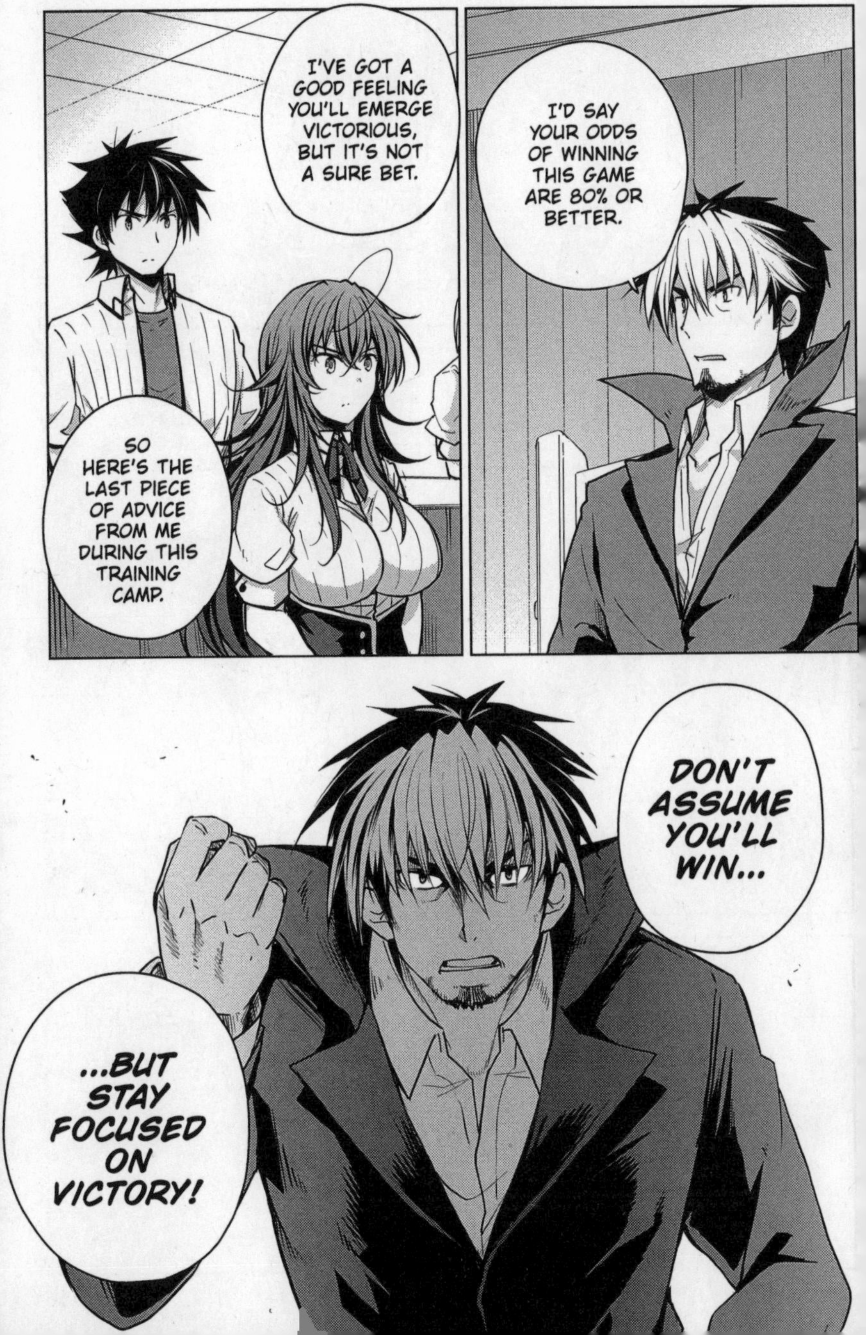
I'D SAY YOUR ODDS OF WINNING THIS GAME ARE 80% OR BETTER.
I'VE GOT A GOOD FEELING YOU'LL EMERGE VICTORIOUS, BUT IT'S NOT A SURE BET.
SO HERE'S THE LAST PIECE OF ADVICE FROM ME DURING THIS TRAINING CAMP.
DON'T ASSUME YOU'LL WIN...
...BUT STAY FOCUSED ON VICTORY!

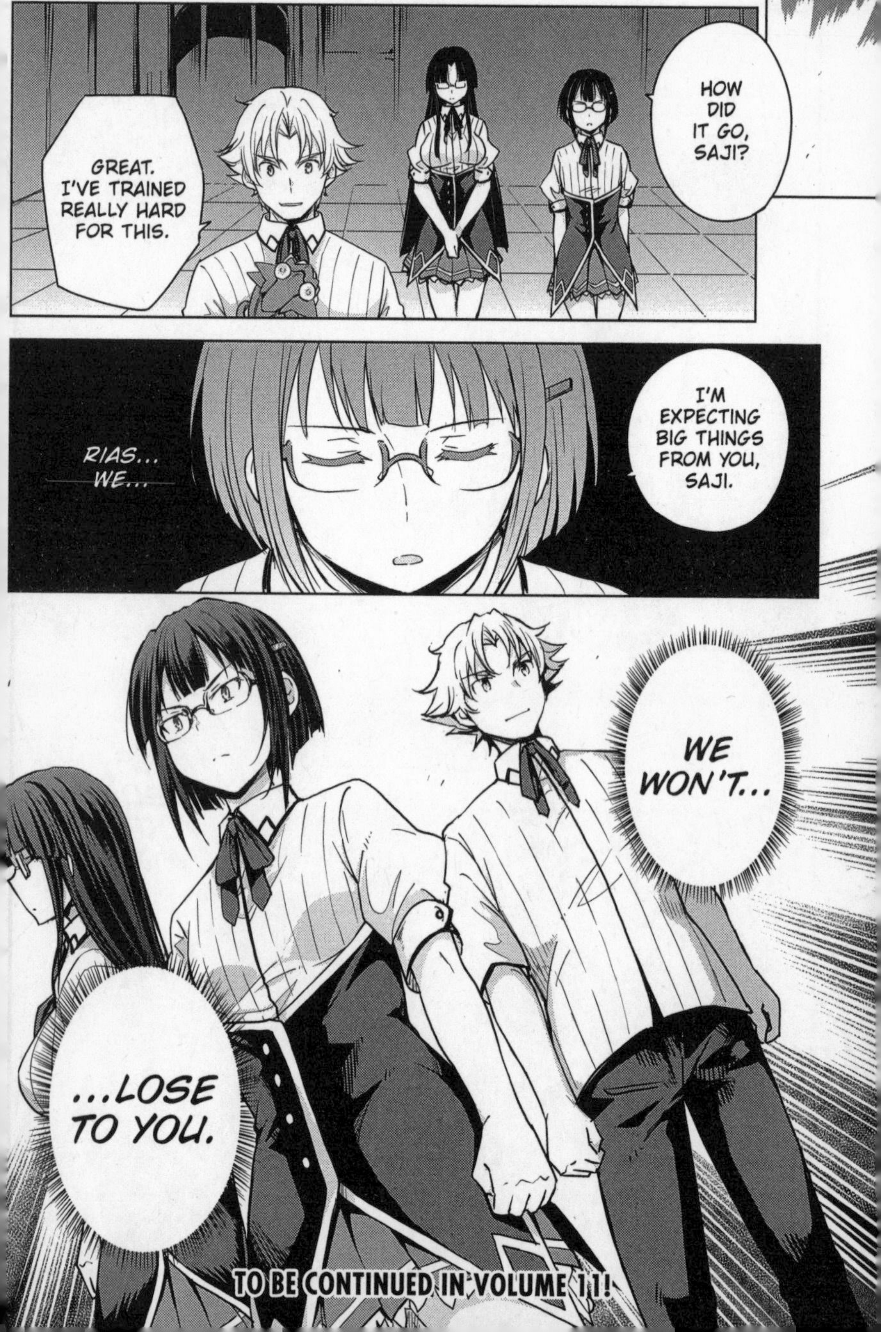
HOW DID IT GO, SAJI?
GREAT. I'VE TRAINED REALLY HARD FOR THIS.
I'M EXPECTING BIG THINGS FROM YOU, SAJI.
RIAS... WE...
WE WON'T...
...LOSE TO YOU.
TO BE CONTINUED IN VOLUME 11!

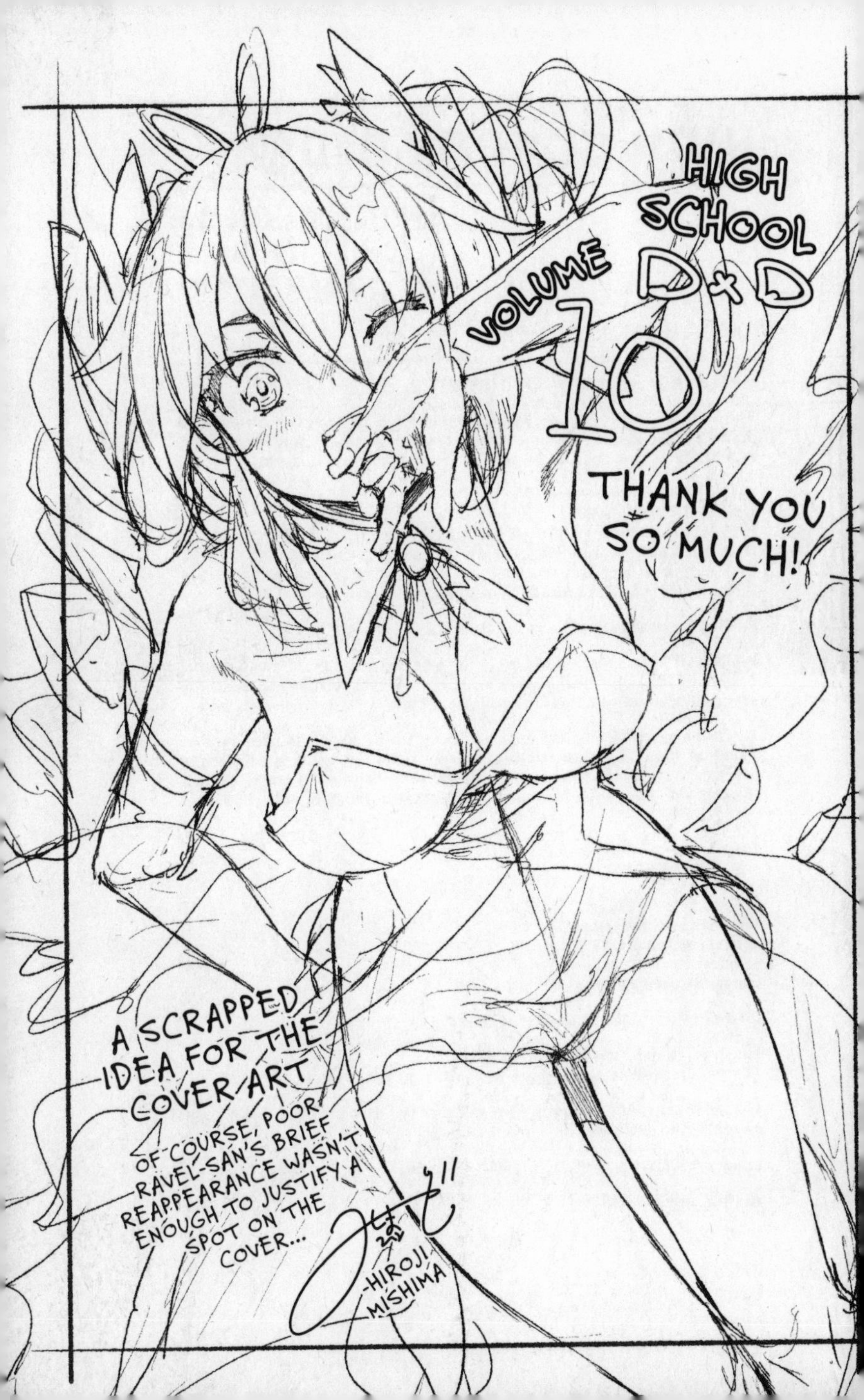
HIGH SCHOOL D×D
VOLUME 10
THANK YOU SO MUCH!
A SCRAPPED IDEA FOR THE COVER ART
OF COURSE, POOR RAVEL-SAN'S BRIEF REAPPEARANCE WASN'T ENOUGH TO JUSTIFY A SPOT ON THE COVER...
-HIROJI MISHIMA

HIGH SCHOOL DxD ⑩

HIROJI MISHIMA
ICHIEI ISHIBUMI
ZERO MIYAMA

Translation: Caleb D. Cook

Lettering: Anthony Quintessenza

HIGHSCHOOL DXD Volume 10
© HIROJI MISHIMA 2017
© ICHIEI ISHIBUMI • ZERO MIYAMA 2017
First published in Japan in 2017 by KADOKAWA CORPORATION, Tokyo.
English translation rights arranged with KADOKAWA CORPORATION, Tokyo, through TUTTLE-MORI AGENCY, INC., Tokyo.

English translation © 2017 by Yen Press, LLC

Yen Press
1290 Avenue of the Americas
New York, NY 10104

Visit us at yenpress.com
facebook.com/yenpress
twitter.com/yenpress
yenpress.tumblr.com
instagram.com/yenpress

First Yen Press Edition: December 2017

Yen Press is an imprint of Yen Press, LLC.
The Yen Press name and logo are trademarks of Yen Press, LLC.

Library of Congress Control Number: 2015960114

ISBN: 978-0-316-41406-7

10 9 8 7 6 5 4 3 2 1

BVG

Printed in the United States of America